Thomas R. Gulledge
William P. Hutzler (Eds.)

# Analytical Methods in Software Engineering Economics

With 45 Figures



Springer-Verlag
Berlin Heidelberg New York
London Paris Tokyo
Hong Kong Barcelona
Budapest

Professor Dr. Thomas R. Gulledge
The Institute of Public Policy
George Mason University
4400 University Drive
Fairfax, VA 22030-4444, USA

Dr. William P. Hutzler
Economic Analysis Center
The MITRE Corporation
7525 Colshire Drive
McLean, VA 22102-3481, USA



ISBN 3-540-55950-7 Springer-Verlag Berlin Heidelberg New York Tokyo
ISBN 0-387-55950-7 Springer-Verlag New York Heidelberg Berlin Tokyo


Printed in the United States of America



2142/7130-543210 - Printed on acid-free paper

# PREFACE

This volume presents a selection of the presentations from the first annual conference on *Analytical Methods in Software Engineering Economics* held at The MITRE Corporation in McLean, Virginia. The papers are representative of the issues that are of interest to researchers in the economics of information systems and software engineering economics.

The 1990s are presenting software economists with a particularly difficult set of challenges. Because of budget considerations, the number of large new software development efforts is declining. The primary focus has shifted to issues relating to upgrading and migrating existing systems. In this environment, productivity enhancing methodologies and tools are of primary interest.

The MITRE Software Engineering Analysis Conference was designed to address some of the new and difficult challenges that face our profession. The primary objective of the conference was to address new theoretical and applications directions in Software Engineering Economics, a relatively new discipline that deals with the management and control of all segments of the software life-cycle. The discipline has received much visibility in the last twenty-five years because of the size and cost considerations of many software development and maintenance efforts, particularly in the Federal Government.

We thank everyone who helped make this conference a success, especially those who graciously allowed us to include their work in this volume.

Thomas R. Gulledge
The Institute of Public Policy
George Mason University
Fairfax, Virginia 22030 USA

William P. Hutzler
Economic Analysis Center
The MITRE Corporation
McLean, Virginia 22102 USA

## TABLE OF CONTENTS

# Economic Analysis of Software Technology Investments

Barry W. Boehm
Defense Advanced Research Projects Agency
University of California, Los Angeles
Computer Science Department
Los Angeles, CA 90024

## 1. Introduction

### 1.1 Background

Many large organizations are finding that:

- Software technology is increasingly critical to their future organizational performance.
- Organizational expenditures on software are increasing.
- Investments in software technology provide opportunities to reduce software costs and increase organizational performance.

The U.S. Department of Defense (DoD) is one such organization. It has embarked on the development of a DoD Software Technology Strategy (SWTS)[Boehm91a] to:

- Identify its current and future software technology needs.
- Analyze and adjust its current software technology investment portfolio to better meet DoD needs.
- Formulate alternative DoD software technology investment portfolios, and analyze them with respect to DoD needs and estimated cost savings.

This paper summarizes one of several analyses undertaken to evaluate alternative DoD software technology investment portfolios. The analysis estimates the DoD software cost savings likely to result from alternative levels of DoD investment and calculates the resulting estimated returns on investment (ROI).

The dollar figures used in this paper represent current and proposed alternative technology investment and savings figures used at one stage of the development of the

SWTS. At this point, they are representative of SWTS data and conclusions, but not necessarily accurate with respect to the final figures to be used in the SWTS.

## 1.2 Overview

The software technology return-on-investment (ROI) analysis presented in this paper considers three alternative programs:

1. A *Baseline*: No significant DoD investments are undertaken to improve DoD software technology. DoD would continue to benefit at the current 4% rate of software productivity improvement resulting from commercial-sector software improvements.

2. A *Current* software technology program: Achieving the best results possible from a program that reflects the current flat-dollar software technology budgets of most DoD organizations. In then-year dollars, the Current Program level used in this analysis is around $195M/year between FY1992 and FY1995. Its level is $192M in FY1996; this $192M is extended for each year between FY1997 and FY2008. In 1992 dollars, the resulting 2008 level of investment would be $88M.

3. An *Achievable* software technology program, described in further detail in the SWTS. This program would: increase the DoD software technology level of investment from $195M to $410M between FY1992 and FY1997, and apply a 3% growth factor to this $410M baseline thereafter. By FY2008, this would be $568M in 2008 dollars and $260M in 1992 dollars, using a 5% deflation rate.

The major questions to be answered by the ROI analysis were:

- Can the Current Program be justified with respect to the no-investment Baseline situation?

- Can the Achievable Program be justified with respect to the Current Program?

- Can the Achievable Program or the Current Program realize the SWTS objective of reducing software unit costs by a factor of two in the year 2000?

The ROI analysis is carried out by estimating a set of 1992-2008 time series of technology fractions-of-time-used (FTs) and fractional-savings (FSs) resulting from the Current and Achievable software technology programs, and using the model presented in Section 2 to calculate the resulting cost savings, net present values, and ROIs.[1]

Section 2 describes the structure of the SWTS ROI model. Section 3 provides a summary of the inputs used to calculate the ROI results, with rationales relating the choice of ROI input quantities to the expected stream of software technology results produced by the Current and Achievable Programs. Section 4 presents and discusses the resulting estimated DoD software cost savings and ROI results. Section 5 presents the resulting conclusions.

## 2. SWTS ROI Model

The SWTS ROI model begins by computing the estimated cost savings resulting from three major sources: "work avoidance" through software reuse technology improvements; "working smarter" through process technology improvements; and "working faster" through improvements in software tools and environments. These cost savings are calculated for both development and maintenance from the years 1992 through 2008.[2]

Achieving the end results of the Current and Achievable software technology programs requires investment in new software technologies to achieve cost savings. To assess the potential worth of these investments, two financial measures of merit are computed. One measure is the ROI mentioned above. The other measure is net present value (NPV). Both measures account for the time value of money.

---

[1]For a complete definition of net present value and ROI, see section 2.4.

[2]This analysis has been automated in a model using Microsoft Excel™ macros by The Institute for Defense Analyses. The resulting tool provides a set of pull-down menus that allow the user to rapidly change a number of assumptions underlying the analysis and obtain graphic output of the resulting savings. See [BOEHM91b].

The remainder of this section describes the model structure and parameters, shows algebraic representations of how cost savings are calculated, and provides examples of how the formulas are applied to the alternative SWTS programs.

## 2.1 Model Structure and Parameters

The Baseline scenario used as the starting point of the analysis represents the estimates of the annual level of DoD software expenditure in the absence of any significant DoD software technology investment. The analysis assumes that for the initial year, 1992, DoD software expenditure will be $24 billion (B). This estimate is conservative: 1990 estimates have ranged from $24B to $32B. The analysis also assumes that this number will increase over time at a 5% rate through the year 2008. This growth rate was calculated assuming that the annual DoD software output will be reduced to a growth rate of 4% by DoD budget limitations. This demand growth would be absorbed by improvements in commercial software technology, which are likely to continue to produce 4% annual productivity gains. Thus, the Baseline scenario represents a constant DoD software work force level; the 5% cost growth rate results from an assumed 5% inflation rate. This estimate is also very conservative. The analysis assumes that the distribution of this expenditure between development and maintenance is 30% for development and 70% for maintenance. Using the information from above, the 1992 baseline would be $7.2B for development and $16.8B for maintenance.

Table 1 below summarizes these parameters and the sources upon which they are based.

The estimated effects of the Current and Achievable DoD technology programs are calculated by adjusting the original cost baseline by annual estimates of the cost saving effects of work avoidance, working smarter, and working faster on both software development and maintenance. Note that the manner in which the baseline costs are computed implies that there will be a 4% gain in productivity whether any of the initiatives are employed or not. The adjustments to the baseline through work avoidance, working smarter, and working faster are in addition to such "natural" productivity trends.

**Table 1: Baseline Parameters**

| Parameter Category | Parameter Value or Name | Source |
|---|---|---|
| Total DoD 1992 Software Spending | $24 billion | EIA90 ($32B)<br>AVWK91 ($31B) |
| Development/Maintenance Split | 30% Development,<br>70% Maintenance | BOEHM81,<br>EIA90 |
| Growth Rates: | | |
| DoD SW Cost | 5% | AVWK91 (7%)<br>EIA90 (1%) |
| Productivity Growth | 4% | MARTIN83,<br>LEVITAN88 |
| Inflation rate | 5% | |

As noted above, the analysis identifies three sources of cost savings caused by the Initiative; these are formally described as end product cost avoidance (EPCA), process cost avoidance (PCA), and process cost reduction (PCR). EPCA represents cost savings from avoiding the need to write more lines of code: via software reuse, application generators, commercial off-the-shelf (COTS) software, Ada generics, and other product-related improvements. PCA represents savings from process-related improvements that enable projects to avoid costly rework by "working smarter." Examples of PCA technology improvements are prototyping and risk management technology, and those captured by the Software Engineering Institute (SEI) software process assessment. PCR represents savings from improvements in software engineering environments (SEEs) and better, more interoperable tools that partially automate software development and maintenance, enabling people to "work faster" on those core portions of the software process remaining, after one has eliminated avoidable product efforts via EPCA and avoidable process efforts via PCA.

Table 2 summarizes the sources of savings used in this analysis.

**Table 2: Savings Sources**

| Source | Formal Name | Abbreviation | Characteristic |
|---|---|---|---|
| work avoidance | end product cost avoidance | EPCA | reuse |
| working smarter | process cost avoidance | PCA | rework avoidance |
| working faster | process cost reduction | PCR | tools & environments |

The analysis is divided into a development and maintenance portion. Cost savings are determined by the multiplicative product of the fraction of time the improvements are used and the fraction of savings realized when the improvements are used.

## 2.2 Calculating Development Savings

As noted above, the analysis estimates the savings resulting from software technology improvements for the years 1992 to 2008. For each year and source of savings (EPCA, PCA, and PCR for both development and maintenance), some value for FS from the use of technologies and some FT value are postulated. The proportion of cost avoidance caused by a given source of savings in a given year is calculated by multiplying FS by FT. The product of FT and FS is then subtracted from 1 and the result is multiplied by the annual baseline cost to give the annual cost under a software technology improvement program.

An example may make this computation clear. If one were to estimate the FS from EPCA in the year 2000 to be 80% and the fraction of software reused rather than being developed (FT) to be 12%, the resulting savings would be 0.80 * 0.12 = 0.096 or 9.6%. Subtracting this value from 1 gives 0.904, which could be thought of as a residual cost fraction (RCF), the fraction of costs left after avoidable end-product costs have been eliminated. Using the baseline development cost for the year 2000, which is computed (assuming 5% compounded growth from a 1992 value of $7.2B) to be $10.6B, the new costs would be $10.6B * 0.904 = $9.6B. This means $1B of savings from development reuse or EPCA would come in the year 2000. Similar calculations would be applied sequentially for PCA and PCR savings. For example, the FT and FS for PCA in 2000 are estimated to be 75% and 16%, respectively. Thus 0.75 * 0.16 = 0.12 or 12%. The RCF would be 1 - 0.12 = 0.88. Applying the RCF to the $9.6B yields $8.45B. Similarly for the PCR, FT and FS for 2000 are 75% and 7%, respectively. The RCF is calculated to be 0.948. Applying this to the $8.45B yields $8.01B. The difference between the baseline development estimate, $10.6B, and the estimated savings from all of the three sources, $8.01B, is the total dollar development savings, in this case, $2.59B in 2000.

The example above is summarized in Table 3.

**Table 3: Algebraic Example of Year-2000 Development EPCA Savings**

| Category | RCF | ADC | RADC | ADS |
|---|---|---|---|---|
| EPCA | 0.904 = 1 - (0.8 * 0.12) | $10.6B | $9.6B = $10.6B * 0.904 | $1.0B = $10.6B - $9.6B |
| PCA | 0.88 = 1 - (0.75 * 0.16) | $9.6B | $8.45B = $9.6B * 0.88 | $1.15B = $9.6B - $8.45B |
| PCR | 0.948 = 1 - (0.75 * .07) | $8.45B | $8.01B = $8.45B * 0.948 | $0.44B = $8.45B - $8.01B |
| Total ADS | | | | $2.59B |

Notes: ADS = annual development savings. RADC = residual annual development cost. ADC = annual development software cost. RCF = residual cost fraction; computed as 1 - (FT x FS) for each component of savings. ADS = ADC - RADC. RADC = ADC x RCF.

## 2.3 Calculating Maintenance Savings

The analysis also estimates the savings for maintenance resulting from software technology improvements for the years 1992 to 2008. For each year, FTs and FSs are estimated. The technologies and processes that cause these savings are listed below.

- EPCA: (1) use of COTS and (2) the megaprogramming technology described in the SWTS: Ada generics, domain-specific software architectures (DSSAs), module composition technology, application generators.

- PCA: (1) improved maintenance process and (2) improved understandability of software.
- PCR: (1) increased use of tools and environments and (2) better structured, easy-to-modify software.

Table 4 presents a similar algebraic example of the maintenance savings for EPCA in the year 2000. The Baseline annual maintenance software cost is computed to be \$24.8B; the three sources of software technology savings reduce this to \$19.1B, for a total savings of \$5.7B.

**Table 4: Algebraic Example of Year-2000 Maintenance EPCA Savings**

| Category | RCF | AMC | RAMC | AMS |
|---|---|---|---|---|
| EPCA | 0.872 = 1 - (0.16 * 0.8) | \$24.8B | \$21.6B = \$24.8B * 0.872 | \$3.2B = \$24.8B - \$21.6B |
| PCA | 0.91 = 1 - (0.65 * 0.14) | \$21.6B | \$19.7B = \$21.6B * 0.91 | \$1.9B = \$21.6B - \$19.7B |
| PCR | 0.97 = 1 - (0.7 * 0.05) | \$19.7B | \$19.1B = \$19.7B * 0.97 | \$0.6B = \$19.7B - \$19.1B |
| Total AMS | | | | \$5.7B |

Notes: AMS = annual maintenance savings. RAMC = residual annual maintenance cost. AMC = annual maintenance software cost. RCF = residual cost fraction, computed as 1 - (FT x FS) for each component of savings. AMS = AMC - RAMC. RAMC = AMC x RCF.

### 2.4 Calculating ROI and NPV

To achieve the software development and maintenance cost savings discussed above, a substantial investment by the DoD would be required. To assess the potential worth of such investments, two financial measures of merit are computed. One measure is the ROI. The other measure is NPV. Both measures are calculated from constant dollars and account for time value of money by "discounting" the benefits (in this case the DoD cost savings) and the costs (i.e., the DoD investment).[3]

The formula used in the NPV computation can be shown as:

$$\text{NPV} = \sum_{t=0}^{m} \frac{(S_t - C_t)}{(1+d)^t}$$

where

$S_t$ = the cost savings for year *t*.

$C_t$ = the dollar value of the investment in year *t*.

d = the discount rate.

m = the number of years over which the calculations are made.

In this case, m = 16, and t = 0 corresponds to the year 1992.

To be consistent with OMB guidelines [OMB72], we assume the discount rate to be 10%. The resulting NPV figure is the present value (or worth today) of the stream of savings derived from the stream of investments made over the period of this analysis.

The ROI computation also is closely related to the NPV figure. The ROI measure is the ratio of the discounted savings to the discounted costs. Algebraically this can be shown as:

$$\text{ROI} = \frac{\sum_{t=0}^{m} \frac{S_t}{(1+d)^t}}{\sum_{t=0}^{m} \frac{C_t}{(1+d)^t}},$$

---

[3]Constant dollars are used so that, after adjusting for inflation, a dollar in the future has the same purchasing power as a dollar in the present. Discounted dollars are used so that, after discounting, a future dollar has the same value to us now as does a dollar in the present.

where the variables are defined as above.

The ROI figure used in this analysis is interpreted as the return for a dollar of investment when adjusted for price-level changes and the time value of money. For example, if the ROI is computed to be 6, then this figure suggests that for every constant, time-discounted dollar invested by the government, 6 constant, time-discounted dollars in savings will be returned.

## 3. Inputs to the Return on Investment Analysis

This section presents the input estimates used in the ROI analysis and the rationales for the numerical values estimated. As the ROI model is automated with adjustable parameters, the effect of alternative estimates can readily be calculated. The input estimates discussed below are:

1. Reuse (EPCA) inputs.
2. Working-smarter (PCA) inputs.
3. Working-faster (PCR) inputs.
4. DoD Baseline software costs.
5. Current and Achievable software technology investment levels.

### 3.1 Reuse (End Product Cost Avoidance) Inputs

The reuse fraction of time FT (EPCA) represents the fraction of DoD software reused across all DoD software development or maintenance activities that would otherwise have involved developing or modifying code at the Ada or COBOL level, or below (e.g., assembly code). As discussed in [BOEHM81] and elsewhere, there are various levels of reuse of code, specifications, and other software artifacts that lead to different levels of savings. For this analysis, FT is defined to cover only situations where essentially all code in a module is reused, or where coding is avoided by using very high level languages (VHLLs) or application generators.

For module reuse, extensive measured experience in the NASA Software Engineering Laboratory has indicated that the average savings fraction FS (EPCA) is

0.8 [BASILI81, SEID89]. Savings from VHLLs or application generators have typically varied from 0.5 to 0.9, depending primarily on the maturity of the technology.

**Development.** Early gains will come primarily from use of commercial off-the-shelf (COTS) software, particularly in the Corporate Information Management (CIM) area. In the mid-90s, module reuse supported by process improvements and repositories (e.g., STARS, RAPID) will boost reuse. In the late 90s, major gains will begin from investments in DoD DSSAs and early module-composition megaprogramming technology. At this point, gains from the reduced-effort Current Program begin to tail off, while gains from the Achievable Program are estimated to increase. These comparative trends are estimated to continue through about 2003-2008, as the additional megaprogramming technology in the Achievable Program matures. Some factors, particularly cultural inertia and the rapid technical change in underlying computer architectures will serve as retardants to progress toward complete, reuse-based software development.

The resulting estimated development EPCA time series are as follows:

**Table 5: Estimated Development EPCA Time Series**

| Current Program | 1992 | 1994 | 1996 | 1998 | 2000 | 2002 | 2004 | 2006 | 2008 |
|---|---|---|---|---|---|---|---|---|---|
| FT (EPCA) | .005 | .02 | .05 | .08 | .12 | .15 | .18 | .20 | .22 |
| FS (EPCA) | .70 | .75 | .78 | .80 | .80 | .80 | .80 | .80 | .80 |
| **Achievable Program** | **1992** | **1994** | **1996** | **1998** | **2000** | **2002** | **2004** | **2006** | **2008** |
| FT (EPCA) | .005 | .02 | .06 | .12 | .20 | .30 | .40 | .47 | .52 |
| FS (EPCA) | .70 | .75 | .78 | .80 | .82 | .84 | .86 | .87 | .88 |

**Maintenance.** Maintenance reuse savings will come from two primary sources:

- Use of COTS software: the net savings will be the difference between the amount of non-COTS modification that would otherwise have been needed, and the COTS maintenance fees.
- Modification avoidance via megaprogramming technology: initially Ada generics and similar capabilities, and eventually maintenance via module replacement based on DSSA and module-composition capabilities, plus life-cycle gains from VHLLs and application generators. These modularity-based savings come both from reengineering existing software and introduction of newly developed module-based software into the downstream maintenance inventory.

Estimated gains in the early 90s come primarily from replacement of DoD-unique software inventory by COTS, particularly in the CIM area. As in the development phase, estimated maintenance gains in the late 90s and 2000s become larger for the Achievable Program than for the Current Program, because of the stronger DSSA, VHLL, application generator, and module composition capabilities made available to DoD via the Achievable Program.

The resulting estimated maintenance EPCA time series are as follows:

**Table 6: Estimated Maintenance EPCA Time Series**

| Current Program | 1992 | 1994 | 1996 | 1998 | 2000 | 2002 | 2004 | 2006 | 2008 |
|---|---|---|---|---|---|---|---|---|---|
| FT (EPCA) | .02 | .061 | .085 | .12 | .16 | .20 | .22 | .24 | .26 |
| FS (EPCA) | .70 | .75 | .78 | .80 | .80 | .80 | .80 | .80 | .80 |

| Achievable Program | 1992 | 1994 | 1996 | 1998 | 2000 | 2002 | 2004 | 2006 | 2008 |
|---|---|---|---|---|---|---|---|---|---|
| FT (EPCA) | .02 | .071 | .12 | .18 | .25 | .32 | .40 | .48 | .56 |
| FS (EPCA) | .70 | .75 | .78 | .80 | .81 | .82 | .83 | .84 | .85 |

### 3.2 Working-Smarter (Process Cost Avoidance) Inputs

A quantitative understanding of the distribution of cost across the various activities involved in the software process is crucial to estimating process cost savings, both for process cost avoidance (PCA) and process cost reduction (PCR). The analysis below is based on a value-chain analysis [PORTER80] of typical process cost distributions, based on a sample of 40 DoD software projects [BOEHM88]. The potential effects of process and tool improvements on each of the canonical software development and maintenance activities (requirements analysis, prototyping, design, etc.) are estimated below, based on their initial value-chain cost distributions.

Table 7 shows the results of the analysis for software development. The first column shows the current cost distribution across development activities: 4% of current costs (assuming an overall system design as starting point) go to software requirements analysis, while 15% goes to coding and related activities such as unit test. Columns two and three show the potential effects of working-smarter process improvements. The effort devoted to requirements analysis is increased from 4% to 6%, while the effort devoted to coding activities is decreased from 15% to 7% (reduced rework caused by better requirements and design, reduced project turbulence because of better, pre-verified interface definitions, and reduced make-work such as full-scale critical design review).

Columns four and five show the potential effects of tools and environmental support to make the remaining essential work go faster. For requirements analysis, better modeling and specification tools could reduce the 6% figure to 5%. For coding-related activities, better tools for automating portions of the coding and unit testing process, and better support of group-coordination and change-effect processing could reduce the 7% figure to 5%. The final column shows the resulting normalized cost percentages: both requirements analysis and code would consume 11% of the reduced total cost.

The total potential working-smarter (or PCA) savings is thus 37% of the original total. This figure is consistent with [JONES86], which has rework costs increasing to 50% for very large projects. The subsequent potential working-faster (or PCR) savings is 30% of the post-PCA costs or 19% of the original total. This figure is conservative with respect to the 33%-50% productivity gains for tool and environment support in software cost estimation models such as the Constructive Cost Model (COCOMO) and Ada COCOMO [BOEHM81, BOEHM89].

Table 8 shows the counterpart cost breakdown and potential working-smarter (PCA) and working-faster (PCR) savings for maintenance. Overall potential PCA savings are 39%; PCR potential savings are 31% of the remainder, or 19% of the original total.

**Table 7: Potential Software Development Savings - Value Chain Analysis**

| Activity | Current Cost % | Work-Smarter Savings | Remainder | Work-Faster Savings | Overall Remainder | Revised Cost% |
|---|---|---|---|---|---|---|
| Rqts. Analysis | 4 | +2 | 6 | -1 | 5 | 11 |
| Prototyping | 3 | +2 | 5 | -1 | 4 | 9 |
| Rqts. Trace | 4 | -1 | 3 | -1 | 2 | 4 |
| Design | 12 | -1 | 11 | -3 | 8 | 18 |
| Code | 15 | -8 | 7 | -2 | 5 | 11 |
| Integration & Test | 14 | -8 | 6 | -1 | 5 | 11 |
| Documentation | 15 | -8 | 7 | -3 | 4 | 9 |
| Config. Mgmt. | 5 | -1 | 4 | -2 | 2 | 4 |
| Management | 16 | -8 | 8 | -2 | 6 | 14 |
| Other* | 12 | -6 | 6 | -3 | 3 | 7 |
| Total | 100 | -37 | 63 | -19 (30% of 63) | 44 | 100 |

* "Other" includes project communications, quality assurance functions, training functions, security management, simulation.

**Development Process Cost Avoidance**. The fraction of time process improvements are used, FT (PCA), is estimated as the fraction of the DoD software performer base that has improved itself at least one level on the five-level Software Engineering Institute (SEI) process maturity assessment scale [HUMPHREY89].

Most contractors and internal DoD software organizations are still at Level 1. The prospect of using maturity level as a contractor source selection criterion, or recent directives for internal CIM organizations to use SEI assessments [STRASSMANN91], will cause relatively rapid early increases in FT (PCA). However, cultural inertia will still leave some DoD software projects at Level 1 in the year 2008.

**Table 8: Potential Software Maintenance Savings - Value Chain Analysis**

| Activity | Current Cost % | Work-Smarter Savings | Remainder | Work-Faster Savings | Overall Remainder | Revised Cost% |
|---|---|---|---|---|---|---|
| Rqts. Analysis | 6 | 0 | 6 | -1 | 5 | 12 |
| Proto-typing | 0 | +2 | 2 | 0 | 2 | 5 |
| Rqts. Trace | 2 | +1 | 3 | -1 | 2 | 5 |
| Design | 11 | -3 | 8 | -2 | 6 | 14 |
| Code | 14 | -7 | 7 | -2 | 5 | 12 |
| Integration & Test | 20 | -10 | 10 | -3 | 7 | 17 |
| Documen-tation | 16 | -9 | 7 | -3 | 4 | 9 |
| Config. Mgmt. | 4 | 0 | 4 | -2 | 2 | 5 |
| Manage-ment | 15 | -7 | 8 | -2 | 6 | 14 |
| Other* | 12 | -6 | 6 | -3 | 3 | 7 |
| Total | 100 | -39 | 61 | -19 (31% of 61) | 42 | 100 |

* "Other" includes project communications, quality assurance functions, training functions, security management, simulation.

The fractional savings FS (PCA) from working smarter is estimated as a function of the average number of process maturity levels that organizations developing DoD software have progressed. Improving one level of maturity is estimated to produce an 0.14 savings fraction; two levels, 0.24; three levels, 0.32; and four levels,

0.37. The SEI is collecting data to provide better quantitative information on the effects of process maturity on software costs.

The resulting estimated development PCA time series are given in Table 9. The FT series are the same for the Current and Achievable Programs, as process maturity adoptions are primarily a function of DoD management initiatives. The FS are estimated to be considerably higher in the out-years for the Achievable Program, because of significantly better technology support of tailorable process models, process programming, prototyping, and knowledge-based risk management aids.

**Table 9: Estimated Development PCA Time Series**

| Current Program | 1992 | 1994 | 1996 | 1998 | 2000 | 2002 | 2004 | 2006 | 2008 |
|---|---|---|---|---|---|---|---|---|---|
| FT (PCA) | .05 | .25 | .50 | .65 | .75 | .80 | .85 | .89 | .92 |
| FS (PCA) | .12 | .13 | .14 | .15 | .16 | .18 | .20 | .22 | .24 |
| **Achievable Program** | **1992** | **1994** | **1996** | **1998** | **2000** | **2002** | **2004** | **2006** | **2008** |
| FT (PCA) | .05 | .25 | .50 | .65 | .75 | .80 | .85 | .89 | .92 |
| FS (PCA) | .12 | .14 | .16 | .20 | .24 | .27 | .30 | .32 | .34 |

**Maintenance.** Estimated FT adoption rates for maintenance process improvements show significant increases similar to those for development. The maintenance rates are somewhat lower, since maintenance processes are more difficult to decouple from their large inventories of existing software. The estimated FS rework-avoidance savings are lower than development savings for similar reasons, but this is compensated for by technology contributions to process cost avoidance. Software understanding and reengineering technology will avoid much of the cost in software maintenance currently devoted to the process of understanding poorly structured and poorly explained software. This cost is estimated to be as high as 47% of the maintenance effort [PARIKH83]. Improving one level of process maturity is estimated to produce a combined rework-avoidance and understanding-improvement savings fraction of 0.10; two levels, 0.18; three levels, 0.26, and four levels, 0.34.

As with development PCA, the FS estimates for the Achievable Program are considerably higher in the out-years than for the Current Program, because of significantly better technology support for software understanding and reengineering. The resulting maintenance PCA time series are given below.

**Table 10: Estimated Maintenance PCA Time Series**

| Current Program | 1992 | 1994 | 1996 | 1998 | 2000 | 2002 | 2004 | 2006 | 2008 |
|---|---|---|---|---|---|---|---|---|---|
| FT (PCA) | .05 | .20 | .40 | .55 | .65 | .70 | .75 | .80 | .84 |
| FS (PCA) | .10 | .10 | .11 | .12 | .14 | .16 | .17 | .18 | .19 |
| **Achievable Program** | **1992** | **1994** | **1996** | **1998** | **2000** | **2002** | **2004** | **2006** | **2008** |
| FT (PCA) | .05 | .20 | .40 | .55 | .65 | .70 | .75 | .80 | .84 |
| FS (PCA) | .10 | .11 | .13 | .16 | .20 | .25 | .30 | .35 | .40 |

### 3.3 Working-Faster (Process Cost Reduction) Inputs

The fraction of time PCR tools and environments are used FT (PCR) is estimated as the fraction of the DoD software performer base that has improved itself at least one level on an ascending computer-aided software engineering (CASE) maturity hierarchy for tools and environment support. The maintenance PCR savings are also enhanced by re-engineering technology improvements and by better-structured software entering the maintenance inventory. The CASE maturity levels and their corresponding savings fractions FS (PCR) for development and maintenance are given in Table 11.

**Table 11: Levels of Tool and Environment Support**

| CASE Maturity Level | Development FS (PCR) | Maintenance FS (PCR) |
|---|---|---|
| 1. Minimal | 0.00 | 0.00 |
| 2. 1991 CASE Tools | 0.07 | 0.06 |
| 3. Integrated CASE Environment | 0.14 | 0.14 |
| 4. Integrated, Fully-Populated CASE Environment | 0.23 | 0.24 |
| 5. Proactive CASE Environment | 0.30 | 0.32 |

The savings fractions at the lower levels are low because CASE tools are frequently purchased and installed without the associated tailoring, training, and process integration needed to make them pay off. In some situations, indiscriminate purchasing of CASE tools has actually reduced productivity.

**Development and Maintenance.** The resulting development and maintenance PCR time series are given in Tables 12 and 13. The comparisons between the Current Program and Achievable Program are similar to those for PCA; the estimated FT (PCR) adoption rates are the same, while the estimated FS (PCR) savings fractions are considerably higher in the out-years because of the significantly higher levels of DoD-responsive advanced CASE technology.

The FS (PCR) are net savings, which have reduced the gross savings by 0.05, reflecting the typical 5% added to the cost of doing business for the purchase, amortization, and maintenance fees for CASE tools and workstations. Thus, the 1992 development savings fraction is not 0.07, as might be expected from Table 11, but rather 0.02.

**Table 12: Estimated Development PCR Time Series**

| Current Program | 1992 | 1994 | 1996 | 1998 | 2000 | 2002 | 2004 | 2006 | 2008 |
|---|---|---|---|---|---|---|---|---|---|
| FT (PCR) | .15 | .35 | .50 | .65 | .75 | .80 | .85 | .89 | .92 |
| FS (PCR) | .02 | .04 | .05 | .06 | .07 | .08 | .09 | .10 | .11 |
| Achievable Program | 1992 | 1994 | 1996 | 1998 | 2000 | 2002 | 2004 | 2006 | 2008 |
| FT (PCR) | .15 | .35 | .50 | .65 | .75 | .80 | .85 | .89 | .92 |
| FS (PCR) | .02 | .04 | .07 | .11 | .15 | .18 | .21 | .23 | .25 |

## 3.4 DoD Baseline Software Costs

The DoD baseline software cost profile from which savings are calculated is that discussed in Section 2.1, in which no significant DoD efforts are undertaken to improve DoD software technology. Past experience indicates that one would expect a

4% per year general improvement in software productivity to apply to the DoD. The Baseline scenario limits DoD software demand growth to 4%.

**Table 13: Estimated Maintenance PCR Time Series**

| Current Program | 1992 | 1994 | 1996 | 1998 | 2000 | 2002 | 2004 | 2006 | 2008 |
|---|---|---|---|---|---|---|---|---|---|
| FT (PCR) | .10 | .30 | .45 | .60 | .70 | .75 | .80 | .84 | .87 |
| FS (PCR) | .01 | .02 | .03 | .04 | .05 | .06 | .07 | .08 | .09 |
| **Achievable Program** | **1992** | **1994** | **1996** | **1998** | **2000** | **2002** | **2004** | **2006** | **2008** |
| FT (PCR) | .10 | .30 | .45 | .60 | .70 | .75 | .80 | .84 | .87 |
| FS (PCR) | .01 | .03 | .06 | .09 | .13 | .17 | .21 | .24 | .27 |

As discussed in Section 2.1, it was assumed that the DoD will spend $24B in 1992 for software and that this $24B can be separated into development (30%) and maintenance (70%). A 5% inflation rate is also assumed, yielding a net growth in DoD software expenditures of 5% per year compounded over the period of the analysis. The results are shown below in Table 14.

**Table 14: Baseline Estimates of DoD Software Expenditures (Billions of Then-Year Dollars)**

| $B | 1992 | 1994 | 1996 | 1998 | 2000 | 2002 | 2004 | 2006 | 2008 |
|---|---|---|---|---|---|---|---|---|---|
| Total DoD Software | $24.0 | 26.5 | 29.2 | 32.2 | 35.5 | 39.1 | 43.1 | 47.5 | 52.4 |
| Maintenance | 16.8 | 18.5 | 20.4 | 22.5 | 24.8 | 27.4 | 30.2 | 33.3 | 36.7 |
| Development | 7.2 | 7.9 | 8.8 | 9.6 | 10.6 | 11.7 | 12.9 | 14.3 | 15.7 |

Note: In this table, as with all tables that report spreadsheet results, the columns do not always add or subtract exactly because of rounding.

To account for the price-level changes over time, the estimates of savings and investments have been deflated to constant 1992 dollars. Hereafter, the results of the analyses will be presented in both then-year and constant dollars.

### 3.5 Investment Levels for Current and Achievable Software Technology Programs

As described in the introduction to this section, the Current scenario assumes that the $219M/year level of funding provided in FY1996 for core software technologies will be continued over the entire time horizon.

The Achievable funding scenario is associated with an enhanced software technology program described in the SWTS. In then-year dollars, it involves a significant boost (to $568M) in DoD spending per year for software technologies for the time period 1992 through 2008. Using a 5% deflation rate, the $568M in 2008 dollars translates to $260M in constant 1992 dollars. The funding profiles are shown in Table 15.

## 4. Estimated Savings and ROIs

Figure 1 and Table 16 present the Baseline scenario results. These results suggest that total DoD spending for software will reach almost $52B by the year 2008. The maintenance fraction of the $52B total is estimated to be approximately $37B by 2008. The estimated expenditure for software development is $16B by the year 2008. In light of the planned decline in the DoD budget over the same period of time, if the software expenditures follow the pattern depicted by Figure 1, software will soon account for nearly 20% of the total DoD budget. Such out-year estimates may appear high, but some estimates of future aircraft and ship development costs have allocated 30% of the costs to software.

Figure 2 and Table 17 show the differences between the Baseline (no SWTS expenditures), the Current Program, and the Achievable Program. The incremental savings are the difference between the Current and Achievable scenarios. These results indicate that the Achievable funding scenario generates a stream of savings that are relatively small in the first several years but increase rapidly in the out years. For example, we estimate the Achievable Program scenario generates savings of approximately $38B then-year dollars or $17.5B constant 1992 dollars by the year 2008.

**Table 15: Investment Profiles for Current and Achievable SWTS Programs**

| Then-Year Dollars ($M) | 92 | 93 | 94 | 95 | 96 | 97 | 98 | 99 | 00 | 01 | 02 | 03 | 04 | 05 | 06 | 07 | 08 |
|---|---|---|---|---|---|---|---|---|---|---|---|---|---|---|---|---|---|
| Current | 194 | 194 | 197 | 195 | 192 | 192 | 192 | 192 | 192 | 192 | 192 | 192 | 192 | 192 | 192 | 192 | 192 |
| Ach. Add-on | 0 | 58 | 110 | 164 | 212 | 218 | 230 | 243 | 256 | 269 | 283 | 298 | 312 | 327 | 343 | 359 | 376 |
| Ada Add-on | | 30 | 20 | 10 | | | | | | | | | | | | | |
| Ach. Total | 194 | 282 | 327 | 369 | 404 | 410 | 422 | 435 | 448 | 461 | 475 | 490 | 504 | 519 | 535 | 551 | 568 |

| Constant 1992 Dollars ($M) | 92 | 93 | 94 | 95 | 96 | 97 | 98 | 99 | 00 | 01 | 02 | 03 | 04 | 05 | 06 | 07 | 08 |
|---|---|---|---|---|---|---|---|---|---|---|---|---|---|---|---|---|---|
| Current | 194 | 185 | 179 | 168 | 158 | 150 | 143 | 136 | 130 | 124 | 118 | 112 | 107 | 102 | 97 | 92 | 88 |
| Ach. Add-on | 0 | 55 | 100 | 142 | 174 | 171 | 172 | 173 | 173 | 173 | 174 | 174 | 174 | 173 | 173 | 173 | 172 |
| Ada Add-on | | 29 | 18 | 9 | 0 | 0 | 0 | 0 | 0 | 0 | 0 | 0 | 0 | 0 | 0 | 0 | 0 |
| Ach. Total | 194 | 269 | 297 | 319 | 332 | 321 | 315 | 309 | 303 | 297 | 292 | 286 | 281 | 275 | 270 | 265 | 260 |

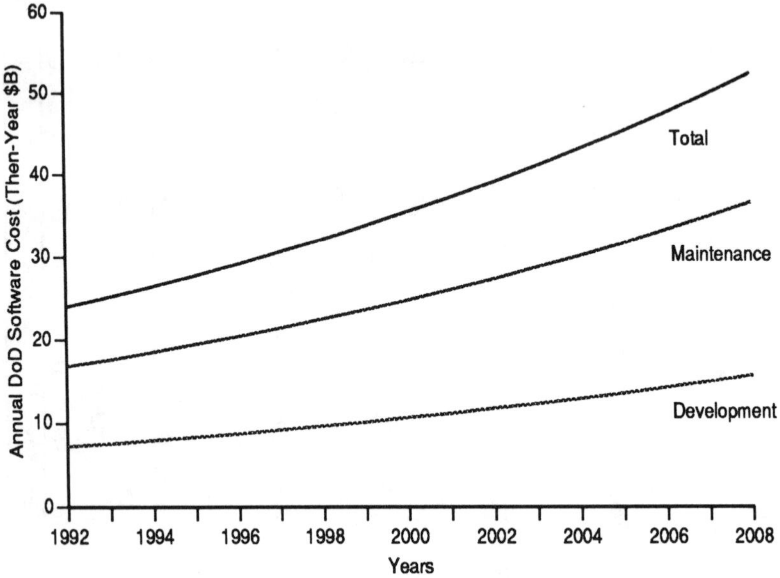


**Figure 1: Then-Year Baseline Software Expenditures by Software Life Cycle**

**Table 16: Baseline Software Expenditures by Software Life Cycle**

| Then-Year Dollars ($B) | 1992 | 1994 | 1996 | 1998 | 2000 | 2002 | 2004 | 2006 | 2008 |
|---|---|---|---|---|---|---|---|---|---|
| Total DoD Software | 24.0 | 26.5 | 29.2 | 32.2 | 35.5 | 39.1 | 43.1 | 47.5 | 52.4 |
| Maintenance | 16.8 | 18.5 | 20.4 | 22.5 | 24.8 | 27.4 | 30.2 | 33.3 | 36.7 |
| Development | 7.2 | 7.9 | 8.8 | 9.6 | 10.6 | 11.7 | 12.9 | 14.3 | 15.7 |
| Constant 1992 Dollars ($B) | 1992 | 1994 | 1996 | 1998 | 2000 | 2002 | 2004 | 2006 | 2008 |
| Total DoD Software | 24.0 | 24.0 | 24.0 | 24.0 | 24.0 | 24.0 | 24.0 | 24.0 | 24.0 |
| Maintenance | 16.8 | 16.8 | 16.8 | 16.8 | 16.8 | 16.8 | 16.8 | 16.8 | 16.8 |
| Development | 7.2 | 7.2 | 7.2 | 7.2 | 7.2 | 7.2 | 7.2 | 7.2 | 7.2 |

Note: In this table, as with all tables that report spreadsheet results, the columns do not always add or subtract exactly because of rounding.

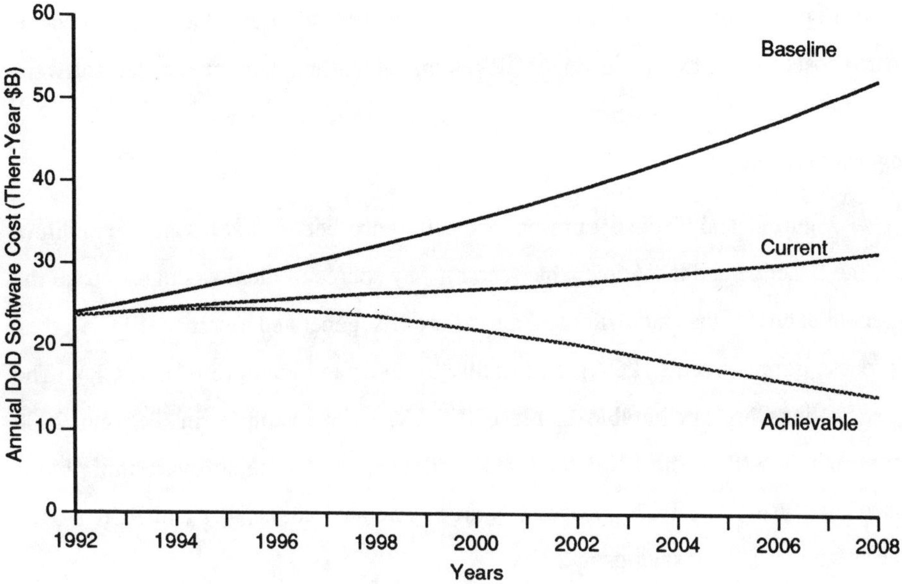


**Figure 2: Then-Year Total Software Expenditures from Baseline, Current, and Achievable Program**

**Table 17: Software Expenditure Savings from Current and Achievable Programs**

| Then-Year Dollars ($B) | 1992 | 1994 | 1996 | 1998 | 2000 | 2002 | 2004 | 2006 | 2008 |
|---|---|---|---|---|---|---|---|---|---|
| Current Scenario Savings | 0.4 | 1.8 | 3.6 | 5.8 | 8.5 | 11.3 | 14.1 | 17.3 | 20.8 |
| Achievable Scenario Savings | 0.4 | 2.0 | 4.7 | 8.5 | 13.3 | 18.7 | 24.9 | 31.3 | 38.1 |
| Incremental Savings | 0.0 | 0.2 | 1.1 | 2.7 | 4.9 | 7.3 | 10.8 | 14.0 | 17.3 |

| Constant 1992 Dollars ($B) | 1992 | 1994 | 1996 | 1998 | 2000 | 2002 | 2004 | 2006 | 2008 |
|---|---|---|---|---|---|---|---|---|---|
| Current Scenario Savings | 0.4 | 1.6 | 2.9 | 4.3 | 5.7 | 7.0 | 7.9 | 8.7 | 9.5 |
| Achievable Scenario Savings | 0.4 | 1.8 | 3.9 | 6.3 | 9.0 | 11.5 | 13.9 | 15.8 | 17.5 |
| Incremental Savings | 0.0 | 0.2 | 0.9 | 2.0 | 3.3 | 4.5 | 6.0 | 7.1 | 7.9 |

Note: In this table, as with all tables that report spreadsheet results, the columns do not always add or subtract exactly because of rounding.

Figure 3 and Table 18 compare the Baseline scenario costs and the Achievable scenario costs for the two main stages (development and maintenance) in the software life cycle. The relative proportion of development and maintenance costs does not change significantly.

Figure 4 and Table 19 present the difference between software expenditure under the Baseline and the Achievable scenarios by source of these savings. Recall the sequential nature of the calculations. Savings are first generated by reuse (EPCA), then by process improvements (PCA), and finally by tools and environments (PCR). The largest savings are attributable to reuse (EPCA). For example, in the year 2000 approximately \$7B of the \$13B then-year dollars saved by the software initiative is caused by reuse. The PCA (process) source generates about \$4B and PCR (tools) generates about \$2B in savings in 2000.

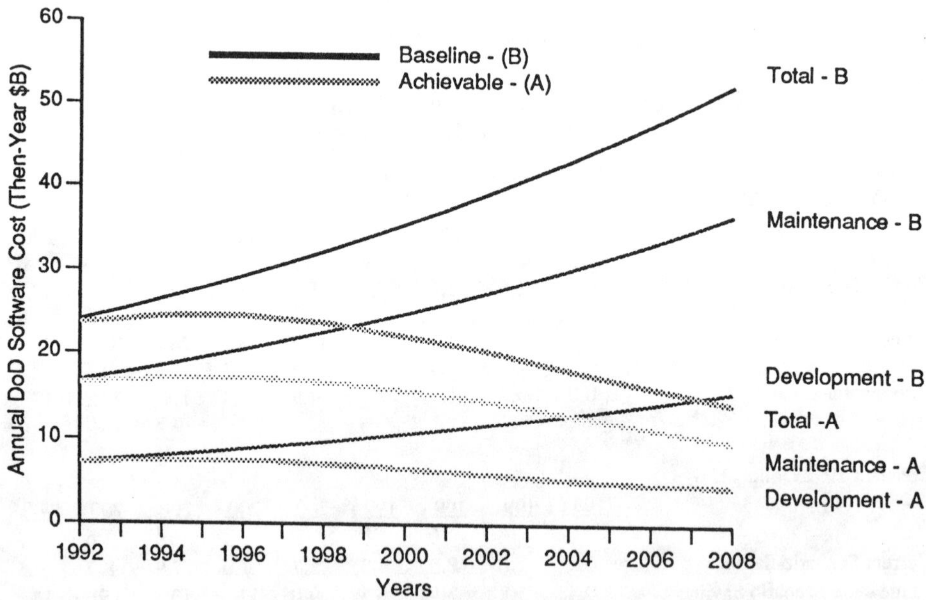


**Figure 3: Then-Year, Life-Cycle Baseline and Achievable Software Expenditures**

**Table 18: Baseline Versus Achievable Software Expenditure Savings by Life Cycle**

| Then-Year Dollars ($B) | 1992 | 1994 | 1996 | 1998 | 2000 | 2002 | 2004 | 2006 | 2008 |
|---|---|---|---|---|---|---|---|---|---|
| Maintenance Savings | 0.3 | 1.5 | 3.3 | 5.9 | 9.2 | 12.8 | 17.2 | 21.8 | 26.9 |
| Development Savings | 0.1 | 0.5 | 1.3 | 2.6 | 4.2 | 5.8 | 7.7 | 9.5 | 11.2 |
| Total Savings | 0.4 | 2.0 | 4.7 | 8.5 | 13.3 | 18.7 | 24.9 | 31.3 | 38.1 |

| Constant 1992 Dollars ($B) | 1992 | 1994 | 1996 | 1998 | 2000 | 2002 | 2004 | 2006 | 2008 |
|---|---|---|---|---|---|---|---|---|---|
| Maintenance Savings | 0.3 | 1.4 | 2.8 | 4.4 | 6.2 | 7.9 | 9.6 | 11.0 | 12.3 |
| Development Savings | 0.1 | 0.5 | 1.1 | 1.9 | 2.8 | 3.6 | 4.3 | 4.8 | 5.1 |
| Total Savings | 0.4 | 1.8 | 3.9 | 6.3 | 9.0 | 11.5 | 13.9 | 15.8 | 17.5 |

Note: In this table, as with all tables that report spreadsheet results, the columns do not always add or subtract exactly because of rounding.

## 4.1 NPV and ROI under Current and Achievable Scenarios

The ROI and NPV figures for the Current scenario are presented in Table 20. We can see that as early as 1994 the investment in software technology is paying back more than $5 for every $1 invested. By the final year the cumulative ROI indicates that the ratio of 27:1 is possible. The NPV figures indicate that the value today of the stream of savings generated by the current set of investments is approximately $34B in constant-1992 discounted dollars.

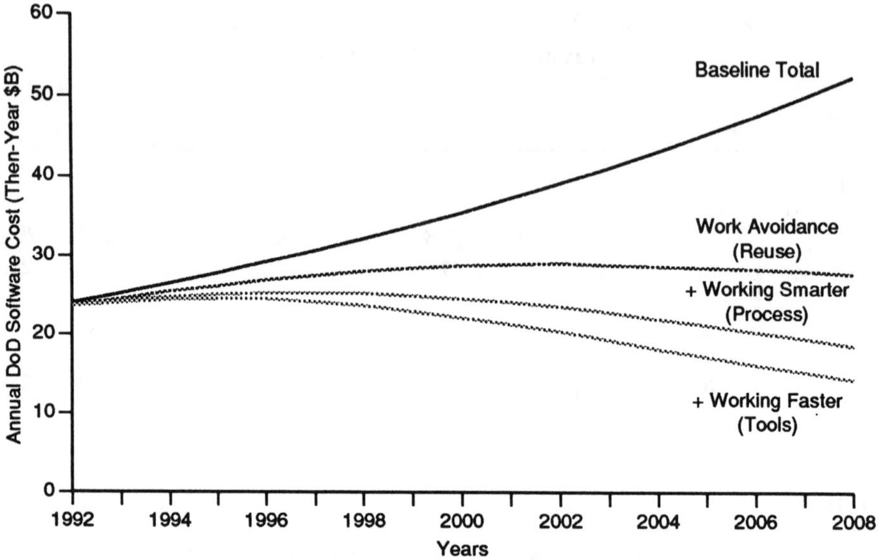


**Figure 4: Then-Year Baseline Versus Achievable Software Expenditure by Source of Savings**

**Table 19: Baseline Versus Achievable Software Savings by Source of Savings**

| Then-Year Dollars ($B) | 1992 | 1994 | 1996 | 1998 | 2000 | 2002 | 2004 | 2006 | 2008 |
|---|---|---|---|---|---|---|---|---|---|
| EPCA Savings | 0.3 | 1.1 | 2.3 | 4.2 | 6.8 | 10.1 | 14.5 | 19.2 | 24.6 |
| PCA Savings | 0.1 | 0.7 | 1.6 | 2.8 | 4.2 | 5.4 | 6.7 | 8.0 | 9.1 |
| PCR Savings | 0.0 | 0.3 | 0.7 | 1.5 | 2.4 | 3.1 | 3.8 | 4.1 | 4.3 |

| Constant 1992 Dollars ($B) | 1992 | 1994 | 1996 | 1998 | 2000 | 2002 | 2004 | 2006 | 2008 |
|---|---|---|---|---|---|---|---|---|---|
| EPCA Savings | 0.3 | 1.0 | 1.9 | 3.1 | 4.6 | 6.2 | 8.1 | 9.7 | 11.3 |
| PCA Savings | 0.1 | 0.6 | 1.3 | 2.1 | 2.8 | 3.3 | 3.7 | 4.0 | 4.2 |
| PCR Savings | 0.0 | 0.2 | 0.6 | 1.1 | 1.6 | 1.9 | 2.1 | 2.1 | 2.0 |

The ROI and NPV figures for the Achievable funding scenario are presented in Table 21. The cumulative ROI indicates that for every $1 dollar invested, $22 dollars are returned. The NPV of this scenario is about $54B.

The ROI for the Achievable Program is smaller then the Current Program ROI. However, the Achievable Program generates significantly larger NPV over the time period analyzed. The NPV and ROI results for both scenarios are summarized in Table 22. Also, two columns are included to show the difference between the NPV in the two scenarios and the ROI of the incremental investment. These columns show the incremental effect of the move from the Current to the Achievable Program. The NPV column indicates that the additional benefit to the Achievable Program over the Current Program is $19B. The ROI column indicates that the return on DoD investment that generates the incremental savings is about 17:1.

## 4.2 Excursions and Sensitivity Analysis

Three excursions from the Current and Achievable scenarios are presented below. They are included here to better illuminate some of the underlying assumptions that generate the results reported above, and the sensitivity of the results to those assumptions.

The three excursions are the effect on expenditures and savings of a 3% increase in the growth rate in software demand, the effect on ROI of large decreases in the predicted FT and FS levels, and the effect of slowing the transfer into use of these software technologies.

**Table 20: ROI and NPV For Current Funding Scenario (NPV in Millions of Constant-1992 Discounted Dollars)**

| Year | NPV | ROI |
|---|---|---|
| 1992 | 229 | 2.2 |
| 1994 | 2,162 | 5.2 |
| 1996 | 5,626 | 8.5 |
| 1998 | 10,126 | 12.0 |
| 2000 | 15,241 | 15.5 |
| 2002 | 20,513 | 18.9 |
| 2004 | 25,547 | 21.9 |
| 2006 | 30,196 | 24.7 |
| 2008 | 34,417 | 27.1 |

Note: NPV reported in millions of 1992 dollars.

**Table 21: ROI and NPV For Achievable Funding Scenario (NPV in Millions of Constant-1992 Discounted Dollars)**

| Year | NPV | ROI |
|---|---|---|
| 1992 | 229 | 2.2 |
| 1994 | 2,247 | 4.3 |
| 1996 | 6,528 | 6.7 |
| 1998 | 12,873 | 9.4 |
| 2000 | 20,721 | 12.3 |
| 2002 | 29,254 | 15.2 |
| 2004 | 37,952 | 17.8 |
| 2006 | 46,252 | 20.2 |
| 2008 | 53,920 | 22.3 |

Note: NPV reported in millions of 1992 dollars.

### 4.2.1 Effects of Additional Demand Growth on Software Expenditure

The results presented here are affected by the assumptions made about the effects of SWTS on software spending. These results are also influenced by the assumptions made about the growth in software demand. This section shows one excursion from the Baseline-Current-Achievable Programs discussed previously.

The excursion shown is to assume in the Baseline case an 8% growth in then-year dollar expenditure on software. Assuming that inflation remains at 5%, this results in a 3% annual growth in the overall work force necessary to develop and maintain DoD software.

Figure 5 and Table 23 show the results of this excursion. Figure 5 can be compared with Figure 2. A major difference between the two figures is that the Current Program in Figure 5 shows pronounced cost growth, while in Figure 2 the growth is just beginning in the later years. Only the Achievable Program is still able to reduce then-year spending on software.

**Table 22: ROI and NPV Comparisons between Current Funding and Achievable Funding Scenarios, in Constant-1992 Discounted Dollars ($M)**

| | Current | | Achievable | | Incremental Effect | |
|---|---|---|---|---|---|---|
| Year | NPV | ROI | Net PV | ROI | Net PV | ROI |
| 1992 | 229 | 2.2 | 229 | 2.2 | 0 | |
| 1994 | 2,162 | 5.2 | 2,247 | 4.3 | 86 | 1.5 |
| 1996 | 5,626 | 8.5 | 6,528 | 6.7 | 901 | 3.2 |
| 1998 | 10,126 | 12.0 | 12,873 | 9.4 | 2,747 | 5.5 |
| 2000 | 15,241 | 15.5 | 20,721 | 12.3 | 5,480 | 8.0 |
| 2002 | 20,513 | 18.9 | 29,254 | 15.2 | 8,740 | 10.5 |
| 2004 | 25,547 | 21.9 | 37,952 | 17.8 | 12,385 | 13.0 |
| 2006 | 30,196 | 24.7 | 46,252 | 20.2 | 16,056 | 15.2 |
| 2008 | 34,417 | 27.1 | 53,920 | 22.3 | 19,503 | 17.1 |

Note: NPV reported in millions of 1992 dollars. Incremental NPVs may not be the difference between Current and Achievable NPV because of rounding.

### 4.2.2 ROI Sensitivity to Decreased Estimates of FT and FS

This section shows the effects on ROI of significant decreases in the FT and FS savings parameters in the model. The conclusion of this analysis is that, even if the FT and FS estimates that generate the results shown in the Current and Achievable scenarios reported above are overestimated by a factor of two, and that the improvement between Current and Achievable programs is halved, both the Current and Achievable SWTS investment programs are still a good buy.

This analysis starts with the Current and Achievable scenarios reported above. Four excursions are calculated. The first excursion hypothesizes that all the FT and FS improvements between the Current and the Achievable case are too large, and deals with this by halving the improvement between Current and Achievable Programs. For example, Table 10 shows the maintenance FS for PCA of 0.14 and 0.20 for the Current and Achievable programs, respectively. This excursion reduces the 0.20 to 0.17.

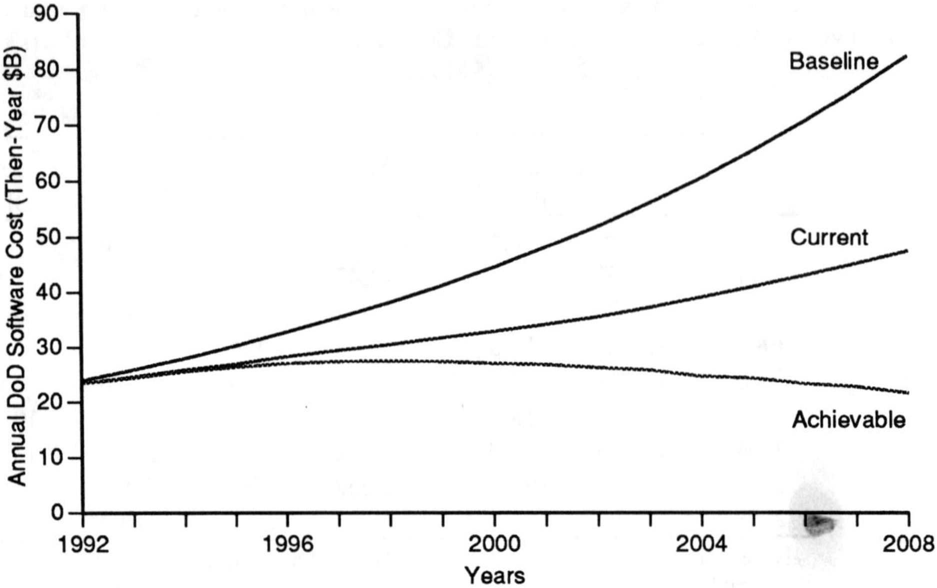


**Figure 5: Then-Year Effects of Additional Demand Growth**

The second excursion starts with the Current and Achievable Programs, and assumes that all FT for both programs are too high by a factor of two. From Table 5, the Development EPCA FT for the Current and Achievable Programs for the year 2000 are 0.12 and 0.20, respectively. In this excursion, they will be reduced to 0.06 and 0.10. This excursion will be used in Section 4.2.3 in the discussion on technology transfer leverage.

**Table 23: Effects of Additional Demand Growth in Then-Year and Constant 1992 Dollars ($Billions)**

| Then-Year Dollars ($B) | 1992 | 1994 | 1996 | 1998 | 2000 | 2002 | 2004 | 2006 | 2008 |
|---|---|---|---|---|---|---|---|---|---|
| Total DoD Software | 24.0 | 28.0 | 32.7 | 38.1 | 44.4 | 51.8 | 60.4 | 70.5 | 82.2 |
| Current Scenario Savings | 0.4 | 1.9 | 4.0 | 6.8 | 10.6 | 15.0 | 19.8 | 25.6 | 32.7 |
| Achievable Scenario Savings | 0.4 | 2.1 | 5.3 | 10.1 | 16.7 | 24.8 | 34.9 | 46.4 | 59.8 |
| Incremental Savings | 0.0 | 0.3 | 1.3 | 3.2 | 6.1 | 9.7 | 15.1 | 20.8 | 27.1 |
| Constant 1992 Dollars ($B) | 1992 | 1994 | 1996 | 1998 | 2000 | 2002 | 2004 | 2006 | 2008 |
| Total DoD Software | 24.0 | 25.5 | 27.0 | 28.7 | 30.4 | 32.3 | 34.2 | 36.3 | 38.5 |
| Current Scenario Savings | 0.4 | 1.7 | 3.3 | 5.1 | 7.2 | 9.3 | 11.2 | 13.2 | 15.3 |
| Achievable Scenario Savings | 0.4 | 1.9 | 4.3 | 7.6 | 11.4 | 15.4 | 19.8 | 23.9 | 28.0 |
| Incremental Savings | 0.0 | 0.2 | 1.0 | 2.4 | 4.2 | 6.1 | 8.6 | 10.7 | 12.7 |

Note: In this table, as with all tables that report spreadsheet results, the columns do not always add or subtract exactly because of rounding.

The third excursion starts again with the Current and Achievable Programs, and assumes that all FS and FT for both programs are too high by a factor of two. For example, from Table 10, the maintenance PCA FT and FS are 0.65 and 0.14 for the Current Program, and 0.65 and 0.20 for the Achievable Program. In this excursion, they will be reduced to 0.325 and 0.07, and 0.325 and 0.10, respectively. This results in the savings proportions (FT * FS) being reduced by a factor of four. The fourth and final excursion sequentially applies the reductions for the first and third excursion. Using the data from Table 10 above, the final values are 0.325 and 0.07, and 0.325 and 0.085, respectively.

The ROI generated by these excursions are shown in Table 24. The Current, Achievable, and Incremental ROI in the first line are reproduced from Table 22. The four excursions are identified numerically. The Incremental ROI for excursion one is calculated from the original Current Program and the excursion one Achievable Program, and the incremental ROI for excursion four is based on the Current ROI from excursion three and the Achievable ROI from excursion four.

These ROI show that the SWTS expenditures are cost-effective even if the FS and FT estimates are high by a factor of two; and that the Achievable Program is cost-effective even in the face of an additional halving of the FS and FT improvements from the Current Program. That is, the worst case Current Program ROI is still 7.5, the worst case Achievable ROI is 5.1, and the incremental ROI between these two is 2.5. As these ROI calculations are based on discounted dollars, any ROI greater than 1 is cost-effective.

**Table 24: ROI for FT and FS Decreases**

| Case | Current Program ROI | Achievable Program ROI | Incremental ROI |
|---|---|---|---|
| Current and Achievable Program | 27.1 | 22.3 | 17.1 |
| 1. Reduce Achievable FT and FS Improvements by 50% of Difference from Current Program | 27.1 | 18.5 | 9.0 |
| 2. Reduce FT Values by 50% | 14.2 | 12.3 | 10.2 |
| 3. Reduce FT and FS Values by 50% | 7.5 | 6.4 | 5.3 |
| 4. Apply Both 1 and 3 above | 7.5 | 5.1 | 2.5 |

Note: ROI is cumulative savings over cumulative DoD investment, both in constant, discounted dollars.

### 4.2.3 Technology Transfer Leverage

Changes in the FT coefficients show changes in the rate of adoption of SWTS technology. Case 2 in Figure 24 indicates that a 50% reduction in these adoption rates corresponds to a roughly 50% reduction in the return on investment in the the Current and Achievable Programs. In these cases, the Current ROI decreases from 27.1 to 14.2 and the Achievable ROI decreases from 22.3 to 12.3. This approximately proportional relationship between changes in FT and resulting changes in ROI is characteristic of the model.

This relationship between changes in FT and changes in ROI points out a tremendous leverage opportunity for technology transition initiatives to reduce the current, typical, 18-year delay [REDWINE85] between the emergence of an enabling software technology and its common operational use. If such initiatives can achieve even a modest reduction of this delay down to 15 years, the DoD ROI would increase roughly by a factor of 20%.

### 4.2.4 Meeting the SWTS Factor-of-Two Objective

Data generated from the ROI analysis can be used to assess whether the SWTS could meet its stated objective of reducing DoD software costs by a factor of two by the year 2000. Table 25 reproduces data from Tables 16 and 17 for the years 2000, 2002, and 2004. The data show the no-investment Baseline, the savings from the Baseline that will occur with the investments in the Achievable program, and the DoD software costs estimated if the Achievable program investments are undertaken.

From these data, a cost reduction factor (CRF) can be generated. This factor is the ratio of the Baseline costs over the remaining costs once the program is implemented. If the CRF is greater than or equal to two, the SWTS investments have met their objective.

With the assumptions in the model, the Achievable Program CRF does not exceed two until slightly after FY2002. With less conservative assumptions, for example the more aggressive technology transition effort discussed in Section 3.5, the factor-of-two cost objective appears reachable by the year 2000 for the Achievable Program. It does not appear reachable by the Current Program, although the cost reductions are still quite large.

**Table 25: Data on Factor-of-Two Cost Reductions**

| Program | Expenditures, Savings, and Cost Reduction Factors by Years | | |
|---|---|---|---|
| | 2000 | 2002 | 2004 |
| Baseline Costs | $35.5 | $39.1 | $43.1 |
| Achievable Program Savings | $13.3 | $18.7 | $24.9 |
| Remaining DoD Costs | $22.2 | $20.4 | $18.2 |
| Achievable Cost Reduction Factor (CRF) | 1.60 | 1.92 | 2.37 |
| Current Program CRF | 1.31 | 1.41 | 1.49 |

Notes: Dollars in then-year billions, CRF is a ratio of baseline costs over remaining DoD costs.

## 5. Summary and Conclusions

The major questions posed in Section 1 have the following answers:

- Can the Current software technology program be justified with respect to the no-investment Baseline situation? Yes. The net present value generated by the Current Program is $34 billion. The return on investment is 27:1.

- Can the Achievable Program be justified with respect to the Current Program? Yes. The incremental net present value is $19 billion. The incremental return on investment is about 17:1. The incremental ROI from the Achievable Program is smaller than the ROI of the Current Program. This is the result of the Current Program's opportunity to work the high-leverage areas first. However, a DoD investment that pays $17 for each dollar invested is extremely cost-effective.

- Can the SWTS meet its objective of reducing software costs by a factor of two by the year 2000?

  Answer: Only with less conservative assumptions than those used in the analysis. Using the conservative assumptions, the Achievable Program has an estimated cost reduction factor of 1.60 by 2000 and reaches a factor of 2 slightly after the year 2002. However, with moderately less conservative but quite responsible assumptions, the objective can be reached by the Achievable Program. The corresponding cost reduction factor for the Current Program is in the 1.3-1.4 range.

An even stronger case for the Achievable Program is evident, once more realistic projections of DoD software demand are used. As seen in Figure 5, with even a 3% increase in software demand over the conservative constant-1992-dollar demand projection, the Current Program is unable to hold the line on out-year DoD software costs, while the Achievable Program continues to reduce out-year DoD software costs.

Excursions are also presented to show that the Current and Achievable Programs are cost-effective even if savings estimates are optimistic. Table 24 summarizes ROI results that indicate that even if the FT and FS for the Current and Achievable Programs are over-estimated by a factor of two, the savings still justify the SWTS investment.

**Acknowledgements:**

I would like to thank Dr. Thomas Frazier of IDA for a number of useful refinements of the model; and Dr. Frazier, Bruce Angier, Elizabeth Bailey, K.L. Wilson, and Catherine McDonald of IDA for generating and refining the automated version of the model. Dr. Jack Kramer of DARPA and Paul Strassman of OSD provided valuable suggestions in applying the model to the DoD STARS program and the DoD Corporate Information Management Initiative.

**References:**

[AVWK91] *Aviation Week & Space Technology*, March 18, 1991, Vol. 134, No. 11.

[BASILI81] Basili, V.R. and Freburger, K., "Programming Measurement and Estimation in the Software Engineering Laboratory," *Journal of Systems and Software*, February 1981.

[BOEHM81] Boehm, B.W., *Software Engineering Economics*, Prentice Hall, Englewood, NJ, 1981.

[BOEHM88] Boehm, B.W. and Papaccio, P., "Understanding and Controlling Software Costs," *IEEE Transactions on Software Engineering*, October 1988, pp. 1462-1477.

[BOEHM89] Boehm, B.W. and Royce, W.E., "Ada COCOMO," *Proceedings of the Fourth COCOMO Users' Group Meeting*, SEI, November 1989.

[BOEHM91a] Boehm, B.W., and Castor, V.L., (ed), "Draft DoD Software Technology Strategy," ODDR&E, December 1991.

[BOEHM91b] Boehm, B.W., Frazier, T.P., Angier, B., Bailey, E.K., and Wilson, K.L., *A User's Guide For The Software Technology Economic Impact Model*, Institute for Defense Analyses, IDA Document D-971, October 1991.

[EIA90] *EIA Information System Forecast for the 1990's: the 2nd Annual Federal Information Systems Conference Final Report*, Requirements Committee, Government Division, Electronics Industry Association, 1990, Alexandria, VA, May 30.

[HUMPHREY89] Humphrey, W. S., Kitson, D. H., and Kasse, T. C., *The State of Software Engineering Practice: A Preliminary Report*, CMU/SEI-89-TR-1 or ESD-TR-89-01, Software Engineering Institute, February 1989.

[JONES 86] Jones, T.C., *Programming Productivity*, McGraw Hill, 1986.

[LEVITAN88] Levitan, K. B., Salasin, J., Frazier, T. P., and Angier, B. N., *Final Report on the Status of Software Obsolescence in the DoD*, IDA Paper P-2136, Institute for Defense Analyses, August 1988.

[MARTIN83] Martin, E., "The Context of STARS," *Computer*, Vol. 16, No. 13, November 1983, pp. 14-17.

[OMB72] Office of Management and Budget, "Discount Rates to be Used in Evaluating Time-Distributed Costs and Benefits," Circular No. A-94, March 27, 1972.

[PARIKH83] Parikh, G. and Zvegintzov, N., "The World of Software Maintenance," *Tutorial on Software Maintenance*, IEEE Computer Society Press, 1983, pp. 1-3.

[PORTER80] Porter, Michael E., *Competitive Strategy*, New York: The Free Press, 1980.

[REDWINE85] Redwine, Samuel T., and Riddle, William E., "Software Technology Maturation," *Proceedings, 8th International Conference on Software Engineering*, IEEE, August 1985.

[SEID89] Seidowitz, E. and Stark, M., "Ada in the SEL: Experience with Operational Ada Projects," *Proceedings of the Second NASA Ada Users' Symposium*, SEL-89-008, NASA/SEL, Goddard Space Flight Center, Greenbelt, MD, November 1989.

[STRASSMANN91] Strassmann, Paul A., Director of Defense Information Memorandum on "Open Systems Implementation," OASD ($C^3I$), May 23, 1991.

# MEASURING THE DEVELOPMENT PERFORMANCE OF INTEGRATED COMPUTER AIDED SOFTWARE ENGINEERING (I-CASE): A SYNTHESIS OF FIELD STUDY RESULTS FROM THE FIRST BOSTON CORPORATION

**RAJIV D. BANKER**
Andersen Chair in Accounting and Information Systems
Carlson School of Management
University of Minnesota
Minneapolis, MN 55455

**ROBERT J. KAUFFMAN**
Associate Professor of Information Systems
Stern School of Business
New York University
44 West 4th Street
New York, NY 10012

## INTRODUCTION

The First Boston Corporation, a large investment bank in New York City, began to build its own integrated computer aided software engineering (I-CASE) tool in 1986. This decision was made following a comprehensive survey of the market for CASE tools available at that time. This resulted in a determination that there would be no tools commercially available within the next few years that would:

(1) enable cost-effective expansion of the firm's current applications to support the demand for increased financial market trades processing in a 24-hour a day, global market;

(2) create high functionality, multi-tiered cooperative processing applications that efficiently utilize the power and flexibility of --

* microcomputers and engineering workstations on the trading platform;

* fault-tolerant minicomputers for intraday trades processing and a link to the financial markets;
* mainframe computers for current account and firm securities inventory management, and historical database queries to support trading analytics; and,

(3) further control costs by paring down the overall level of developer expertise that needed to be brought together to create the firm's applications.

Following in-house development of "High Productivity Systems" (**HPS**), an I-CASE tool set that supports the development of reusable software, First Boston's next step was to rebuild and roll out the core applications that formed its investment banking software architecture.

A number of research questions were on our and management's agenda when we began to examine software development using HPS at First Boston. These included:

(1) To what extent did I-CASE support the software development process, leading to improved productivity and higher quality applications?

(2) Did software reuse drive the results?

(3) Are the gains recognizable in small-scale experimental project development?

(4) If so, can they also be replicated in large-scale application development?

This paper provides some insights to these questions by presenting the results of two phases of a multi-year field study that was carried out at the First Boston Corporation. The *first* phase involved three exploratory I-CASE development experiments in which we closely examined development performance. The *second* phase involved data collection to support an empirical study of twenty large-scale software development projects representing the bank's I-CASE-built *New Trades Processing Architecture* (**NTPA**).

We first turn to a more in-depth discussion of the results of the three experimental development projects. Thereafter, we will examine the results of the development in the second phase of the project. We conclude with some ideas on measurement and management approaches to improve the performance of I-CASE development activities.

## EVIDENCE FROM SMALL-SCALE EXPERIMENTAL PROJECTS DEVELOPED USING I-CASE

A useful approach to measuring the potential productivity impacts of automated software engineering techniques is to examine how the process of development proceeds in an experimental setting. The reasons for this are threefold:

(1) When a software project is developed as an experiment, the analyst has the opportunity to carefully craft the specifications for the project. This ensures that the developer will focus on developing the kind of system using the tools that management wishes to understand better.

(2) Since the specifications of the product can be controlled and the developer's work can be closely monitored, it is possible to get a more accurate measurement of development productivity for an experimental project than for a real one.

(3) Monitoring the developer also helps the analyst to understand the process behind the product. This enables the analyst to go one step farther: to gain an understanding of what factors drive the level of software development productivity that is subsequently observed.

We applied this approach to estimate the productivity gains that First Boston's HPS delivered for development of three small experimental applications:

(1) a retail industry information system that offers store, district and head office query and data processing capabilities;

(2) an investment banking executive information system; and,

(3) an investment banking trading workstation front-end.

Each was designed to exhibit a high level of user functionality and also require at least two-tier (microcomputer and mainframe) cooperative or client-server processing. Based on surveys of project managers in related work we conducted at First Boston, we learned that developing a system with high functionality and two-tier cooperative processing would require less than twice the effort when compared to development using traditional means, even when project teams were staffed with the most able developers. We were interested to see the extent to which HPS affected development performance, even for a developer with relatively little software engineering experience.

**Experiment #1: A Retail Sales Tracking System**

*Application Description.* The experimental development project was a sales tracking system designed for broad use by large firms operating in multiple locations in the retailing industry. The report and inquiry capabilities of the system were meant to serve the needs of two levels of management: senior management at the firm's head office and store managers in the field. The firm's computer architecture was expected to consist of a large mainframe computer at the head office and minicomputers at each of the stores. Management's interest in obtaining on-line, real-time and batch reports based on intra-day and historical sales necessitated cooperative processing, because all data were uploaded to the firm's head office at the end of each business day for long-term storage. The system's high functionality was distinguished by the pull down menus and mouse-driven input screens of the friendly user interface.

*Function Point Analysis.* We performed a function point analysis to determine the relative size of the application. Function points measure the functionality of an application, as opposed to source lines of code (**SLOC**) (Albrecht and Gaffney, 1983). This metric is increasingly accepted as a meaningful and reliable measure upon which to base an estimate of development effort (Kemerer, 1990; Symons, 1988). We estimated the size of the application at about 373 function points. Table 1 shows the breakdown by task of the function point total.

*Task Description.* The functional specifications for the experimental development project were designed in cooperation with First Boston Corporation staff members in advance of engaging the experimental developer. The project consisted of six development tasks. Four of these were primary tasks, which were presented in detail at the beginning of the development period. The final two tasks were enhancements. The enhancements were only discussed with the developer following successful completion of the first four tasks.

| EXPERIMENT #1: DEVELOPMENT TASKS | SIZE IN FUNCTION POINTS |
|---|---|
| *Primary Tasks* | |
| Task #1 | 72 |
| Task #2 | 80 |
| Task #3 | 75 |
| Task #4 | 70 |
| *Enhancement Tasks* | |
| Task #5 | 50 |
| Task #6 | 26 |
| *Overall Project* | |
| Tasks #1-#6 | 373 |

**TABLE 1. FUNCTION POINTS BY DEVELOPMENT TASK, EXPERIMENT #1 -- RETAILING APPLICATION**

*Project Manager Perceptions of HPS Development Productivity.* There were insufficient time or resources available during the study period to develop the experimental system in parallel using traditional 3GL tools for comparison purposes. Therefore, we sought to obtain development effort estimates from two knowledgeable sources to support our conclusions about the productivity gains associated with using HPS.

The first estimates were obtained in formal estimation sessions that we moderated involving two teams of First Boston's project managers. The second source was an external consulting firm to whom we gave detailed documentation on the experimental application.

The two formal estimation sessions involved seven project managers overall. They were requested to gauge how long the technical design, construction and testing-implementation phases would take if the application were built:

(1) without HPS and using minimal 3GL development tools;

(2) using HPS to construct a two-tiered cooperative processing application; or,

(3) using HPS to construct a three-tiered cooperative processing application.

Project managers estimated that traditional development of the project would take about ten weeks, even if the system were redefined to incorporate less functionality. Two-tiered HPS development (similar to the experimental system that was later developed), on the other hand, was estimated to require only six weeks total. Increasing the requirements specifications to make the experimental development project a three-tiered system was estimated to take approximately eight weeks.

When project managers were asked to estimate the effort required using traditional methods to provide the minimal functionality of the experimental development project in a single-tiered environment, they reported at least four months would be required. When they considered what would be involved in duplicating the full functionality provided by HPS development using traditional methods across the micro, mini and mainframe computer environments, that estimate rose to two years of development effort. This estimate parallels what we learned from project managers in another set of structured interviews conducted at First Boston.

For a second independent and unbiased opinion, we provided the functional specifications for the experimental development project to an external consulting firm. They had no knowledge of any other aspects of this project. Their estimates indicated that duplicating the system with minimal functionality in a 3GL development environment would have taken at least two years, while use of commercially available 4GL productivity tools would have required about eight months. These estimates are summarized in Table 2.

*Experimental Setting and Subject.* HPS Version 2.61 was used for the duration of this experimental development project. During this time, the developer worked in a technically stable development environment. The subject of the experimental application was a First Boston employee with an average knowledge of HPS, based on a little more than six months of experience, and somewhat greater than average programming ability. This person participated in the project on a full-time basis, with the exception of one brief interruption.

*Experimental Results.* This project was actually completed in six weeks, matching the average of the two estimates provided by First Boston's project managers. Table 3 reports actual productivity levels in function points per person month for each experimental task. The developer observed that HPS Version 2.61 development involving an IBM S/88 minicomputer benefitted the least from HPS; apparently there were few facilities in place at that time to support minicomputer software development. The developer also observed that development time for on-line, real-time screens was greatly reduced due to the implementation of a new screen painting facility.

| PROJECT MANAGER PRODUCTIVITY ESTIMATION CATEGORIES | High Functionality, Single-tiered Comparison: HPS to Traditional | High Functionality, Cooperative Processing Comparison: HPS to Traditional |
|---|---|---|
| *Overall Life Cycle Productivity* | 30% gain | 100% gain |
| *Average of Productivity for Selected Subtasks* | 70% gain | 130% gain |
| *Maintenance/Enhancement Productivity* | 80% gain | 120% gain |

**TABLE 2. PROJECT MANAGER ESTIMATES OF DEVELOPMENT PRODUCTIVITY GAINS IN TWO DEVELOPMENT SCENARIOS -- RETAILING APPLICATION (EXPERIMENT #1)**

Throughout the experiment, we observed no explicit reuse of objects that were constructed in other projects and stored in the repository. However, the developer "templated" a great many new objects, by making slight modifications to objects that she had built. Nevertheless, the productivity results, averaging 149 function points per person month across the six experimental tasks, compared favorably with national estimates of software development productivity in the United States that are presented near the end of this paper (Bouldin, 1989).

We also noted that productivity increased when the developer performed the second of two inter-related tasks. This is indicated by the relatively higher productivity levels observed for the enhancement tasks. We also observed that the developer's productivity declined following the brief, mid-project switch after Task #3 to another job. Finally, we observed that the developer pushed the limits of

HPS' high productivity in completing the final task. We believe that this did not represent normal output, however, because the developer was due to go on vacation at the end of the week the project was completed. Table 3 summarizes these results.

| EXPERIMENTAL DEVELOPMENT TASKS | UNADJUSTED ACTUAL PRODUCTIVITY (Function points/ person month) | ADJUSTED ACTUAL PRODUCTIVITY (Function points/ person month) |
|---|---|---|
| *Primary Tasks* | | |
| Task #1 | 230 | 138 |
| Task #2 | 240 | 144 |
| Task #3 | 420 | 252 |
| Task #4 | 200 | 120 |
| *Enhancement Tasks* | | |
| Task #5 | 360 | 216 |
| Task #6 | 775 | 465 |
| *Overall Project* | | |
| Tasks #1-#6 | 248 | 149 |

**Note:** We report both unadjusted and adjusted actual productivity estimates. Adjusting the actual productivity estimates downward by about 40% makes them comparable to development in other First Boston Corporation projects.

The actual development effort we observed commenced at the technical design phase, whereas in most software development shops, strategic planning, business analysis and functional design account for a substantial amount of effort that we have not measured in the experiment.

**TABLE 3. PRODUCTIVITY BY DEVELOPMENT TASK -- RETAIL APPLICATION (EXPERIMENT #1)**

Clearly, these figures are only estimates; they could not be substantiated at the time because the CASE tool was so new. In addition, the experimental project was small, and one could argue that commercial development of larger systems would be an order of magnitude or two more complex. Still, the results prompted us to look into HPS-based development performance more deeply, to attempt to understand what factors led to the high level of observed productivity.

**Experiment #2: An Executive Information System**

*Application Description.* This experimental application was meant to greatly extend the core functionality of a system that previously had been built using 4GL tools at a large financial institution. The application was intended to offer executives the opportunity to make queries about the content of business relationships with important customers.

*Function Point Analysis.* This application measured 1509 function points, and was broken into two modules:

(1) a customer reporting module, representing about 1056 function points, or 70% of the application's functionality, derived primarily from external interfaces and input types;

(2) a customer account maintenance module, representing the remaining 30% of the functionality, or 453 function points, derived primarily from input and output types.

The complexity multiplier for the application was 1.03, suggesting that it was of normal complexity, and in fact, the application exhibited a somewhat lower level of functionality than we saw in other systems developed using HPS. Yet, this application was a cooperative processing application, as the experiment was designed to demonstrate three-tiered development productivity. User query databases were located on a mainframe. The front-end graphics were generated by a microcomputer, and employed data that were downloaded from a mainframe and updated in real-time by a fault-tolerant minicomputer.

*Task Description.* The design specifications of this experimental project were created with the idea of testing the development of an application that incorporated many features that were believed to be well-supported by various elements of the HPS tool set. Thus, the resulting application included the basic functionality of its 4GL-developed predecessor, but emphasized on-line, real-time functionality.

*Estimate of Labor Required.* The core elements of the application were estimated by the developers to take about 4 to 5 person months to code using CICS screens and mainframe COBOL. However, we were unable to perform a function point analysis to determine the size of the 4GL-developed system. The developers indicated that the new version of the system that was to be built experimentally could not have been developed without HPS.

*Experimental Setting and Subjects.* Experimental development was carried out under similar technical conditions as in Experiment #1. HPS Version 2.61 was used and the tool was stable during the time the application was under development. In addition to the design specifications, the primary difference between this experiment and Experiment #1 was that this development was undertaken by a team of seven developers, instead of just one person. Among the members of the experimental project team, only one had more than six months experience in the use of HPS, however, none of the participants was a novice in software development.

*Experimental Results.* Total observed work effort for the project was 918 hours, or about 5.18 person months, however, work on the project was not continuous for all the developers. Each person spent an average of about 135 hours on the project, with one person spending 10% more and another 10% less. These estimates reflect the fact that the developers were also spending time in demonstrations of the tool, in meetings and in other non-project related activities for 40 hours over the five-week period. This level of effort is consistent with the production of 175 function points per person month for the project overall.

The developers uniformly reported that becoming adept at HPS development did not take very long. The application was developed in a series of increasingly complex prototypes, with developers alternately playing the role of critical users. The core functionality of the 4GL-developed system was in place within the first two weeks, and developers reported that team members had reused a significant number of objects built by the team members for the project. However, we did not have a measurement approach in place at that time to capture the levels of reuse that were occurring.

**Experiment #3: A Trader Workstation Front-end**

*Application Description.* Experiment #3 involved the re-creation and expansion of the functionality of a trader workstation front-end that previously had been built at a large financial institution. The application was re-developed to demonstrate that HPS could support a set of cooperative processing functions that were evenly distributed across the mainframe, minicomputer and microcomputer platforms.

*Function Point Analysis.* The size of the application was 1389 function points. The functionality was distributed as follows:

(1) 691 function points represented minicomputer functionality; and,

(2) the remainder, 698 function points, ran on the mainframe and microcomputer.

When we examined the function point results more closely, we found that approximately 37% of the functionality was derived from interfaces and 25% was derived from inputs.

This experiment occurred about four months after Experiments #1 and #2, and by that time, we had begun to make progress in understanding that tracking productivity alone would not tell the whole story of development performance with HPS. Thus, for this project we began to measure reuse more directly, in terms of a metric called "reuse leverage". Reuse leverage is defined as follows:

*#_HPS_OBJECTS_CALLED / #_UNIQUE_HPS_OBJECTS_BUILT*

In addition to the overall level of reuse leverage, we also tracked the greatest observed level of reuse leverage for an object, and individual reuse leverage ratios for 3GL components, and HPS screens and rules.

*Experimental Setting and Subjects.* HPS Version 2.61 again was used and the tool was stable during the time the application was under development. The team of developers that worked on this experiment had been involved in the development of a 3GL version of the same system at another financial institution.

*Experimental Results.* Table 4 reports the reuse leverage results for Experiment #3. When examining these results, the reader should keep in mind that all objects (except existing 3GL components) used by the developers were also built by them during the course of their experimental development work.

The reuse leverage results indicated that the developers extensively reused objects that they built themselves. The overall level of reuse leverage of 3.35 times indicates that only about 30% (1/3.35) of the functionality had to be built from scratch, indicating significant potential for a productivity gain to be observed.

Trader workstation software normally requires many calls to well-tested 3GL components that provide specialized functions related to the pricing and trading of financial instruments. In most investment banks such library routines are normally available right off the shelf, so the reuse leverage observed for 3GL components is quite realistic.

| REUSE LEVERAGE CATEGORY | REUSE LEVERAGE |
|---|---|
| Overall Reuse Leverage | 3.35 times |
| Greatest Observed Reuse Leverage for a Specific Object | 17.00 times |
| 3GL Component Reuse Leverage | 11.10 times |
| HPS Screen Reuse Leverage | 3.43 times |
| HPS Rule Reuse Leverage | 2.72 times |

**TABLE 4. REUSE LEVERAGE RESULTS FOR TRADER WORKSTATION FRONT-END (EXPERIMENT #3)**

The greatest observed level of reuse leverage for a single object was about 17 times, and this object was one that was built by the developers as an HPS object during the project. Such high levels of reuse often occur in financial analytics software, for example, when date or interest rate-related computations must be performed in order to compute the present value of a series of cash flows related to a financial instrument.

More interesting to us was the evidence that two kinds of HPS objects -- "rules" and "screens" -- offer significant reuse opportunities. Rules can be thought of in COBOL as statements in the procedure division. Screens, on the other hand, enable users to interact with the application, input trade-related data and see the results of specific trades. In on-line, real-time applications, these two object types are the most labor-consuming to build. (Batch applications involve the creation of HPS "report" objects, while both batch and on-line applications require developers to build "files" and other less labor-intensive objects.)

A reuse leverage of 2.72 times for rules is consistent with only having to build about 37% (1/2.72) of the procedure division, if development had occurred using COBOL. Screens tended to be reused even more, 3.43 times, which means that developers only built about 30% (1/3.43) of all application screens from scratch.

Table 5 presents productivity results for Experiment #3, and breaks them out across the minicomputer function points and the combined PC-mainframe function points. The application required 502 person-hours of effort, for an aggregate productivity level of about 272 function points per person month.

| DEVELOPMENT ACTIVITY | FUNCTION POINTS | FUNCTION POINTS/ PERSON MONTH |
|---|---|---|
| *Minicomputer Software Functionality* | 691 | 222 |
| *PC and Mainframe Software Functionality* | 698 | 336 |
| *Overall Application* | 1389 | 272 |

**Note:** The actual productivity estimates were adjusted downward by about 40% to make them comparable to development in other First Boston Corporation projects. The actual development effort we observed commenced at the technical design phase, whereas in most software development shops, strategic planning, business analysis and functional design account for a substantial amount of effort that we have not measured in the experiment.

**TABLE 5. PRODUCTIVITY RESULTS FOR TRADER WORKSTATION FRONT-END (EXPERIMENT #3)**

The results that were observed in the development of the trader workstation front-end (perhaps to a greater extent than the results observed in the first two experiments), confirmed that software reuse has the power to play a major role in the realization of improved productivity results. Although some of our preliminary questions about the extent of the productivity gains that might be observed in HPS development were answered, many more new questions emerged that would require additional study. These questions included the following:

(1) Would the order of magnitude of the software development productivity results hold when the project was scaled up from an experiment to the creation of larger, more complex systems?

(2) Would differences in software reuse leverage levels appear in larger projects? In projects that performed predominantly on-line, real-time processing versus batch processing?

(3) How would software development performance change as the use of the I-CASE tool and the tool set itself matured? How rapidly could developers come up to speed to enable large productivity gains to be achieved?

(4) What modifications to standard models in the software engineering economics literature would be needed to capture the impact of reuse on productivity? Does the creation of "reuse leverage" represent a separate "production process"?

## EVIDENCE FROM LARGE-SCALE DEVELOPMENT USING I-CASE: FIRST BOSTON'S NEW TRADES PROCESSING ARCHITECTURE (NTPA)

The recent trend in software development in the investment banking industry has been in the direction of applications that deliver a higher level of functionality for the user. Such applications are exemplified by workstation displays that present historical pricing data, graphical analytics and up-to-date prices for financial instruments, in addition to a capability to effect a trade. In this section we will examine the First Boston Corporation's experience with respect to I-CASE-based software development of such applications. The software development performance results that we present emphasize the close relationship between software reuse and the firm's ability to achieve high levels of development productivity.

**First Boston's New Trades Processing Architecture: Background**

During the latter half of the 1980s, First Boston Corporation's senior IS management believed that to effectively support the firm's investment banking business increasingly sophisticated software applications and growing computer hardware power for high speed securities and money market transactions processing would be needed. This also would require immediate access to large mainframe databases whose contents could be processed in real-time using highly complex financial analysis software. Such applications would require local access and customized analysis of distributed databases for financial market traders, and management and control of the firm's cash balances and securities inventory.

Similar to other firms in the industry, First Boston's systems would soon need to operate 24 hours a day across three platforms -- microcomputers, minicomputers and mainframes -- in support of global investment banking and money market trading activities. Much of the power that such software/hardware combinations would deliver was aimed at giving traders a few minutes (or even seconds) worth of time, an advantage that would help them to realize a profit in highly competitive markets. Such *high functionality software* was believed to offer a trader the ability to:

(1) obtain improved information access, through consolidation of multiple digital data feeds of market information on a single trader workstation;

(2) utilize real-time computer-based financial optimization analytics to support trading decisions with respect to existing and newly created financial instruments, and that would take advantage of the consolidated digital feeds; and,

(3) customize a user-friendly, windowing interface to suit a specific need.

In addition, senior management believed that higher functionality software could pay off in other ways. For example, through the delivery of consolidated and unbundled information on customer accounts and trader positions, it might be possible to improve global and local financial risk management.

The firm's senior management also recognized that it was not possible to bring high functionality systems into production rapidly with traditional development methods. The only way to avoid this "software trap" was to consider automating software development (Feder, 1988). Following a survey of the available technologies then on the market, it was decided that an integrated CASE tool would be built in-house (Clemons, 1991). The result was the commitment of $100 million over the course of the next several years to create a new software development methodology and a new architecture of investment banking software applications. This investment would lay the foundation for *High Productivity Systems* (**HPS**), the firm's I-CASE tool set, and the infrastructure of investment banking applications for the firm that came to be known as the *New Trades Processing Architecture* (**NTPA**).

**HPS and the Reusable Software Approach**

The approach that the firm implemented emphasized *software reuse*. The technical vision involved rebuilding the firm's information systems architecture in a way that their basic building blocks -- objects and modules -- could be reused repeatedly. The methodology also would help to reduce the bank's reliance on costly language-specialized programmers by making it possible to develop software that could run on any of the three platforms with a single "rules language." This rules language would be defined within the HPS I-CASE tool. Code generators would then process this HPS code so that run-time COBOL, PL/1 and C and other code would be generated for each of the three major development platforms. The automated generation of run-time code was meant to screen developers from the complexity of the development environment. Most developers could focus on development by employing the HPS rules language, instead of traditional 3GLs.

HPS supports reuse because it operates in conjunction with an *object-based centralized repository*. The object types are defined within the rules language and include programs, rules, output screens, user reports, data fields and 3GL components, among others. The centralized repository is the key enabling technology that supports the firm's reuse methodology. Specifications for the objects used to construct an application are stored in the repository and are widely available to other developers. The repository includes all the definitions of the data and objects that make up the organization's business.

The motivation for having a single repository for all such objects is similar to that for having a single database for all data: all objects need only be written once, no matter how many times they are used. When they are used and reused in various combinations, repository objects form the functionality that represents the information systems processing capability of the firm.

At the time we conducted this study, HPS provided application entity relationship diagramming and screen prototyping facilities for enterprise modeling and analysis and design. It also offered code generators for several development languages, as well as tools for debugging code and managing versions of the same application. Table 6 presents an overview of some of the capabilities of HPS in the first two years that it was deployed.

**Data Collection**

Data were gathered on the development of twenty NTPA applications (some of which were broken in sub-projects), representing substantially all I-CASE development at First Boston during the first two years following the deployment of HPS. Table 7 presents information that will provide the reader with some understanding of the functions these applications provided for the bank's information processing infrastructure.

We obtained data in the following ways:

(1) examination of records on labor charges to projects;

| LIFE-CYCLE PHASE | ACTIVITY SUPPORTED | SPECIFIC TOOL SET CAPABILITY |
|---|---|---|
| *Requirements* | Enterprise modeling | Information engineering-based data modeling package |
| | Information engineering | Diagramming tools to represent:<br>* entity-relationships<br>* business function hierarchies<br>* object-functionmatrixmapping |
| *System Analysis and Design* | Detailed support for enterprise modeling and information engineering | Capabilities of diagramming tools mentioned above apply here also<br><br>Data dependency diagramming |
| *Construction* | Code development for cooperative processing on mainframes, minis and PCs | Languages include: C, COBOL, assembler, PL1 and SQL |
| | Code generation from HPS "rules language" | Specific generators for: Windows and OS/2; COBOL CICS/MVS batch; IBM S/88 batch and on-line COBOL; IBM 3270 terminal screens; Windows and OS/2 PresentationManager menusand HELP screens; DB2 databases |
| *Implementation and Testing* | Application code debugging | Debugging tool for generated code |
| | Installation support | Tool capabilities include:<br>* autoversioninstallationcontrol<br>* repository migration control<br>* system rebuild |
| *Production and Maintenance* | Miscellaneous | Production version management facilty; software distribution control; debuggers for maintaining code |

**TABLE 6. THE HPS TOOL SET IN YEARS 1 AND 2 FOLLOWING IMPLEMENTATION**

| | |
|---|---|
| Broker Master | Product Master |
| Trade Inquiry | Dividend Interest Redemption |
| Dealers' Clearance | Real-Time Firm Inventory |
| Producer Master | Affirmation |
| Trading Account | Mortgage-Backed Securities |
| Trade Entry | Overnight Firm Inventory |
| Figuration | Floor/Desk/Breaksheet |
| Cash Management | Firm Price Management |
| Customer Account | General Ledger Interface |

**Note:** In some instances, applications were subdivided forming the "projects" that we tracked. This led to the identification of multiple projects for a small number of the applications. In addition, the data set we examined did not actually include all of the applications listed above; some were excluded due to unavailable documentation or labor expense data.

**TABLE 7. APPLICATIONS IN THE NEW TRADES PROCESSING ARCHITECTURE -- SOFTWARE FOR THE OPERATING INFRASTRUCTURE OF AN INVESTMENT BANK**

(2) function point analysis based on examination of documentation describing NTPA applications;

(3) interviews with project managers and project team members; and,

(4) object analysis based on DB2 queries to the object repository and manual examination of application documentation.

*Estimates of labor consumed.* We obtained disaggregated and detailed reports on the hours for each developer assigned to an application project. Although this data was relatively complete, the bank did not have a productivity reporting system in place (nor did it track productivity in terms of function points).

As a result, in some cases it was necessary to apply second checks to ensure that we had captured all (or substantially all) of the labor hours expended on a project. In other cases where we believed that the data were too sketchy or likely to be in error, we omitted the project from further consideration in the study.

*Function point analysis.* To perform function point analyses for NTPA applications, we collected application documentation for as many applications as we could. In some cases, no documentation was yet available. These had been built using HPS prior to the time that application documentation was an automated by-product of system analysis and design procedures.

Function point analyses performed by members of the research team were double-checked for accuracy, and all members of the team were thoroughly trained to reduce the likelihood that the results would be different for different analysts. Project managers offered information about the extent to which the application development environment differed from the norm, making application development more complex.

*Interviews with project managers and team members.* These interviews were conducted by two members of the research team over the course of two months. The primary purpose of the interviews was to gain assistance with interpreting the labor charges that were made to the projects, how to break those charges out over sub-projects (where they were defined and software developers were broken into smaller teams), and other aspects of a project that might result in different levels of observed productivity. For example, project managers assisted us by specifying the "environmental modifiers" that are applied in function point analysis. In many cases, we learned that I-CASE development tended to reduce environmental complexity for development.

Because the research team was on-site at the bank, the interview process allowed for an initial meeting and then multiple follow-up interviews, when necessary. In many cases, project managers played a crucial role in helping to ensure that the data we collected were accurate. They also offered advice and guidance that helped us to shape a new modeling perspective that reflects the related activities of reusing software and improving productivity.

Project team members provided useful information to enable us to better understand how the reusable software approach was applied in specific software projects. Through interviews with these developers, we learned about some of the advantages and disadvantages of the approach, and how smaller and larger projects might be affected differently.

The key issue that was discussed had to do with the *incentive compatibility* of software developers to build objects that would be widely reusable by other software developers. In the first two years of software development under HPS, developers "owned" objects that they developed first. Thus they had some measure of responsibility to ensure that the objects performed well in their own and in other developers' applications.

Because guaranteeing the performance of a software object in multiple contexts was difficult for individual developers, an *agency problem* developed which resulted in developers encouraging one another to make slight modifications to existing objects, and then to rename them. This had the effect of shifting ownership from the original developer to the developer who modified the object.

*Object analysis.* In order to obtain information about software reuse levels in each of the projects, research team members conducted "object analyses" to enable the estimation of project reuse leverage. This proved to be more difficult than we envisioned for two reasons:

(1) It was necessary to ensure that the documented application matched the content of the application that was actually built; and,

(2) the documentation varied in quality, in some cases enabling function point

analysis, but not a detailed count of application objects.

In view of these difficulties, a compromise was necessary. We found this compromise in follow-up interviews with project managers, who informed us that some HPS objects required very little effort to build, while others would be likely to act as the primary cost drivers. This enabled us to focus data collection efforts on the key cost driver objects (rules, screens, files, reports and 3GL components). As it turned out, much of this data was available from the documentation, and was quite accurate.

(More recently, we have been attempting to implement an automated object analysis procedure to confirm the quality of the NTPA project reuse leverage levels that we report in this paper and elsewhere (Banker and Kauffman, 1991). Our attempts to carry out automated object analysis for the NTPA projects have been hampered as the I-CASE tool has evolved. Further analysis requires the migration of prior versions of the applications to the centralized object repository that operates under the current version of HPS.)

**Software Reuse Results**

Table 8 presents the results obtained for reuse leverage in the twenty NTPA projects. The results contrast software development under HPS in Years 1 and 2 following implementation. They show how reuse leverage differed for on-line, real time versus batch processing application development. The table also shows the distribution of the application projects across these categories.

The observed levels of reuse leverage were lower in Year 1 (1.82 times) than they were in Year 2 (3.95 times). This is a very likely outcome. The lower reuse leverage in Year 1 was probably caused by one of several factors. These include:

| CASE TOOL EXPERIENCE CATEGORIES | WEIGHTED AVERAGE REUSE LEVERAGE BY APPLICATION TYPE | | |
|---|---|---|---|
| | ON-LINE (# PROJECTS) | BATCH (# PROJECTS) | BOTH (# PROJECTS) |
| YEAR 1 PROJECTS ONLY | 2.95 (5) | 1.41 (8) | 1.82 (13) |
| YEAR 2 PROJECTS ONLY | 4.11 (6) | 3.05 (1) | 3.95 (7) |

Note: The average reuse leverage results are weighted for project size in terms of the total number of objects in an application.

**TABLE 8. REUSE LEVERAGE FOR ON-LINE AND BATCH APPLICATIONS BY CASE TOOL EXPERIENCE CATEGORY**

* lack of familiarity on the part of developers with the reusable software approach;
* difficulty in finding the appropriate objects to reuse;
* the practice (discussed earlier and interpreted as a response to the agency problem of object "ownership") of templating and renaming nearly matching software objects to avoid having to debug them; and,
* the small number of objects available in the repository for reuse.

In the Year 1 results, it is also interesting to note that on-line, real-time application development evidenced higher reuse leverage (2.95 times) than batch processing applications (1.41 times). In Year 1, the HPS tool set was biased to support on-line, real-time development to a greater extent than batch processing applications. Although the developers of the HPS I-CASE tools had a year or more lead time to develop its capabilities, the functionality of the tools was still limited. Management decided to focus efforts to create HPS tools that would support on-line, real-time development earlier. Facing substantial risks associated with the large investment in building an I-CASE tool set, it was important to enable the delivery of applications that would be visible to users early on and whose impact would be felt in the business. In addition, the higher cost of developing more complex on-line, real-time applications made the focus natural.

By Year 2 the HPS tool set increasingly treated on-line, real-time and batch development on equal terms. Year 2 reuse leverage for batch processing application (3.05 times) exceeded the Year 1 level observed for on-line, real-time applications (2.95 times). This improvement can be attributed (in part) to changes in the HPS tool set. For example:

* batch development activities were made more productive through the deployment of a "report painting" facility; this enabled developers to nearly match the productivity that they could obtain for on-line, real-time applications when using a screen painter; and,
* when communication between platforms was required for both batch and on-line applications, highly specialized 3GL components (frequently called "middleware" by the developers we interviewed) had now become available that could be "plugged in".

Developers indicated that they were learning how to use HPS, and in the process, how to reuse more code more often. This perhaps best explains the level of reuse observed for Year 2 on-line, real-time application development (4.11 times). This level of reuse is consistent with building just 24% of an application from scratch, while the remaining 76% results from reused objects.

**Large Application Development Productivity**

Table 9 presents the function point productivity levels that were observed for the twenty NTPA projects. Similar to our presentation of the reuse leverage results, we include results for Years 1 and 2 to indicate the extent of the learning that was occurring about how to develop software using HPS. We also include separate productivity figures for on-line, real-time and batch processing applications.

| CASE TOOL | PRODUCTIVITY BY APPLICATION TYPE OF PROJECT IN FUNCTION POINTS PER PERSON-MONTH | | |
|---|---|---|---|
| EXPERIENCE CATEGORIES | ON-LINE (# PROJECTS) | BATCH (# PROJECTS) | BOTH (# PROJECTS) |
| YEAR 1 PROJECTS ONLY | 32.1 (5) | 9.4 (8) | 15.6 (13) |
| YEAR 2 PROJECTS ONLY | 135.4 (6) | 38.4 (1) | 121.6 (7) |

**Note:** The average productivity results are weighted for project size in function points.

**TABLE 9. PRODUCTIVITY COMPARISONS FOR ON-LINE AND BATCH APPLICATIONS BY CASE TOOL EXPERIENCE CATEGORY**

The productivity results in Year 1 suggest the power associated with software reuse. Productivity for Year 1 on-line, real-time application development was on the order of 32 function points per person month (FP/M), while Year 1 batch processing application development was only 9.4 FP/M. The reuse leverage associated with the on-line projects was 2.95 times (only 34% of the total functionality of the applications had to be built), and batch projects was a more modest 1.41 times (71% of application functionality had to be built from scratch).

By Year 2 productivity for both on-line and batch application development was substantially improved. Year 2 productivity for batch projects (38.4 FP/M) now exceeded Year 1 productivity for on-line, real-time applications. When these results were reviewed with project managers and software developers, most indicated that the increase in reuse leverage for batch development was responsible, and that the improved capabilities of the I-CASE tool set was a major factor. (Recall that Year 2 reuse leverage of 3.05 times for batch processing application exceeded the Year 1 level of 2.95 times observed for on-line, real-time applications.)

Meanwhile, Year 2 productivity for on-line, real-time projects improved to 135.4 FP/M, four times better than in Year 1. Developers that we interviewed indicated that the primary factors responsible for this result were the availability of a larger pool of reusable repository objects, and the knowledge of how to locate them. In Year 2 developers became more familiar with a facility in HPS that provided key word search for objects. The key words were taken from the object name, still a relatively weak method on which to develop a complete set of candidate objects for reuse, but apparently very useful.

(Since the time that we did this analysis, we have learned much about the process of reusing software in the HPS I-CASE development environment. Banker, Kauffman and Zweig (1992) reported that reuse is often biased towards reuse of "owned" objects or objects created by project team members. Apparently the key word search facility was not the only, and probably not even the primary mechanism that developers used to identify objects that could potentially be reused.)

**Comparison of Productivity Results with National Averages**

Table 10 summarizes the productivity results obtained in the study and compares them with estimates of national averages of software development productivity made by Capers Jones. The present results compare favorably with the estimated national averages, and suggest the potential for order of magnitude productivity gains that may become possible when I-CASE development tools are used.

| PROJECT COMPARISON CATEGORIES | FUNCTION POINTS/ PERSON-MONTH | COMMENTS |
|---|---|---|
| *Intra-firm Estimates of Year 2 Performance* | | |
| BATCH PROCESSING ONLY | 38.4 | Productivity influenced by lack of 3GL component handling facility in earlier version of CASE tool. Batch report painter and SQL query support added to boost productivity in Year 2. |
| ON-LINE, REAL-TIME ONLY | 135.4 | Productivity enhanced by use of rapid, on-line screen painter, and high levels of reuse. |
| *External World Estimates* | | |
| MILITARY/ DEFENSE DEPARTMENT | 3.0 | Large, technically complex development efforts. |
| TRADITIONAL 3GL | 5.0 | Averages initial development and subsequent maintenance. |
| MIS BUSINESS APPLICATIONS | 8.0 | Averages development activities conducted with and without CASE tools. |
| MATURE CASE, NO REUSE | 15.0 | "Mature" defined as a minimum of two years of experience with a relatively stable tool set. |
| MATURE CASE, WITH REUSE | 65.0 | A projected target for firms using an I-CASE tool. |

**Note:** The external world figures are found in Bouldin (1989), who attributes them to Capers Jones.

**TABLE 10. COMPARISONS BETWEEN INTRA-FIRM AND EXTERNAL WORLD SOFTWARE DEVELOPMENT PRODUCTIVITY**

## CONCLUSION

This paper provided evidence of the extent to which software reuse and I-CASE tools that operate in conjunction with a centralized repository have the potential to influence software development performance. Clearly, the results of this study can only be generalized to a limited extent. The research examined one I-CASE tool set at one site over two time periods, just following deployment of the tools. Nevertheless we learned much about the process of modeling software development productivity in this kind of development environment and the kinds of new metrics that management will want to track to better understand I-CASE development. In this concluding section, we first offer some preliminary answers to questions that were posed earlier. Finally, we end this paper by offering some thoughts about what implications our work may have for researchers and managers.

Did the order of magnitude of the software development productivity results observed in the experiments hold for larger-scale development? Apparently they did not. Although development productivity was at least one order of magnitude better (135.4 FP/M for I-CASE on-line, real-time application development versus Capers Jones' estimate of 8.0 FP/M for business MIS applications developed using traditional methods) than if 3GL methods had been used, it was evident that the results only held in a limited scenario. Moreover, nowhere did we observe in the NTPA development the 200+ FP/M productivity levels observed in experimental development.

Were the levels of software reuse different in the experimental and large-scale development projects? Here we had just one data point among the experimental projects to make our comparison. The results suggest that they were similar, especially in Year 2. (The comparison is between the overall reuse leverage (3.35 times) observed for Experiment #3, the trader workstation front-end, and the reuse leverages observed for NTPA on-line (4.11 times) and batch processing (3.05 times) applications in Year 2.) Increasing software reuse as project size increases involves planning, coordination and search costs that were not evident for the experimental projects or for smaller projects. But larger projects may offer more opportunities for reuse, despite their complexity. The relationship between project scale and software reuse observed is an issue that must be addressed in future research.

Did development performance change as the use of the I-CASE tool and the tool set itself matured? There is no doubt from the results that we report and the interpretations offered to us by First Boston Corporation project managers that learning played a very important role in the outcome. Developers were learning to use the new tools as they became available. They were learning to be better at reusing code simultaneously. We observed a very steep learning curve for productivity and reuse leverage between Years 1 and 2 in the use of HPS to develop NTPA. The extent of the potential impact of future learning remains an open issue, however.

What was learned from this study that will assist other researchers in their attempts to model I-CASE development performance? Our research suggests that software development labor is transformed into software outputs (objects, modules or function points in this case) in the presence of a second production process that leads to observed reuse. From what we have seen, reuse leverage is created through a separate production process that involves labor, an existing pool of software objects and significant capital invested in a tool that supports the reusable software approach. Although detailed consideration of the factors that may drive higher levels of software reuse is beyond the scope of this paper, the reader should recognize that such factors must be considered to understand how to manage projects to generate higher levels of software reuse, paving the way for order of magnitude of gains in development productivity.

From a software engineering economics perspective, the well-accepted concept that software outputs are based on a single "software development production function" may need to be re-evaluated. We have made initial attempts along these lines by estimating two separate production functions using seemingly unrelated regression estimation. For additional details, see Banker and Kauffman (1991).

The implications of this research for managers in I-CASE environments are as follows:

(1) Because software reuse appears to constrain the potential for software development productivity, it makes sense to implement measurement systems that track software reuse, as well as software development performance. Problems with software development productivity may be due to insufficiently high levels of reuse.

(2) If managers believe that it is worthwhile to measure software reuse, they should also recognize the potential difficulties that such measurement may entail. The metric that is discussed in this paper, reuse leverage, is probably new to the reader. There are no widely implemented standards at present, though the IEEE has written a standards document and made it widely available for comment. In addition, measuring reuse leverage manually was very labor and time-consuming. The only real solution is to automate such analysis. (In fact, very little work has been done to date in this area also. One exception is the work of Banker, Kauffman, Wright and Zweig (1992), who proposed a taxonomy of software reuse metrics and suggested an approach to their automation.)

(3) The levels of observed reuse are likely to be influenced by the set of incentive mechanisms that managers devise to overcome the "agency problem" that we described. In the development environment that we studied it is likely that a one-time (if minor) gain in reuse leverage could be obtained by placing objects, once they have been developed and tested, on neutral ground, so that the original developer would no longer be required to guarantee their performance. Other gains could be achieved by implementing incentive mechanisms to increase more directly the observed

levels of reuse.

A natural new owner would be an "object administrator", whose primary roles would involve:

(1) ensuring that a broad base of reusable repository objects is available for other developers to use;

(2) planning for a minimal subset of "reusable objects" to provide the kind of functionality that is needed in many different kinds of projects; and,

(3) proposing incentive mechanisms for senior management review that will assist in the achievement of higher levels of reuse leverage to support improved productivity.

Our call for "object administration" is meant to achieve the same kinds of payoffs in I-CASE development in the 1990s that database administration has delivered since the 1970s.

## REFERENCES


[Albrecht and Gaffney, 1983] Albrecht, A.J. and Gaffney, J.E. "Software Function, Source Lines of Code, and Development Effort Prediction: A Software Science Validation," *IEEE Transactions on Software Engineering*, 9:6, November 1983.

[Banker and Kauffman, 1991] Banker, R. D, and Kauffman, R. J. "Reuse and Productivity: An Empirical Study of Integrated Computer Aided Software Engineering (ICASE) Technology at the First Boston Corporation," *MIS Quarterly*, September 1991.

[Banker, Kauffman and Zweig, 1992] Banker, R. D., Kauffman, R. J., and Zweig, D. "Monitoring the 'Software Asset' Using Repository Evaluation: An Empirical Study." Forthcoming in *IEEE Transactions on Software Engineering.*

[Banker, Kauffman, Wright and Zweig, 1992] Banker, R. D., Kauffman, R. J., Wright, C., and Zweig, D. "Automating Reuse and Output Measurement Metrics in an Object-Based Computer Aided Software Engineering Environment." Forthcoming in *IEEE Transactions on Software Engineering.*

[Bouldin, 1989] Bouldin, B. M. "CASE: Measuring Productivity -- What Are You Measuring? Why Are You Measuring It?" *Software Magazine*, 9:10, August

1989.

[Clemons, 1991] Clemons, E. "Evaluating Investments in Strategic Information Technologies," *Communications of the ACM*, January 1991.

[Feder, 1988] Feder, B. "The Software Trap: Automate -- Or Else," *Business Week*, May 9, 1988.

[Kemerer, 1990] Kemerer, C. F. "Reliability of Function Points Measurement: A Field Experiment," Working Paper, Sloan School of Management, MIT, December 1990.

[Symons, 1988] Symons, C. R. "Function Point Analysis: Difficulties and Improvements," *IEEE Transactions on Software Engineering*, 14:1, January 1988.

## ACKNOWLEDGEMENTS

Special thanks are due Mark Baric, Gene Bedell, Gig Graham, Tom Lewis and Vivek Wadhwa of Seer Technologies. They provided us with access to data on software development projects and managers' time throughout our field study at the First Boston Corporation. We also appreciated the efforts of Eric Fisher, Charles Wright, Vannevar Yu and Rachna Kumar, who assisted in the data collection. An earlier version of this research was presented at the "Software Engineering Economics I Conference," sponsored by the MITRE/Washington Economic Analysis Center, June 1991. Jean Kauffman provided helpful editorial comments to improve the readability of the paper. All errors are the responsibility of the authors.

# RETURNS-TO-SCALE IN SOFTWARE PRODUCTION: A COMPARISON OF APPROACHES

Patricia E. BYRNES
School of Public Policy and Management
Ohio State University
Columbus, Ohio 43210 USA

Thomas P. FRAZIER
Institute for Defense Analyses
1801 N. Beauregard Street
Alexandria, Virginia 22311 USA

Thomas R. GULLEDGE
The Institute of Public Policy
George Mason University
Fairfax, Virginia 22030 USA

## I. INTRODUCTION

The literature on the software development industry (summarized in [2]) contains references to returns-to-scale as a factor in software development productivity. As noted in [2], most studies have typically related project size to labor productivity. A general finding is that software development tools and more specialized labor are usually employed on larger, in terms of project size, software projects. However, this observation does not necessarily imply increasing returns to a particular input, such as software development tools or more specialized labor. The confusion in the literature stems from the use of the term *scale* and the more general observation that large projects rarely have the same capital-labor mix as their smaller counterparts. In this paper returns-to-scale estimates are allowed to vary with both project capital-labor mix and project size.

We estimate returns-to-scale in both parametric and nonparametric production models[1] for a sample of Department

---

[1] See [11] for a comparison of parametric and nonparametric methods for measuring productive efficiency.

of Defense (DoD) Automated Information Systems (AIS) software development projects. We demonstrate that when input mix is believed to be an important determinant of economies-of-scale, the typical approach of relating labor productivity to project size may be inappropriate for determining the true nature of returns-to-scale and the effect of economies-of-scale on productivity. We also confirm the Banker and Kemerer [2] observation that as project size increases, diminishing returns eventually prevail. However, we extend the Banker and Kemerer results by showing that when labor and productivity tools are both included as production inputs, efficient project size is, in general, larger than when only a labor input is considered.

## A. The Concept of Returns-to-Scale

A production technology defines the technical means whereby materials and services (designated inputs) may be combined to produce one or more goods or services (the outputs of the process). Economists have chosen to represent these technical relationships with production functions which express the maximum level of output(s) produced for each given level of inputs[2]. Graphically the production function can be represented by the isoquant (constant product locus) in Figure 1. In Figure 1 we assume that two inputs, capital (K) and labor (L), are used to produce one output, Q. It should be noted that while point A lies on the isoquant; point A′ does not; that is, point A′ does not represent a technically efficient means of producing a given output level $Q_0$. Mathematically, a production function can be written as:

---

[2] The neoclassical theory of production economics is presented by Ferguson [9]. More modern treatments of the subject are presented by Shephard [12] or Färe [7].

$$Q = F(x_1, x_2, \ldots, x_n),$$

where Q is the maximum output rate and the x's are the input rates of the *n* production factors. One characteristic of the production technology is returns-to-scale.

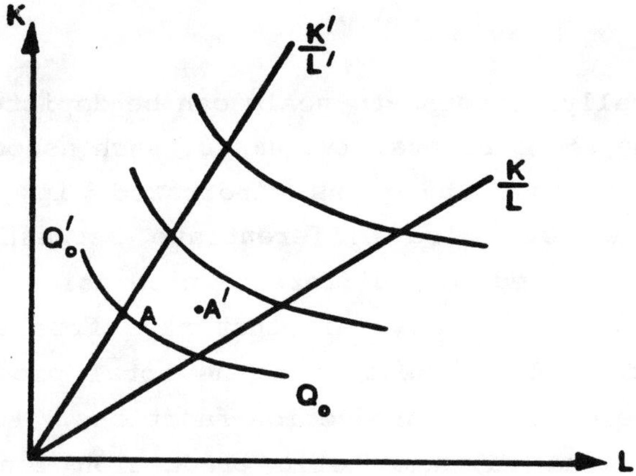


Figure 1. Software Production Function.

Returns-to-scale is defined as the relative increase in output as all inputs are increased proportionally so that the relative factor mix does not change. The returns-to-scale elasticity, $\epsilon$, is given by:

$$\epsilon = \frac{dQ}{d\lambda} \bullet \frac{\lambda}{Q},$$

where $\lambda$ is the proportionate expansion in all inputs, and is equal to $dF/dx_i$ for all i. By definition, $|\epsilon| > 1$ indicates increasing returns-to-scale, $|\epsilon| = 1$ indicates constant returns-to-scale, and $|\epsilon| < 1$ indicates decreasing returns-to-scale. Alternatively, total differentiation of the production function yields an equivalent expression that allows the returns-to-scale elasticity to be expressed in terms of the partial factor output elasticities as:

$$\epsilon = \frac{\partial F}{\partial x_1} \bullet \frac{x_1}{Q} + \frac{\partial F}{\partial x_2} \bullet \frac{x_2}{Q} + \ldots + \frac{\partial F}{\partial x_n} \bullet \frac{x_n}{Q}.$$

Graphically, returns-to-scale can be depicted in terms of the spacing among several isoquants, each associated with a different output rate as indicated in Figure 1. Furthermore, we can also differentiate between different scale effects based on different production functions. Following [6], consider two distinct rays from the origin, K′/L′ and K/L. Along these rays the total product curves differ for the different production functions. For the most general case, the ray-homothetic production function, the total product curves associated with K′/L′ and K/L may differ both with respect to factor intensity and output level. Another case, the ray-homogeneous production function allows the total product curves to vary with factor proportions, but they are monotone; that is, the degree of homogeneity is constant for each K/L. Or equivalently, scale elasticity is constant along a particular K/L but may differ between K′/L′ and K/L. For the homothetic production function, the total product curves are also identical, however, they need not be monotone; that is, scale elasticity may vary with output.

Homothetic production functions and their corresponding scale effects can be explained in another way. Define the marginal rate of technical substitution (MRTS) as the negative of the rate at which one input substitutes for another along an isoquant (i.e., holding output rate constant). Using the general production function, the MRTS is defined as

$$MRTS = \frac{\partial x_2}{\partial x_1}\Big|_{Q=\bar{Q}},$$

where $\bar{Q}$ is a given output rate. For homothetic technologies the MRTS remains unchanged as we move from one isoquant to another keeping input proportions constant; that is, the MRTS along a ray K′/L′ is constant. Thus, a homothetic technology implies that the returns-to-scale elasticity, $\epsilon$, is a function of only output since it will be invariant to changes in input proportions.

A further decomposition of homothetic technologies defines the most restrictive production function, the homogeneous production function. Homogeneous production functions are characterized by a constant returns-to-scale elasticity; that is, $\epsilon$ is invariant to changes in Q (as well as input proportions). This means that the total product curves associated with the two factor proportions K′/L′ and K/L are identical and monotone.

## B. Software Productivity Literature Review

Much of the literature relevant to scale estimation in new software development is summarized by Banker and Kemerer [2]. In most of these studies regression analysis is used to estimate returns-to-scale, and in most cases a global estimate is obtained for each software project data set. Banker and Kemerer extend this research by applying nonparametric linear programming methods to compute a most productive scale size for new software projects (see [1] for a presentation of most productive scale size). Since the linear programming approach provides a scale estimate for each software project, it is possible to examine how scale varies with project size. Given our understanding of the software development process, a reasonable hypothesis is that small projects are characterized by increasing returns, while large projects are characterized by diminishing returns. This hypothesis was not rejected by Banker and Kemerer after examining numerous new software project data sets.

### C. An Extended Hypothesis

This paper extends and refines the work of Banker and Kemerer. We confirm, using a DoD software development project data set, that increasing returns are associated with small projects and decreasing returns are associated with larger projects. In addition, we hypothesize that the software productivity tools identified by Boehm [3] delay the inevitable occurrence of diminishing returns. That is, given the tools, increasing returns are observed for larger projects than when ignoring the tools. If this hypothesis cannot be rejected, there are obvious implications for software development practitioners. Our data set also suggests that higher-level productivity tools have larger marginal productivity with respect to potential output.

## II. THE DATA

The data were taken from a stratified survey sample of 90 Department of Defense Automated Information Systems supported by general purpose automated data processing and developed by both in-house and contractor personnel [10]. Since there is no completely documented inventory of DoD AIS, the sampling strategy involved collecting data on software development projects that are consistent in age, function, and DoD component within the known DoD hardware inventory. The DoD computer hardware inventory is contained in the Automated Resources Management System maintained by the Defense Logistics Agency [5].

In order to account for differences in computer languages, code reuse, and straight conversion from existing code; the selected sample contains only those COBOL projects for which the algorithms and logic design were almost entirely created from scratch. There were 37 projects that fulfilled these requirements. This data set is homogeneous in the sense that all projects are sized in standardized COBOL lines of code (described further below).

To model software development in a production framework, the inputs and outputs must be specified. We introduce the following notation which is used in the tables and models that follow:

$Q$ = software project output; i.e., thousands of source lines of code,

$L$ = labor measured in man-months of effort required to complete the main software build. This is defined to include effort on detailed design, coding, integration, quality assurance, configuration management, publications, and management,

$K_1$ = number of low-level productivity tools employed per software project,

$K_2$ = number of nominal-level productivity tools employed per software project,

$K_3$ = number of high-level productivity tools employed per software project.

Table 1 contains descriptive statistics of these variables.

Table 1. Variable Descriptive Statistics

| Variable | Mean | St. Dev. | Minimum | Maximum |
|---|---|---|---|---|
| $Q$ | 287.5 | 472.2 | 5.0 | 2000.0 |
| $L$ | 609.7 | 1050.6 | 10.5 | 5000.0 |
| $K_1$ | 2.9 | 1.5 | 1.0 | 7.0 |
| $K_2$ | 4.8 | 2.2 | 1.0 | 10.0 |
| $K_3$ | 4.2 | 3.0 | 1.0 | 14.0 |

The output measure, thousands of source lines of code ($Q$), is taken from the survey. The respondents were instructed to follow the code counting convention used in

[3]. Lines of code are defined to include all program instructions created by project personnel and processed into machine code by some combination of preprocessors, compilers, and assemblers. The measure excludes comment instructions and unmodified utility software, but includes job control language, format statements, and data declarations. The definition of lines of code also excludes non-delivered support software such as test drivers. However, if these are developed with the same care as delivered software, with their own reviews, test plans, documentation, etc.; then they were included in the count.

Turning to the specification of the inputs. The labor variable (L) was taken directly from the survey as defined above. We specified three *capital* variables based on a software tools classification and rating scheme defined by Boehm [3]. Each respondent in the survey indicated the availability and usage of the software productivity tools as described in Table 27-7 of [3], plus several additional tools that were developed and employed subsequently. In order to ensure definitional consistency across all respondents, a glossary of terms concerning each of the tools was provided with the survey instrument. We used a modification of Boehm's rating classification scheme. Those tools that were described as being *low* and *very low* were aggregated into a single rating category. The same grouping strategy was executed for those tools that Boehm labeled *high* and *very high*. Hence, we have three tool categories: low, nominal, and high. The tools and the groupings are listed in Table 2.

## III. MODELS OF RETURNS-TO-SCALE

To analyze returns-to-scale for the sample of new software projects, we estimate several models. First, we estimate the parameters of a ray-homothetic production function [8]. This specification is flexible, and it permits returns-to-scale to vary with respect to output and input mix (i.e., the tools/labor ratio).

Table 2. Software Tools Rating Scale

| Ratings | Tools[a] |
|---|---|
| Low | Assembler, Chief Programmer Team, Configuration Management, Database Aids, Batch Debuggers, Programming Support, Time Sharing Operating System, Performance Measurement and Analysis Tools. |
| Nominal | HOL Compiler, Project and Data Entry Control Systems, Data Dictionaries, Interactive Debuggers, Source Code Formatters, Report Generators, Screen Generators, Reusable Source and Object Code Library System, Virtual Memory operating System, Macro Assembler, Text Editorand Manager. |
| High | Cross Compiler, Conversion Aids, Database Design Aids, DBMS, Distributed Processing, Active Documentation Tools, Failure Analyses Tools, Formal Verification, Display Formatters, Code Generators, Application Generators, Integrated Computer Assisted Software Engineering Environments, Local Area Networks, Program Design Language and Tools, Requirements Specification Language and Analyzer, Interactive Source Editor, Automated Verification System, Expert Systems Applications to Software Engineering, Instruction Set Simulators, Regression Testing, Restructing Tools and Test Coverage Analyzers. |

[a]This listing contains the tools presented in [3], plus tools developed subsequent to Boehm's original work.

There is no assumption that larger projects require a larger number of unique tools. Optimal project size varies with input mix. However, we expect the capital/labor ratio to be high for smaller projects; if for no other reason, because tools may be shared on larger projects. We could make a stronger statement about scale if we have more information about how the tools were actually used, but our data is not sufficiently rich to *match* unique tools to unique labor units. This is a standard problem in production function specification and parameter estimation.

We demonstrate with the ray-homothetic model that the software productivity tools have an impact on scale. We also confirm this result with a less restrictive nonparametric linear programming approach (see [1] and [6]). In section IV we use the results of these analyses to define results which are of use to software development project managers. We also show that there is significant variation in tool marginal productivity, a result that has implications about which tools to employ.

A. The Ray-Homothetic Model

The ray-homothetic production function can be written as:

$$Q = \ln\left(\theta \bullet K^{a_L \frac{L}{S}} \bullet K_1^{a_{K_1}\frac{K_1}{S}} \bullet K_2^{a_{K_2}\frac{K_2}{S}} \bullet K_3^{a_{K_3}\frac{K_3}{S}}\right),$$

where $S = K_1 + K_2 + K_3 + L$ and $\theta$, $a_L$, $a_{K1}$, $a_{K2}$, and $a_{K3}$ are parameters to be estimated. The general properties of the above equation are discussed by Färe [8]. Most importantly, this function is ray-homothetic and contains homothetic and homogeneous production functions as special cases.

To examine returns-to-scale and optimal output, the elasticity definition of returns-to-scale is applied to the production function to obtain the following expression for returns-to-scale:

$$RTS = \frac{a_L \bullet \frac{L}{S} + a_{K_1}\frac{K_1}{S} + a_{K_2}\frac{K_2}{S} + a_{K_3}\frac{K_3}{S}}{Q}.$$

As usual, RTS > 1 indicates increasing returns-to-scale, RTS = 1 indicates constant returns-to-scale, and RTS < 1, decreasing returns-to-scale. Optimal or ideal scale is obtained when constant returns-to-scale prevails, i.e., when RTS = 1. Thus, optimal scale is given by

$$OPTQ = a_L \bullet \frac{L}{S} + a_{K_1} \bullet \frac{K_1}{S} + a_{K_2} \bullet \frac{K_2}{S} + a_{K_3} \bullet \frac{K_3}{S}.$$

These measures indicate that returns-to-scale and optimal scale (from the ray-homothetic production function) vary with output level and input mix. For example, if the estimated parameter for a particular input is less than zero, then the magnitude of scale economies declines with increases in the corresponding input's proportion of the total inputs. To estimate the parameters of the ray-homothetic production function we augment the function with an error term, u, as:

$$Q = \ln\theta + a_L \bullet \frac{L}{S} \bullet \ln L + a_{K_1} \bullet \frac{K_1}{S} \bullet \ln K_1 + a_{K_2} \bullet \frac{K_2}{S} \bullet \ln K_2 + a_{K_3} \bullet \frac{K_3}{S} \bullet \ln$$

## B. The Linear Programming Model

For the linear programming approach a reference technology is constructed from observed inputs and outputs. Let **X** be a (nxm) matrix of observed inputs (n inputs for m software projects) and **Q** be a (1xm) vector of observed output rates for each of the m software projects. Let superscript i define a particular software project contained in **X** and **Q**. Let $\mathbf{X}^i$ be a (nx1) vector of observed inputs on project i. The maximum potential output is defined by:

$$F(\mathbf{X}^i) = \text{Max } \mathbf{Q}\bullet\mathbf{Z}$$
$$\text{ST: } \mathbf{X}\bullet\mathbf{Z} \le \mathbf{X}^i$$
$$\mathbf{Z} \ge 0$$

The (mx1) vector **Z** contains the intensity variables. This linear program is solved once for each software project. The linear programs only differ in the right-hand-side vector which contains the observed inputs on a particular software project, i.

If $\mathbf{Z}^* = (Z_1, Z_2, \ldots., Z_m)$ is the optimal intensity variable vector, then following Banker [1], a project exhibits Constant Returns-to-Scale (CRS), Increasing Returns-to-Scale (IRS), or Decreasing Returns-to-Scale (DRS) according to the following:

$$CRS\ iff \quad SCALE = \sum_{i=0}^{m} Z_i^* = 1,$$

$$IRS\ iff \quad SCALE = \sum_{i=0}^{m} Z_i^* < 1,$$

$$DRS \ iff \quad SCALE = \sum_{i=0}^{m} Z_i^* > 1.$$

## IV. EMPIRICAL RESULTS

### A. Ray-Homothetic Model

The production function model can be estimated using ordinary least squares without simultaneous equation bias if we assume that the observed data were generated under the conditions of expected profit maximization (see [4] and [13]). The least squares regression results are given in Table 3.

Table 3. Regression Results

| Parameter | Estimate | t-ratio |
|---|---|---|
| $\theta$ | -1011.55 | -2.97 |
| $a_L$ | 232.60 | 4.31 |
| $a_{K1}$ | 1571.57 | 1.54 |
| $a_{K2}$ | 959.09 | 0.66 |
| $a_{K3}$ | 1496.06 | 0.65 |
| | n = 37 | $R^2$ = .45 |

In addition to the intercept, the coefficients on labor and the low-level productivity tools are significant. All of the estimated input coefficients are positive, indicating that increasing the relative importance of any one input has a positive effect on optimal size.

Using the parameter estimates and the input/output data, we computed RTS and OPTQ for each software development project. These estimates are given in Table 4, along with the observed output rate and the capital-labor ratio. From these estimates of returns-to-scale we observe that 8 projects operate under decreasing returns-to-scale, while 29 are operating under increasing returns-to-scale; i.e., actual output is less than optimal. To examine the relationship between RTS and the characteristics of software projects, descriptive statistics for output, optimal output, and the observed input mix, K/L, are given in Table 5.

Table 4. Results for the Ray-Homothetic Model

| Project | Q | OPTQ | Scale | Type | K/L |
|---|---|---|---|---|---|
| 1 | 130.0 | 299.8 | 2.3 | IRS | .055 |
| 2 | 400.0 | 302.1 | .8 | DRS | .059 |
| 3 | 68.0 | 470.3 | 6.9 | IRS | .458 |
| 4 | 75.0 | 281.4 | 3.8 | IRS | .025 |
| 5 | 12.0 | 512.6 | 42.7 | IRS | .611 |
| 6 | 20.0 | 324.7 | 16.2 | IRS | .100 |
| 7 | 45.0 | 395.8 | 8.8 | IRS | .250 |
| 8 | 75.0 | 279.8 | 3.7 | IRS | .022 |
| 9 | 200.0 | 277.0 | 1.4 | IRS | .018 |
| 10 | 147.0 | 292.8 | 2.0 | IRS | .043 |
| 11 | 1098.0 | 268.7 | .2 | DRS | .004 |
| 12 | 1500.0 | 288.9 | .2 | DRS | .037 |
| 13 | 1500.0 | 267.2 | .2 | DRS | .002 |
| 14 | 300.0 | 276.2 | .9 | DRS | .016 |
| 15 | 22.0 | 566.2 | 25.7 | IRS | .857 |
| 16 | 45.0 | 303.8 | 6.8 | IRS | .062 |
| 17 | 114.5 | 270.6 | 2.4 | IRS | .007 |
| 18 | 194.0 | 283.9 | 1.5 | IRS | .029 |
| 19 | 102.0 | 269.1 | 2.6 | IRS | .005 |
| 20 | 250.0 | 283.6 | 1.1 | IRS | .028 |
| 21 | 212.0 | 267.7 | 1.3 | IRS | .003 |
| 22 | 84.0 | 297.1 | 3.5 | IRS | .050 |
| 23 | 41.2 | 342.1 | 8.3 | IRS | .133 |
| 24 | 37.9 | 428.4 | 11.3 | IRS | .333 |
| 25 | 200.0 | 344.9 | 1.7 | IRS | .138 |
| 26 | 5.0 | 395.8 | 79.2 | IRS | .250 |
| 27 | 194.0 | 395.8 | 2.0 | IRS | .250 |
| 28 | 50.0 | 311.7 | 6.2 | IRS | .076 |
| 29 | 20.0 | 482.7 | 24.1 | IRS | .500 |
| 30 | 90.0 | 354.6 | 3.9 | IRS | .158 |
| 31 | 10.0 | 350.5 | 35.1 | IRS | .150 |
| 32 | 140.0 | 307.8 | 2.2 | IRS | .069 |
| 33 | 30.0 | 535.6 | 17.9 | IRS | .708 |
| 34 | 700.0 | 277.5 | .4 | DRS | .018 |
| 35 | 25.0 | 406.0 | 16.2 | IRS | .275 |
| 36 | 2000.0 | 273.2 | .1 | DRS | .012 |
| 37 | 500.0 | 270.3 | .5 | DRS | .007 |

Projects characterized by increasing returns are, on average, the smaller (in terms of Q); the largest project with increasing returns has 250 thousand lines of code. The projects characterized by increasing returns have, on average, higher capital-labor ratios than the eight projects which operate under decreasing returns.

Table 5. Statistics by RTS Results for the Ray-Homothetic Model

| Variable | Mean | St.Dev. | Minimum | Maximum |
|---|---|---|---|---|
| IRS (n=29) | | | | |
| SCALE | 13.010 | 18.760 | 1.000 | 84.800 |
| Q | 90.980 | 72.700 | 5.000 | 250.000 |
| OPTQ | 377.410 | 139.300 | 236.300 | 713.300 |
| K/L | .195 | .224 | .003 | .857 |
| DRS (N=8) | | | | |
| SCALE | .390 | .270 | .120 | .840 |
| Q | 999.750 | 621.000 | 300.000 | 2000.000 |
| OPTQ | 253.600 | 189.800 | 235.300 | 293.400 |
| K/L | .019 | .018 | .002 | .059 |
| TOTAL (N=37) | | | | |
| SCALE | 10.290 | 17.370 | .120 | 84.770 |
| Q | 287.470 | 472.170 | 5.000 | 2000.000 |
| OPTQ | 350.640 | 133.560 | 235.280 | 713.330 |
| K/L | .157 | .211 | .002 | .857 |

B. Nonparametric Linear Programming Approach

In order to isolate the effects of the software development tools, the 37 linear programs were analyzed two ways. The models were solved with four factor inputs: labor, high-level tools, nominal tools, and low-level tools. For the second approach the models were solved using only labor as an input. This specification was basically for comparison with Banker and Kemerer [2] and some of the earlier literature that they cite. In the analysis that follows, the four input model is called the full model, while the single input model is called the reduced model. The scale estimates from the 37 linear programs are summarized in Tables 6 and 7, and the individual estimates are presented in Table 8.

Table 6. Statistics by RTS Results for the Full Model

| Variable | Mean | St. Dev. | Minimum | Maximum |
|---|---|---|---|---|
| | IRS (n=24) | | | |
| SCALE | .550 | .194 | .213 | .921 |
| Q | 93.525 | 83.463 | 5.000 | 300.000 |
| K/L | .189 | .251 | .003 | .857 |
| | DRS (N=8) | | | |
| SCALE | 1.260 | .307 | 1.005 | 1.966 |
| Q | 394.125 | 364.741 | 25.000 | 1098.000 |
| K/L | .092 | .094 | .005 | .275 |
| | CRS (N=5) | | | |
| SCALE | 1.000 | .000 | 1.000 | 1.000 |
| Q | 1047.800 | 873.246 | 45.000 | 2000.000 |
| K/L | .110 | .128 | .250 | .057 |

Table 7. Statistics by RTS Results for the Reduced Model

| Variable | Mean | St .Dev. | Minimum | Maximum |
|---|---|---|---|---|
| IRS (n=7) | | | | |
| SCALE | .550 | .137 | .292 | .667 |
| Q | 27.843 | 20.764 | 5.000 | 68.000 |
| K/L | .531 | .212 | .250 | .857 |
| DRS (N=28) | | | | |
| SCALE | 22.172 | 31.917 | 1.111 | 138.889 |
| Q | 364.382 | 520.626 | 10.000 | 2000.000 |
| K/L | .058 | .063 | .003 | .275 |
| CRS (N=2) | | | | |
| SCALE | 1.000 | .000 | 1.000 | 1.000 |
| Q | 119.500 | 105.359 | 45.000 | 194.000 |
| K/L | .250 | .000 | .250 | .250 |

The results are quite different for the two models (which is expected), but in either case increasing returns are usually associated with the smaller projects, just as Banker and Kemerer hypothesized.

The tools delay the onset of diminishing returns. The average size of projects exhibiting constant returns-to-scale is 119.5 when labor is the only productive input. The average size increases to 1047.8 when the tools are included in the production specification.

Table 8. Returns-to-Scale Results for the Linear Programming Model

| Project | Q | Scale Estimate (Full Model) | Type | Scale Estimate (Reduced Model) | Type |
|---|---|---|---|---|---|
| 1 | 130.0 | .583 | IRS | 4.500 | DRS |
| 2 | 400.0 | 1.307 | DRS | 8.861 | DRS |
| 3 | 68.0 | .667 | IRS | .667 | IRS |
| 4 | 75.0 | .363 | IRS | 10.000 | DRS |
| 5 | 12.0 | .500 | IRS | .500 | IRS |
| 6 | 20.0 | .548 | IRS | 1.667 | DRS |
| 7 | 45.0 | 1.000 | CRS | 1.000 | CRS |
| 8 | 75.0 | .294 | IRS | 8.667 | DRS |
| 9 | 200.0 | .504 | IRS | 16.972 | DRS |
| 10 | 147.0 | .682 | IRS | 8.889 | DRS |
| 11 | 1098.0 | 1.025 | DRS | 90.278 | DRS |
| 12 | 1500.0 | 1.000 | CRS | 20.833 | DRS |
| 13 | 1500.0 | 1.000 | CRS | 138.889 | DRS |
| 14 | 300.0 | .426 | IRS | 15.000 | DRS |
| 15 | 22.0 | .292 | IRS | .292 | IRS |
| 16 | 45.0 | .643 | IRS | 4.000 | DRS |
| 17 | 114.5 | .410 | IRS | 24.611 | DRS |
| 18 | 194.0 | .346 | IRS | 8.611 | DRS |
| 19 | 102.0 | .312 | IRS | 24.917 | DRS |
| 20 | 250.0 | .772 | IRS | 19.444 | DRS |
| 21 | 212.0 | .213 | IRS | 25.000 | DRS |
| 22 | 84.0 | .653 | IRS | 6.000 | DRS |
| 23 | 41.2 | .796 | IRS | 1.667 | DRS |
| 24 | 37.9 | .667 | IRS | .667 | IRS |
| 25 | 200.0 | 1.005 | DRS | 2.000 | DRS |
| 26 | 5.0 | .557 | IRS | .557 | IRS |
| 27 | 194.0 | 1.000 | CRS | 1.000 | CRS |
| 28 | 50.0 | .891 | IRS | 4.000 | DRS |
| 29 | 20.0 | .500 | IRS | .500 | IRS |
| 30 | 90.0 | 1.966 | DRS | 3.333 | DRS |
| 31 | 10.0 | .921 | IRS | 1.667 | DRS |
| 32 | 140.0 | 1.151 | DRS | 6.000 | DRS |
| 33 | 30.0 | .667 | IRS | .667 | IRS |
| 34 | 700.0 | 1.216 | DRS | 40.000 | DRS |
| 35 | 25.0 | 1.111 | DRS | 1.111 | DRS |
| 36 | 2000.0 | 1.000 | CRS | 41.667 | DRS |
| 37 | 500.0 | 1.302 | DRS | 82.222 | DRS |

The relationship between size and scale is further examined in Table 9 where Spearman's correlation coefficient (r) between size and scale is estimated for both models. The values in the parentheses are the probabilities of observing a larger estimated r (in absolute value) under the null hypothesis that the population correlation coefficient is zero.

Table 9. Spearman Correlation Estimates Between Size and Scale

| Full Model | Reduced Model |
|---|---|
| r = .434 (.0073) | r = .843 (.0001) |

We note that these results are not uniform over the complete data set. The projects were sorted on size and split into two groups. The small group contains the 18 smallest projects, and the large group contains the 19 largest projects. The correlation results for these data sets are presented in Table 10.

Table 10. Spearman Correlation Estimates Between Size and Scale

| | Full Model | Reduced Model |
|---|---|---|
| Small | r = .037 (.8850) | r = .687 (.0016) |
| Large | r = .454 (.0510) | r = .586 (.0084) |

With the reduced model, the linear relationship between size and scale cannot be rejected, but in the presence of the productivity tools the relationship *breaks down* for the small projects.

C. The Effects of Hardware

None of the models examine the way that hardware affects scale. A more detailed model would include capital inputs that relate to hardware. These measures should consider peripheral devices as well as central processing units. In a production sense, if hardware were a limiting factor, it should create a *congestion* effect on the production process. One would expect these effects to show up more in the peripherals then in the processors, but we have no way to measure congestion effects in either case.

However, we do have some information about hardware effects. In the survey [10], several questions were asked that give some insight into hardware effects. Each respondent was asked the following question: "Does your hardware limit what software can be employed?" If the answer to this question is affirmative, then this measure could be considered a proxy for congestion. A second question related to hardware classification. Each respondent was asked to classify hardware as satisfactory, obsolescent, or obsolete. In the survey glossary, obsolescent was defined as "becoming obsolete," and obsolete was defined as "outmoded."

Only one respondent classified the hardware as obsolete, so for the analyses that follows, the obsolete and obsolescent data were combined. Table 11 provides a description of the sample according to the classification based on the two hardware questions. We note that 28 of the 37 projects have consistent responses to the two questions in the sense that if hardware is obsolete, then there is a limit on software, or if hardware is satisfactory, then there is no limit on software. The observations in the off-diagonal classes are not necessarily inconsistent. For example, hardware could be considered obsolete but not a limiting factor in software development. We do, however, analyze the returns-to-scale results for both questions. This comparison is provided in Table 12. In general, there is no consistent pattern in the relationship between classifying observations based on returns-to-scale status and the classification by responses to hardware status questions.

Table 11: Responses to Hardware Survey Questions

| Status of Hardware | Hardware Limit on Software: Yes | No | Total |
|---|---|---|---|
| Obsolete/Obsolescent | 9 | 2 | 11 |
| Satisfactory | 7 | 19 | 26 |
| Total | 16 | 21 | 37 |

Table 12. Returns-to-Scale Results and Hardware Status

| | Number of Observations With: IRS | CRS | DRS | Average Scale |
|---|---|---|---|---|
| Hardware Limit | | | | |
| Yes | 10 | 3 | 3 | .79 |
| No | 14 | 2 | 5 | .74 |
| Hardware Status | | | | |
| Obsolete | 6 | 3 | 2 | .85 |
| Satisfactory | 18 | 2 | 6 | .73 |

The obvious extension is to determine which tools have larger marginal productivity with respect to potential output. This is accomplished by examining the dual variables from the 37 linear programs. Let $Y_1$, $Y_2$, $Y_3$, and $Y_4$ represent the dual variables for labor and tool categories 1-3 respectively. Also let U represent the dual variable for labor in the single input model. The descriptive information on the optimal dual variables is presented in Table 13.

Table 13. Linear Programming Dual Variables

| Variable | Mean | St. Dev. | Minimum | Maximum |
|---|---|---|---|---|
| $Y_1$ | 1.48 | 1.47 | .00 | 5.38 |
| $Y_2$ | 19.87 | 43.14 | .00 | 161.50 |
| $Y_3$ | 13.53 | 30.12 | .00 | 166.67 |
| $Y_4$ | 56.68 | 82.27 | .00 | 227.94 |
| U | 5.38 | .00 | 5.38 | 5.38 |

The surprising characteristic of this table is the large marginal productivity of the higher-order tools. The marginal change in potential output for these tools is (on the average) larger. In our future research we are studying the characteristics of the projects for which additional higher-order tools generate large increases in potential output.

## V. CONCLUSIONS

The results of this paper are two-fold. First, we confirm earlier research that suggests that increasing returns-to-scale are associated with small software development projects and decreasing returns-to-scale are associated with larger projects. Second, our results indicate that when software productivity tools are included in the model, the project size that is associated with the onset of diminishing returns is much larger. Our results also indicate that in general the higher level tools have larger marginal productivity with respect to potential output.

## VI. REFERENCES

[1] Banker, R.D., Estimating Most Productive Scale Size Using Data Envelopment Analysis, *European Journal of Operational Research*, Vol. 17 (1984), 35-44.

[2] Banker, R.D. and C.F. Kemerer, Scale Economies in New Software Development, *IEEE Transactions on Software Engineering*, Vol. 15, 1199-1205.

[3] Boehm, Barry W. *Software Engineering Economics*. Englewood Cliffs: Prentice-Hall, 1981.

[4] Boyd, G., Factor Intensity and Site Geology as Determinants of Returns-to-Scale in Coal Mining, *Review of Economics and Statistics*, Vol. 69 (1987), 18-23.

[5] Defense Logistics Agency. *DoD Automated Resources Management System (ARMS)*, Users Guide, April, 1985.

[6] Byrnes, P., R. Färe, and S. Grosskopf, Measuring Productive Efficiency: An Application to Illinois Strip Mines, *Management Science*, Vol. 30 (1984), 671-681.

[7] Färe, R., *Fundamentals of Production Theory*. Berlin: Springer-Verlag,1988.

[8] Färe, R., On Scaling Laws for Production Functions, *Zeitschrift für Operations Research*, Vol. 17 (1973), 195-205.

[9] Ferguson, C.E., *The Neoclassical Theory of Production and Distribution*. Cambridge: Cambridge University Press, 1969.

[10] Levitan, K.B., J. Salasin, T.P. Frazier, and B.N. Angier, *Final Report on the Status of Software obsolescence in the DoD*, P-2126, Institute for Defense Analyses, 1988.

[11] Lovell, C.A.K. and P. Schmidt, A Comparison of Alternative Approaches to the Measurement of Productive Efficiency, In A. Dogramaci and R. Färe, Editors, *Applications of Modern Production Theory: Efficiency and Productivity*. Boston: Kluwer Academic Publishers, 1988.

[12] Shephard, R.W., *Theory of Cost and Production Functions*. Princeton: Princeton University Press, 1970.

[13] Zellner, A., J. Kmenta, and J. Dreze, Specification and Estimation of Cobb-Douglas Production Function Models, *Econometrica*, Vol. 34 (1966), 784-795.

# AN ECONOMICS MODEL OF SOFTWARE REUSE

R.D. Cruickshank and J.E. Gaffney, Jr.
Software Productivity Consortium
2214 Rock Hill Road
Herndon, VA 22070

## INTRODUCTION

Much attention has been paid to software reuse in recent years because it is recognized as a key means for obtaining higher productivity in the development of new software systems (Gaffney and Durek 1988; Gaffney and Durek 1991; and Gaffney 1989). Also, software reuse has provided the technical benefit of reduced error content and thus higher quantity. The primary economic benefit of software reuse is cost avoidance. Reuse of an existent software object generally costs much less than creating a new software object.

The reuse economics model presented here should be regarded as a tool to aid in the exploration of the economic benefits of software reuse but not as an algorithm that covers all possible cases of reuse. The framework provided will aid the analyst and the project manager in making decisions about software reuse. The model covers various topics, including the effect of various strategies of investing in the creation of reusable software objects (RSOs), the cost effects of reusing requirements or design in addition to the costs of reusing code, and the effects of reuse on software quality.

## OVERVIEW

Software reuse can occur at many levels, ranging from the reuse of small granules of function (small software objects) within an application system to the reuse of large granules of software function (large software objects) across many application systems. For example, in an antiballistic missile system, the filtering routine in the signal processing function is a small granule while the location and tracking function is a large granule. The reuse methodology covers a wide range, from the ad hoc level of reuse of code to the systematic reuse of software based on an application domain.

Reuse within an application system often takes place as the multiple use of a unit (or granule as above), such as a routine to implement a sine function or a finite impulse response filter, in a number of the major functions of that system. This type of reuse or multiple use of a software object has been common since FORTRAN began to be used. Multiple use within a system is facilitated in Ada through the use of the with and include constructs.

The reuse economics model presented here focuses on the systematic reuse of RSOs having a relatively large amount of functionality. These RSOs are not typically used more than once in a given application system. Systematic reuse is concerned with defining and establishing a domain of software systems, i.e., a family of software systems having similar descriptions (Parnas 1976). Such a family is a set of systems with similar requirements that can be (or are) satisfied by a common architecture and represent a set of closely related design choices at the detailed level. A domain is a coherent business area and the application area corresponding to the family of systems. A domain model characterizes an application family.

The benefits of establishing such a software domain are that software engineering and domain expertise are captured in a manageable form, and this knowledge can be used to produce families of similar application systems. As shown by Parnas, large (functional scale) RSO reuse can be sequential (from one application system to another) or parallel. In the latter case, a common set of RSOs may be used by several application systems which could be developed in parallel or sequentially. This type of reuse might actually be better termed multiple use. The Synthesis development methodology (Campbell 1990; Campbell, Faulk, and Weiss 1990) is concerned with this type of reuse.

The principal economic benefits of software reuse are:

- Lower development costs.
- Higher software product quality due to multiple testing and error removal opportunities reused over a number of application systems.
- Reduced development schedule due to a reduced amount of development work.
- Lower maintenance costs due to lower levels of error creation.
- Reduced life-cycle costs due to reduced development and maintenance costs.

Systematic reuse views software maintenance as a series of redevelopments (i.e., incremental refinements) of application systems.

**SYSTEMATIC REUSE**

The reuse economics model presented here focuses on the systematic reuse of large-scale functional units. Systematic reuse in the reuse economics model is viewed as consisting of two principal activities: domain engineering and application engineering. Domain engineering is the set of activities that are involved in creating RSOs that can be employed as a plurality of specific software systems or application systems. Application engineering is the set of activities that are involved in creating a specific application system.

Domain engineering is regarded in the economic model presented here as covering the capital investment required to create a set of RSOs. Thus, domain engineering includes the capital investment activities necessary to produce a family of application systems. In domain engineering, the requirements for the family of software systems are identified, and the reusable structure to implement the family members is developed.

Capital investment here means the initial investment in terms of effort to create the means to produce application systems before those application systems are actually produced. This investment may be made all at once for the entire domain investment, or it may be made incrementally over the life of the domain, i.e., as long as the domain is used to produce application systems. The effort spent in domain engineering is a capital investment in creating the domain, including the domain definition and models, the application modeling language, and the reuse library. The term capital investment here does not imply any specific contractual arrangement.

### Domain Engineering

Domain engineering is the capital investment process for creating the RSOs for a family of similar systems. It may be done up-front, all at once, or incrementally, over part or all of the time period. The family of application systems, which include some of the RSOs created by the domain engineering processes, is created in this same time period. Domain engineering includes all of the activities associated with identifying a target family of application systems, describing the variation among these systems, constructing an adaptable design, and defining the methods for translating requirements into application systems composed of reusable components.

Domain engineering may not occur in some modes of reuse. One such mode is the ad hoc reuse of software objects that were created for another system. Such objects can include requirements and/or design and/or test plans as well as code. Alternatively, although domain engineering may occur, its cost may not be a consideration to the application system developer because it is borne by someone else. An example of this is when a government agency provides the RSOs produced by one contractor to another contractor tasked with developing an application system.

As shown subsequently, the costs of domain engineering may be amortized in different ways. The simplest way is to spread them across all of the application systems. Other methods include spreading some of them over one subset of the application systems or another part over another subset. The latter scheme is probably the more realistic. It is often difficult if not impossible to anticipate all of the possible variations that might occur across a set of application systems before any are built. In addition, it may be difficult to obtain sufficient funding to cover all of the domain engineering required for the family of application systems.

### Application Engineering

Application engineering is the process of composing a particular application software system which is a member of the family of systems defined in the domain engineering process. Application engineering consists of composing the specific application system with RSOs and any new software needed, reengineering existent software required, and testing the system. Thus, application engineering is a process for producing quality software from reusable components. The application systems are generated from reusable components to implement all of the associated requirements definitions.

Application engineering may be summarized as:

- Transforming the customer's input into a requirements specification for the specific application system to be developed.

- Generating new software objects specific to this application system, some of which may be reusable in other application systems and which may be entered into the reuse library.

- Composing the application system by integrating the new software objects and the reusable software objects obtained from the reuse library. The reuse economics model presented here considers any modified code to be in the new code category.

## THE BASIC ECONOMICS MODEL OF SOFTWARE REUSE

This section presents the basic model of software reuse. It describes the basic model with up-front domain engineering. The version of the model which covers incremental domain engineering is described later.

### Model Assumptions

The assumptions implicit in the reuse economics model are:

- Costs may be measured in labor months (LM) or labor hours (LH) which can be converted to dollars as appropriate.

- The true development cost for a new application system consists of the investment costs in domain engineering (apportioned over the expected number of application systems to which it applies) plus the cost of application engineering specific to the given application system.

  It is important to note that a development organization under some circumstances may not take the cost of domain engineering into account. One such situation is when a government agency provides the results of domain engineering to a contractor developing new application system as government-furnished information.

- A new application software system is composed of two categories of code, new and reused.

- A variety of software objects, including requirements, design, code, test plans, and test steps, may be reusable.

- The cost (in LM) of software development activities can be calculated as the product of a labor rate (LM divided by the size of the software product) and the size (in thousands of source statements) of the software product. Algebraically, this concept is represented by:

$$LM = (LM/KSLOC)(KSLOC)$$

### Reuse Economics Model With Up-Front Domain Engineering

The reuse economics model is designed to reflect the total costs of applying a reuse scheme. The model treats the cost of an application system as the cost of the capital investment in domain engineering apportioned over the expected N application systems plus the cost of application engineering (the cost of creating that particular system). Thus, the cost of an application system, $C_S$, equals the prorated cost of domain engineering plus the cost of application engineering. Further, the cost of application engineering is the cost of the new plus the cost of the reused code in the new application system. Then:

$$C_S = C_{DP} + C_A$$

$$C_S = C_D/N + C_N + C_R$$

where:

$$C_{DP} = C_D/N \text{ and } C_A = C_N + C_R$$

$C_D$ = The total cost of domain engineering.

$C_{DP}$ = The pro rata share domain engineering borne some by each of the N application systems.

$C_A$ = The cost of an application system.

$C_N$ = The cost of the new code in the application system.

$C_R$ = The cost of the reused code in the application system.

Now, each of the costs, $C_D$, $C_N$, and $C_R$, is the product of a unit cost (LM/KSLOC) and an amount of code (KSLOC). Note that all costs are in LM.

Then:

$$C_D = C_{DE} \cdot S_T$$

$$C_N = C_{VN} \cdot S_N$$

$$C_R = C_{VR} \cdot S_R$$

Therefore the basic reuse cost equation is:

$$C_S = C_{US}\, S_S = C_{DE}\, S_T/N + C_{VN}\, S_N + C_{VR}\, S_R$$

where:

$C_{US}$ = Unit cost of the application system.

$C_{DE}$ = Unit cost of domain engineering.

$C_{VN}$ = Unit cost of new code developed for this application system.

$C_{VR}$ = Unit cost of reusing code from the reuse library in this application system. It represents the unit cost of reused code in the case where the library components can be instantiated directly into the application system with no modification.

$S_T$ = Expected value of the unduplicated size of the reuse library, i.e., the available, reusable functionality (source statements) in the library.

$S_N$ = Amount of new code in source statements developed for this application system.

$S_R$ = Amount of reused code (from the reuse library) incorporated into this application system in source statements.

$S_S$ = Total size of the application system in source statements.

Code sizes $S_N$, $S_R$, $S_S$, and $S_T$ are nominally denominated in source statements, either physical or logical (see Gaffney and Cruickshank 1991a; Gaffney and Cruickshank 1991b). These code sizes could be denominated in function points (Albrecht and Gaffney 1983) or their variations, such as feature points. The important thing is that consistent units of code size be employed.

Let $S_N/S_S = 1 - R$ and $S_R/S_S = R$, where R is the proportion of reuse.

Dividing through by $S_S$ and rewriting:

$$C_{US} = \frac{C_{DE}}{N}\frac{S_T}{S_S} + C_{VN}(1-R) + C_{VR}R$$

Now let $S_T/S_S = K$, the library relative capacity. Thus:

$$C_{US} = \frac{C_{DE}}{N} \cdot K + C_{VN} - (C_{VN} - C_{VR}) \cdot R$$

This is the basic reuse unit cost equation. It presumes a single reuse of $S_R$ units (SLOC, KSLOC, function points) in each of the N application systems, on the average. Thus, this equation is most applicable to systematic reuse of units of code having a relatively large amount of functionality.

Some of the software developed for a given application system, of amount $S_N$, might be deemed reusable on other application systems. Such software may be treated as resulting from a portion of an incremental domain engineering investment.

Although not treated further here, the unit cost parameters ($C_{VN}$, $C_{VR}$, and $C_{DE}$) can be considered to be time-variant. Thus, they can represent the effects of technology change (methodology and tools) over time. These parameters are considered to be time-invariant here.

### Library Efficiency

This section discusses some aspects of the structure of a reuse library from an economics point of view.

A reuse library may be constructed so that there are a number of duplicate or alternative objects to cover the expected variation of a unit of function. Alternatively, there may be just object per function, but with the expected variation to be covered by the (application engineer's selection of the) values of one or more parameters to cover that variation.

$S_T$ is the "unduplicated" size of the library or its capacity. There may well be alternate or duplicate implementation functionality in the reuse library (source code, as just stated), but that alternate or duplicate functionality will not add to the size of $S_T$. The case of alternative implementation of source code or all of the functionality of size $S_T$ is covered in the cost model by an appropriate selection of the value of the unit cost parameter, $C_{DE}$.

The factor K (= $S_T$ / $S_S$), the library relative capacity, represents the average proportion (over the N application systems) of an application system in the family of systems that the library covers. Thus, if $S_S$ represents the average application system size in the domain of interest, K is the upper bound for R, or $R \leq K \leq 1$.

The efficiency of the library infrastructure, E, is the ratio of the amount of reused code in the application system to the available reusable code:

$$E = \frac{R}{K} = \frac{S_R \;/\; S_S}{S_T \;/\; S_S} = \frac{S_R}{S_T}$$

where $0 \leq E \leq 1$.

The factor E indicates the extent to which the developer of a new application system has been able to make use of the library of reusable components in the new system. For example, the reuse library may contain a Kalman filtering program and a navigation program that contains a Kalman filtering routine. If the Navigation program is selected (perhaps because it contains a Kalman, filtering routine) to be be used in an application system, then the efficiency of the library for that specific application system is less than 1.0 because the alternate (or duplicate) Kalman filtering program was not used.

E is a measure of the efficiency of the systematic reuse application process. Normally, E is 1.0 or slightly less than 1.0, since application engineers on average are expected to reuse as much code as possible when composing an application system.

If K is assumed to be equal to R, or $S_R = S_T$ (which means E = 1), then the basic reuse unit cost equation can be rewritten as:

$$C_{US} = \frac{C_{DE}}{N} \cdot R + C_{VN} - (C_{VN} - C_{VR}) \cdot R$$

Consolidating terms obtains:

$$C_{US} = C_{VN} - \left( C_{VN} - C_{VR} - \frac{C_{DE}}{N} \right) R$$

This equation is the standard reuse unit cost equation.

### Some Example Applications of the Model

This section provides three example applications of the basic reuse unit cost equation. The three examples are an Ada aerospace system, a real-time command and control (RTCC) application, and a management information system (MIS) application. These applications have the values $C_{DE}$, $C_{VN}$, and $C_{VR}$ given in LM/KSLOC appropriate to a specific instance of domain and application engineering. The labor rates for $C_{VN}$ and $C_{VR}$ are derived from actual RTCC, MIS, and Ada development experience. The labor rates for $C_{DE}$ are based on analysis of the functions included in domain engineering for the RTCC and MIS applications. In the case of the Ada aerospace application, a value of 1.5 for the ratio of $C_{DE}$ to $C_{VN}$ is assumed. The RTCC labor rates (unit costs) are derived from experience based on a DOD-STD-2167A model translated to a systematic reuse model. The MIS labor rates (unit costs) are based on experience with SPECTRUM* and with function points translated to the systematic reuse model derived above.

Table 1 shows the unit costs (in LM/KSLOC) of the two cost configurations.

Table 1. Cost Parameter Applications

| Cost Parameters | Application (LM/KSLOC) | | |
|---|---|---|---|
| | **RTCC** | **MIS** | **Ada Aerospace** |
| $C_{DE}$ | 5.305 | 2.122 | 15.000 |
| $C_{VN}$ | 2.072 | 1.012 | 10.000 |
| $C_{VR}$ | 0.514 | 0.271 | 1.000 |

Thus, the two parametric configurations of the systematic reuse unit cost equations are:

$$\text{RTCC:}\ C_{US} = \frac{5.305}{N} \cdot K + 2.072 - 1.558 \cdot R$$

* Trademark of Software Architecture and Engineering Inc.

$$\text{MIS: } C_{US} = \frac{2.122}{N} \cdot K + 1.012 - 0.741 \cdot R$$

$$\text{Ada aerospace: } C_{US} = \frac{15.000}{N} \cdot K + 10.000 - 9.000 \cdot R$$

Table 2 shows the productivities (in SLOC/LM) resulting from these configurations under the assumption that E = 1 or K = R.

Table 2. Reuse Economics Model Application Productivities

| (E = 1.0) | | Application (SLOC/LM) | | |
|---|---|---|---|---|
| **N** | **R** | **RTCC** | **MIS** | **Ada Aerospace** |
| 2 | 0.7 | 352 | 809 | 112 |
| 2 | 0.9 | 327 | 769 | 116 |
| 3 | 0.7 | 451 | 1,011 | 139 |
| 3 | 0.9 | 442 | 1,018 | 156 |
| 4 | 0.7 | 524 | 1,156 | 158 |
| 4 | 0.9 | 537 | 1,215 | 190 |
| 5 | 0.7 | 580 | 1,265 | 172 |
| 5 | 0.9 | 615 | 1,375 | 217 |
| 10 | 0.7 | 739 | 1,557 | 211 |
| 10 | 0.9 | 872 | 1,864 | 308 |
| 15 | 0.7 | 814 | 1,687 | 227 |
| 15 | 0.9 | 1,012 | 2,115 | 357 |

Table 2 illustrates the cost and productivity benefits to be gained from systematic reuse. Available data shows industry productivities for new software development (design through integration test) to be in the range of 80 to 180 SLOC/LM (12.500 to 5.556 LM/KSLOC). The reuse productivities in Table 2 show a considerable improvement over these performances.

Also note that, where the value of R increases in Table 2, the productivity actually decreases for certain values of N. This result is contrary to intuition, which would expect increasing productivity to accompany increasing values of R. However, where the number of expected application systems is less than the break-even number of systems, decreasing productivity accompanies an increasing proportion of reuse. This phenomenon is discussed later, where the concept of break-even number of systems is introduced.

## Some Recent Reuse Experience

This section provides some data on recent reuse experience. Because no formal domain engineering was done in the composition of these systems, the value for $C_{DE}$ was set at zero. The systems were done in sequence, with software objects being reused (and modified in some cases) from a prior system in creating a new software application system.

### Management Information Systems

Allan Albrecht (Albrecht 1989) provided some worldwide reuse experience from IBM in the development of MIS applications during the period of 1984 to 1988. The data is in the form of function point and productivity measurements on software created for internal IBM applications such as billing and ordering. The applications were written in PL/1. One function point (Albrecht and Gaffney 1983) is equivalent to about 80 lines of PL/1 or 106 lines of COBOL. The 1988 reuse data analyzed here was determined from about 0.5M function points from more than 50 development sites, worldwide.

Figure 1 presents this function point data on overall product productivity, new code productivity, and average percent reuse. The overall product productivity and the percent code reuse figures are for the years 1984 to 1988. The new code productivity figures are for 1986 to 1988; data for the 1984 to 1985 period was not available. Note that overall productivity is equal to total function points in the software system divided by total LM, while new code productivity is equal to function points of new code per LM for new function points. Table 3 shows the data to which the histograms correspond.

Table 3. Productivity and Reuse Experience

| Year | Overall Productivity (P) Function Points/LM | New Code Productivity (N) Function Points/LM | Average Percent Code Reuse (R) |
|---|---|---|---|
| 1984 | 22 | — | — |
| 1985 | 20 | — | — |
| 1986 | 25 | 14 | 31.5 |
| 1987 | 32 | 18 | 40.0 |
| 1988 | 49 | 23 | 67.2 |

Table 4 shows the partial correlations for the years 1986 to 1988 among the three variables shown in Table 3 and the corresponding figures for $100r^2$, the percentage variation of one variable "explained" by its relationship to the other and corrected for the third. Partial correlations indicate the correlations between two variables while holding the third constant, i.e., correcting for the third.

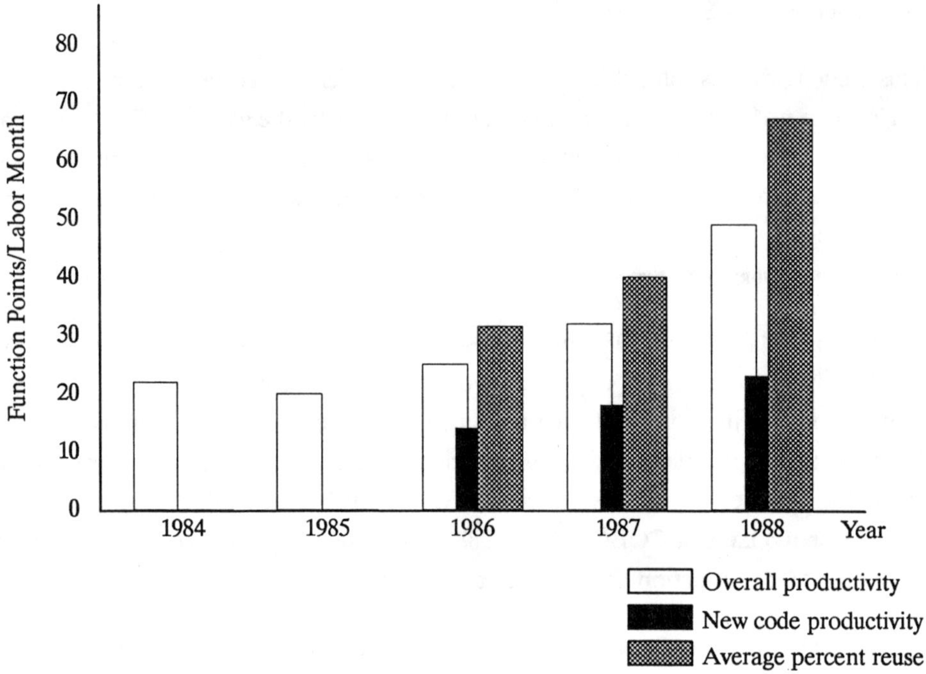


Figure 1. Worldwide Productivity and Reuse Experience

Table 4. Partial Correlations Among Variables, 1986 to 1988

| Variables | | | |
|---|---|---|---|
| Correlated | Held Constant | Correlation r | $100r^2$ |
| P,R | N | 0.9982 | 98.36 |
| P,N | R | 0.9854 | 97.10 |
| R,N | P | -0.9736 | 94.79 |

The strong partial correlations indicate that both the new code productivity (N) and the percent code reuse (R) had a strong influence on the increase in overall productivity (P) in the years 1986 to 1988. Table 5 shows the percent increase in each variable.

There was an increasing degree of code reuse over the period shown, both from the reuse of code and from the new code. This was partially based on the reuse of existing requirements or design so that the increase in overall productivity was strongly associated with both types of reuse.

Table 5. Percent Increase of Variables, 1986 to 1988

| Variable | Percent Increase |
|---|---|
| P | 96 |
| N | 64 |
| R | 113 |

Figure 2 presents a plot of unit cost, $C_{US}$, in LM per function point multiplied by 100, versus the proportion of code reuse for the software development sites reporting in 1988. The data was grouped into six ranges of reuse plus the point (0.0,5.41), as presented in Table 6.

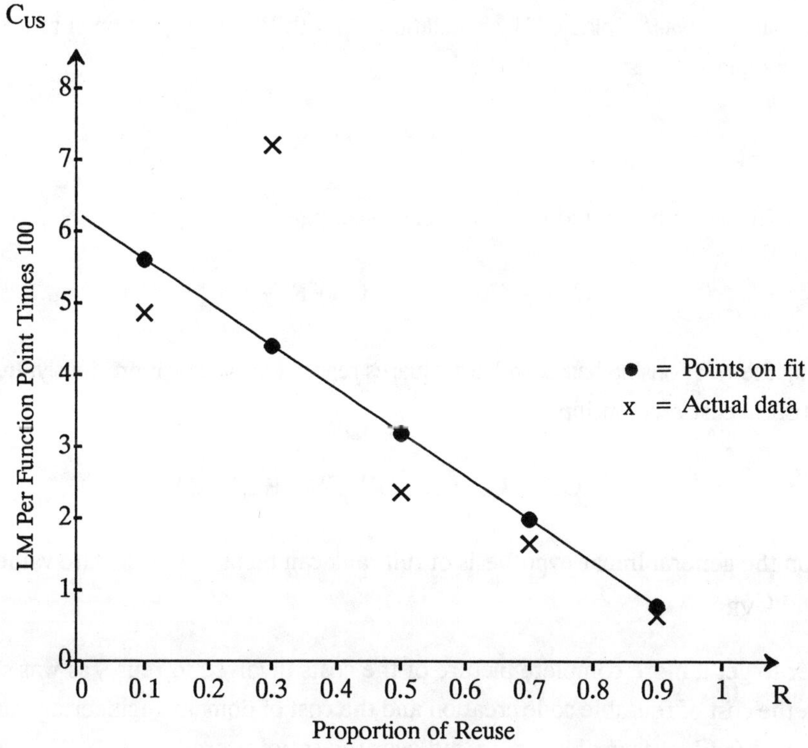


Figure 2. Cost Per Product Unit for 1988

Table 6. 1988 Product Unit Costs Versus Proportion of Code Reuse

| Proportion of Reuse, R | (LM/Function Point) Times 100 |
|---|---|
| 0.0 | 5.41 |
| 0.1 | 4.85 |
| 0.3 | 7.19 |
| 0.5 | 2.35 |
| 0.7 | 1.63 |
| 0.9 | 0.63 |

The product moment sample correlation of $C_{US}$ and R was found to be –0.832 (significant at the 5 percent level) which means that 69.16 percent of the variation in $C_{US}$, the overall product unit cost, was "explained" by its relationship with R, the proportion of reuse. The regression equation was:

$$C_{US} = 6.188 - 6.027^{*}R$$

$C_{VR}$ should not be estimated from the relationship:

$$C_{USi} = C_{VN} - (C_{VN} - C_{VR})^{*}R + \epsilon_i$$

i.e., using the relationship based on least squares regression as shown previously. Instead the statistical cost relationship:

$$C_{Ai} = C_{VN} \cdot S_{Ni} + C_{VR}{}^{*}S_{Ri} + \epsilon_i$$

based on the general linear hypothesis of full rank can be used to calculate values for $C_{VN}$ and $C_{VR}$.

In order to get a more complete picture of the costs involved in reuse, as was stated earlier, the cost of reusable code creation and the cost of domain engineering must be determined (and, presumably, amortized over the set of users).

**Aerospace**

Figure 3 shows the total unit cost in LH/SLOC, $C_{US}$, plotted against the percent of code reuse, R, for eight aerospace applications. (The 0 percent data point is the average of five points, 0.6433 LH/SLOC.) A straight line has been fitted using linear regression, and the fitted equation is:

$$C_{US} = 0.7850 - 0.009435^{\bullet}R$$

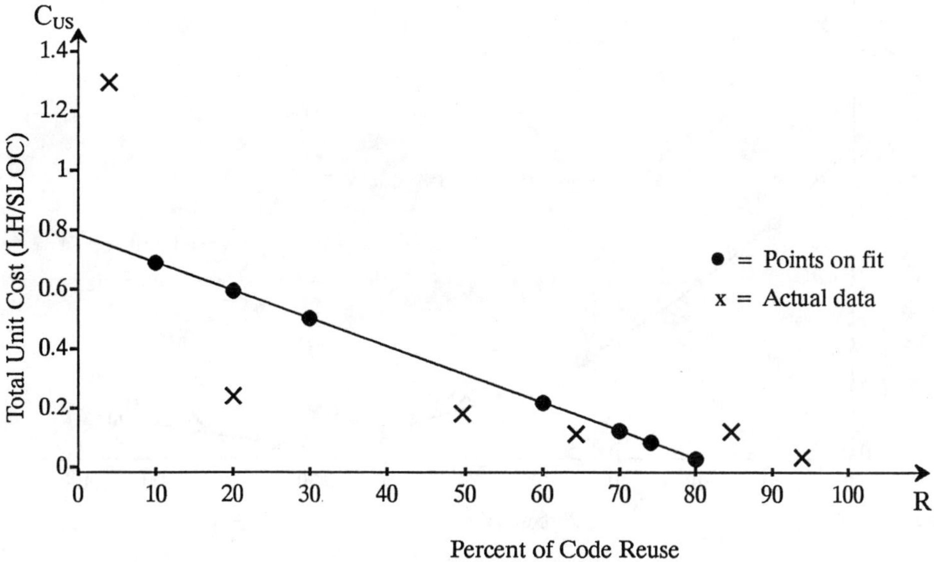


Figure 3. Unit Cost as a Linear Function of Percent Reuse

The correlation of $C_{US}$ and R is r = –0.785, which means that $100r^2 = 61.54$ percent of the variation in $C_{US}$ is explained by its relationship with R. It is obvious from this data and from the fitted line that unit cost declines with an increasing proportion of reuse.

Figure 4 shows the same data as in Figure 3 with a quadratic form fitted. The equation is:

$$C_{US} = 0.920 - 0.0239^{\bullet}R + 0.00016114^{\bullet}R^2$$

Here the multiple correlation of $C_{US}$ with R and $R^2$ is r = –0.846. Thus, the quadratic equation in R provides a better fit than shown in Figure 3 since only $100r^2 = 71.6$ percent of the variation in $C_{US}$ is explained by its relationship to R and $R^2$ in that case. The goodness of this relationship suggests that, in some reuse regimes, the unit cost of software products decrease with increasing levels of reuse but then increase beyond a certain level of reuse. Perhaps the nature of the reuse process becomes less efficient beyond this point.

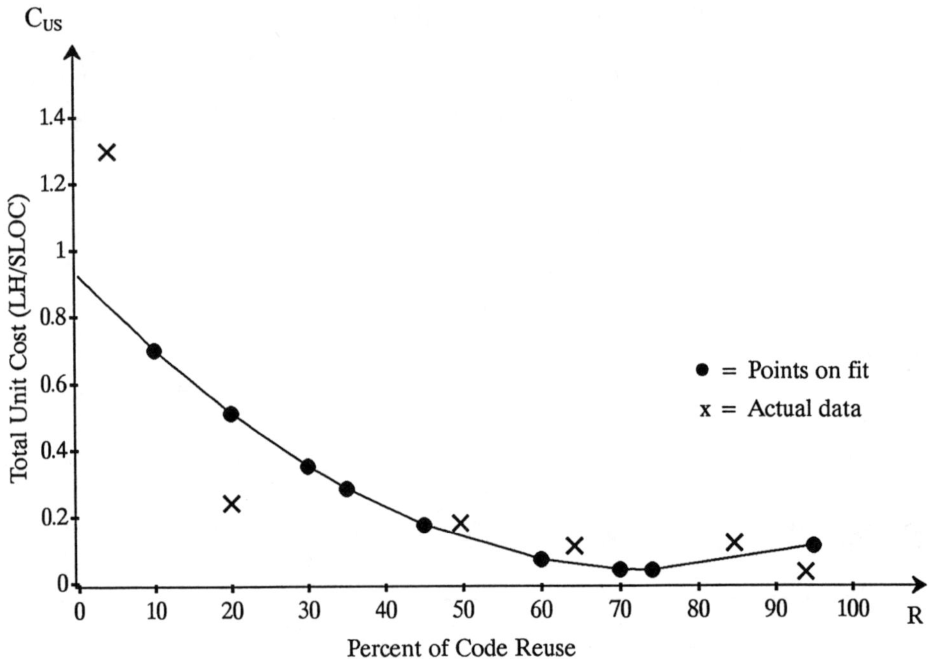


Figure 4. Unit Cost as a Quadratic Function of Percent Reuse

## RETURN ON INVESTMENT

This section defines the break-even number of systems for the case in which all of the domain engineering is done "up front" as assumed in the basic reuse unit cost equation.

### Break-Even Number of Systems

Reuse pays off when the unit cost of an application system which includes reused software is less than or equal to the unit cost of an implementation in all new software. Therefore, the break-even number of systems, $N_0$, is the value of N when $C_{US} = C_{VN}$. Using the basic reuse unit cost equation previously developed:

$$C_{US} = C_{VN} - (C_{VN} - C_{VR})R + K\frac{C_{DE}}{N}$$

and dividing through by $C_{VN}$ produces:

$$C = \frac{C_{US}}{C_{VN}} = 1 - \left(\frac{C_{VN} - C_{VR}}{C_{VN}}\right)R + \frac{C_{DE}}{C_{VN} \cdot N}K$$

The break-even point occurs when C = 1. Let the number of application systems required to break- even be $N_0$. Then:

$$0 = -\left(1 - \frac{C_{VR}}{C_{VN}}\right)R + \frac{C_{DE}}{C_{VN} \cdot N_0}K$$

$$N_0 = \frac{C_{DE}}{(C_{VN} - C_{VR}) \cdot E}$$

where E = R/K is the efficiency in the use of the library content, R = $S_R/S_S$ and K = $S_T/S_S$, $S_T \leq S_S$, $R \leq K$, and $S_R \leq S_T$. Table 7 shows the break-even number of systems for values of E and for two applications previously discussed.

Table 7. Break-Even Number of Systems

| E = R/K | RTCC | MIS | Ada Aerospace |
|---|---|---|---|
| 0.7 | 4.86 | 4.09 | 2.39 |
| 1.0 | 3.40 | 2.86 | 1.67 |

The situation of decreasing productivity with increasing R (in Table 2) occurred when the expected number of application systems, N, was less than $N_0$ (for a particular application type). This phenomenon can be explained by a restatement of the basic unit cost system as:

$$C_{US} = C_{VN} + [-(C_{VN} - C_{VR}) + C_{DE}/EN]R$$

As R increases, $C_{US}$ will increase as long as:

$$C_{DE}/EN - (C_{VN} - C_{VR}) > 0$$

That is, the labor rate $C_{US}$ in LM/KSLOC with increasing R will increase, but productivity in SLOC/LM will decrease as long as the above inequality is true. Solving this inequality for N:

$$N < C_{DE}/[(C_{VN} - C_{VR})E] = N_0$$

As long as the expected number of application systems is less than the break-even number of systems, productivity will decrease with increasing R.

Since $E = S_R/S_T$, if $S_R = S_T$, the amount of reuse is the maximum possible, and $E = 1$. In this case, $K = R$. When $K = R$, the basic reuse unit cost equation becomes:

$$C_{US} = C_{VN} - (C_{VN} - \frac{C_{DE}}{N} - C_{VR})^{*}R$$

In this case, the break-even number of systems, $N_0$, is found by setting $C_{US} = C_{VN}$, as before. Then:

$$N_0 = \frac{C_{DE}}{C_{VN} - C_{VR}}$$

This is exactly the equation derived above but with $E = 1$.

Figure 5 shows the RTCC cost model application data from Table 3 plotted as productivity in SLOC/LM versus the number of application systems for proportions of reuse $R = 0.7$ and $R = 0.9$. This figure illustrates the phenomenon of higher reuse producing lower productivity when the number of application systems is below the break-even point. The MIS data from Table 3 could also be used to illustrate this phenomenon.

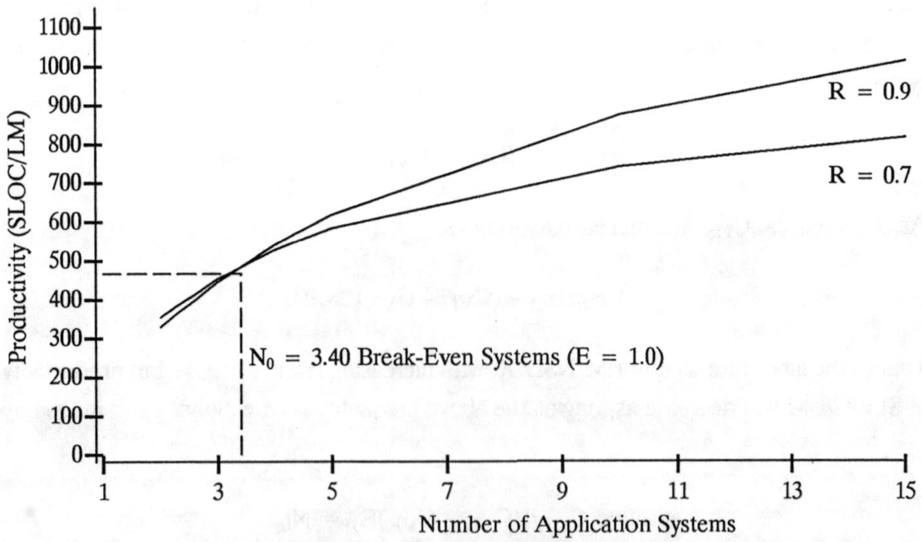


Figure 5. Number of Application Systems Versus Productivity at Two Levels of Reuse

Table 7 shows that when $E = 1.0$, the break-even number of systems for the real-time cost model application is 3.40. Since $E = R/K = 1.0$, $K = 0.9$. Substituting these values into the basic unit cost equation for the real-time application:

$$C_{US} = (5.305/3.40)(0.9) + 2.072 - 1.558(0.9) = 2.07 \text{ LM/KSLOC}$$

and $1{,}000/2.07 = 483$ SLOC/LM. Therefore the 3.40 break-even systems correspond to a productivity of 483 SLOC/LM and whenever N is greater than 3.40, reuse pays off. Note that in the example case of Ada aerospace systems, the break–even number of systems, also when $E = 1.0$, is 1.67. That is, for $N = 2$ systems, reuse pays off.

**Calculating Return on Investment**

As was stated previously, the cost of domain engineering activities represents an investment in the creation of RSOs to make possible a high degree of reuse over a family of application systems. The return on this investment is the difference in costs between the cost of N application systems in which there is no reuse and the cost of N application systems in which there is an average reuse of R. If the cost (in LM/KSLOC) of domain engineering is denoted as $C_{DE}$, the cost (in LM/KSLOC) of new software is denoted as $C_{VN}$, and the cost of reused software (in LM/KSLOC) is denoted as $C_{VR}$, then it can be shown that the percent return on investment (ROI) is:

$$\text{ROI} = [(N)(E)(C_{VN} - C_{VR})/C_{DE} - 1]\ 100$$

where N is the number of application systems and E is the efficiency factor discussed above.

The number of systems, $N_0$, at which the ROI is zero may be termed the break-even number of systems. It is determined by setting:

$$((N_0)\ (E)\ (C_{VN} - C_{VR})\ /\ C_{DE} - 1) = 1$$

Thus:

$$N_0 = \frac{C_{DE}}{(C_{VN} - C_{VR})E}$$

This is the same equation for $N_0$ derived above from a different point of view.

Therefore the expression for ROI may be written as:

$$\text{ROI} = \left(\frac{N}{N_0} - 1\right)100$$

In the case of ROI, the emphasis is on determining when an investment in domain engineering pays off. This can be the case for relative productivity calculations as well. In addition, productivities relative to those of current industry practice may also be of interest, especially to those who wish to understand how systematic reuse compares with current practice.

Table 8 shows the comparison of return on investment for selected values of N. The negative values of percent return on investment are caused by the number of systems (N) being below the break-even number of systems.

Table 8. Percent Return on Investment (E = 1.0)

| N | RTCC | MIS |
|---|---|---|
| 2 | -41.3 | -30.2 |
| 3 | -11.9 | 4.7 |
| 4 | 17.5 | 39.6 |
| 5 | 46.9 | 74.5 |
| 10 | 193.7 | 249.1 |
| 15 | 340.6 | 423.6 |

The equation for return on investment can be restated in terms of the following expression:

$$N = \left(\frac{ROI}{100} + 1\right)\left(\frac{C_{DE}}{C_{VN} - C_{VR}}\right)\left(\frac{1}{E}\right)$$

Figure 6 shows that, for both cost model applications, MIS and real-time (RT), the higher the library efficiency, the greater the return on investment.

Suppose that a 20 percent return is the least return on investment that is acceptable, and suppose that a 50 percent return is considered the highest return that is possible. Let $C_{DE} = 5.305$, $C_{VN} = 2.072$, and $C_{VR} = 0.514$ as with the RTCC example discussed earlier. Then N•E has the value 4.09 for the 20 percent return case and 5.11 for the 50 percent return case. The relationship between N and E then becomes as shown in Figure 7, and the 20 to 50 percent operating region is the area between the lines. Note that the cost of money was not taken into account in this calculation. A later section of this paper discusses cost of money.

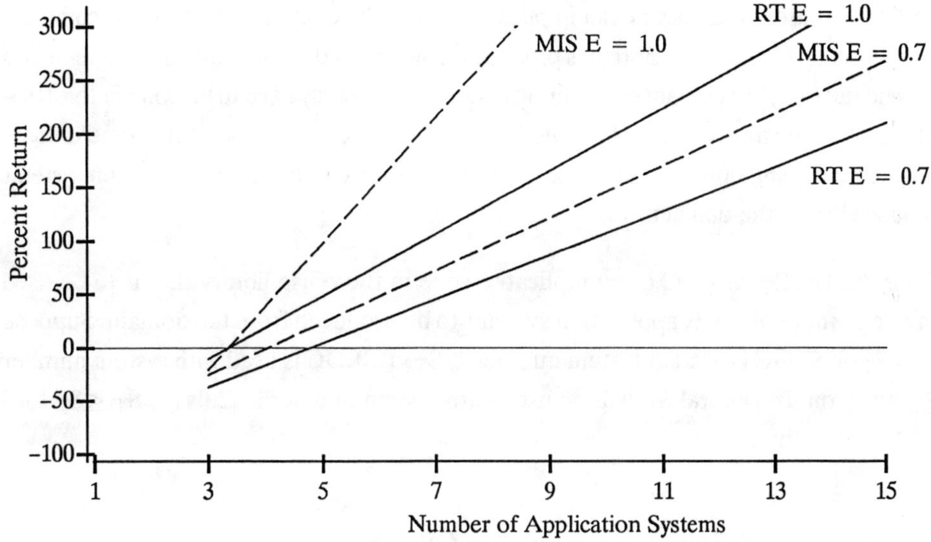


Figure 6. Number of Application Systems Versus Return on Investment

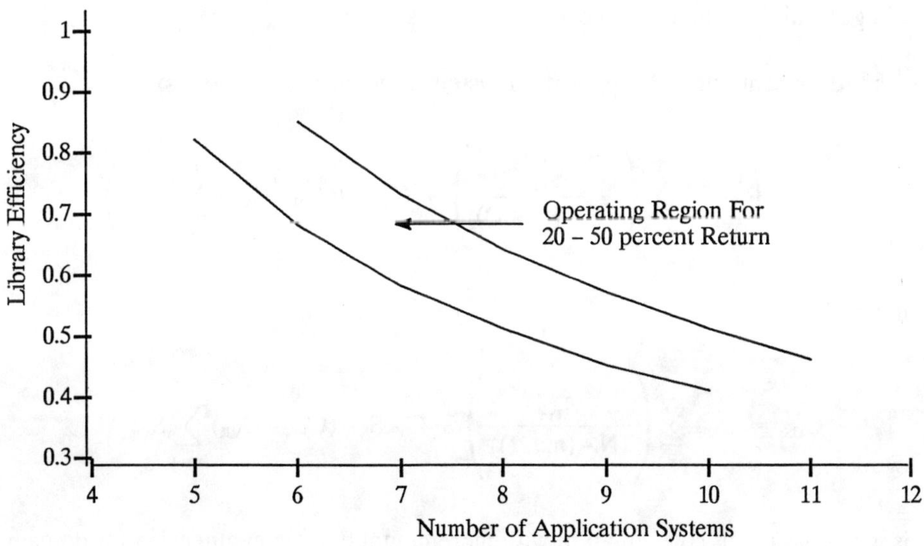


Figure 7. Number of Application Systems Versus Library Efficiency

## Reuse Economics Model With Incremental Domain Engineering

This section generalizes the basic reuse economics model presented earlier to cover the case in which the domain engineering is not done entirely at once, up front.

The basic reuse economics model implies that all of the domain engineering is complete before the first application system is produced. For certain domains and environments this may be the case, but domain engineering does not necessarily have to be done in this fashion. Domain engineering may be done incrementally (i.e., piecewise), with some domain engineering being done in conjunction with more than one of the N application systems produced from the domain.

Consider the $S_T$ KSLOC of unduplicated code in the reuse library that is to be used in one or more of the N application systems to be produced from the domain. Suppose that $S_{T1}$ KSLOC is used in system number 1, $S_{T2}$ KSLOC is used with system number 2, and so on. In general $S_{Ti}$ will be used with system number i. Thus $0 \leq S_{Ti} \leq S_T$ for i = 1,...,N so that:

$$S_T = \sum_{i=1}^{N} S_{Ti}$$

Thus $S_{T1}$ is amortized over N application systems, $S_{T2}$ is amortized over N – 1 systems, and in general $S_{Ti}$ is amortized over N – (i – 1) systems.

For the *i*th system out of N application systems, the unit cost, $C_{USi}$, is:

$$C_{USi} = \left(\frac{C_{DE}}{S_S}\right) \sum_{m=1}^{i} \left(\frac{S_{Tm}}{(N-(m-1))}\right) + C_{VN} - (C_{VN} - C_{VR}) \sum_{m=1}^{i} \left(\frac{S_{Tm}}{S_S}\right)$$

which reduces to:

$$C_{USi} = C_{DE} \sum_{m=1}^{i} \left(\frac{S_{Tm}}{(N-(m-1))}\right) + C_{VN}S_S - (C_{VN} - C_{VR}) \sum_{m=1}^{i} S_{Tm}$$

This is the basic unit cost equation with incremental domain engineering for domain engineering occurring in more than one period of time. This equation assumes that the efficiency, E, is equal to one. Thus:

$$R_i = \sum_{m=1}^{i} \left(\frac{S_{Tm}}{S_S}\right)$$

which is the maximum amount of reuse possible for system i.

If $S_{T1} = S_T$ and if $S_{Ti} = 0$ for $i = 2,3,\ldots,N$, then the basic reuse unit cost equation for incremental domain engineering reduces to:

$$C_{USi} = \left(\frac{C_{DE}}{N}\right)\left(\frac{S_T}{S_S}\right) + C_{VN} - (C_{VN} - C_{VR})\left(\frac{S_T}{S_S}\right)$$

which is the same form as the basic unit cost equation with $K = R$, for the cost of up-front domain engineering.

For the *i*th system to break-even, its cost must be less than or equal to that for the case in which the entire system of size $S_S$ were to be made from entirely new code:

$$C_{DE}\sum_{m=1}^{i}\left(\frac{S_{Tm}}{(N-(m-1))}\right) - (C_{VN} - C_{VR})\sum_{m=1}^{i} S_{Tm} \leq 0$$

If, as before, $S_{T1} = S_T$ and $S_{Ti} = 0$ for $i = 2,3,\ldots,N$ the above equation reduces to:

$$\frac{C_{DE}}{(C_{VN} - C_{VR})} \leq N_0$$

which is identical to the break-even number of systems calculated from the basic unit cost equation with $E = 1$.

Similarly, for N systems as a whole to break-even:

$$C_{DE}\sum_{i=1}^{N}\sum_{m=1}^{i}\left(\frac{S_{Tm}}{(N-(m-1))}\right) - (C_{VN} - C_{VR})\sum_{i=1}^{N}\sum_{m=1}^{i} S_{Tm} \leq 0$$

Now:

$$\sum_{i=1}^{N}\sum_{m=1}^{i}\frac{S_{Tm}}{(N-(m-1))} = N\left(\frac{S_{T1}}{N}\right) + (N-1)\left(\frac{S_{T2}}{(N-1)}\right) + \ldots + S_{TN} = S_{T1} + \ldots + S_{TN} = S_T$$

and:

$$\sum_{i=1}^{N}\sum_{m=1}^{i} S_{Tm} = NS_{T1} + (N-1)S_{T2} + (N-2)S_{T3} + \ldots + S_{TN}$$

Therefore, for the N application systems in the domain to break–even overall:

$$\frac{C_{DE}}{(C_{VN} - C_{VR})} \leq \frac{(NS_{T1} + (N-1)S_{T2} + \dots + S_{TN})}{S_T}$$

and the break-even number of systems, $N_0$,, is found by solving the above equation for N. Let:

$$S_{Ti} = a_i S_T, \qquad \sum_{i=1}^{N} a_i = 1$$

Then the right side of the above equation becomes:

$$Na_1 + (N-1)a_2 + \dots + (N-(N-1))a_N = N - P$$

where:

$$P = \sum_{i=1}^{N} (i-1)^{\bullet} a_i = \sum_{i=1}^{N} i^{\bullet} a_i - 1$$

Thus the break-even number of systems, $N_0$, is given by

$$N_0 = \frac{C_{DE}}{C_{VN} - C_{VR}} + P$$

where P is the incremental spending penalty. It is clear that doing domain engineering incrementally has the effect of increasing the number of systems required to break–even as compared with doing domain engineering all at once.

### Calculating Return on Investment for the Incremental Domain Engineering Case

Now, four cases of incremental funding of domain engineering investment are presented. The value of P, the additional number of application systems required for the break-even point to occur, is calculated for each case:

Case 1: $S_{T1} = S_T$

$$\frac{(NS_{T1})}{S_T} = N - 0, \quad \text{or} \quad P = 0$$

Case 2: $S_{T1} = S_{T2} = \frac{S_T}{2}$

$$\frac{(NS_{T1} + (N-1)S_{T2})}{S_T} = N - \frac{1}{2}, \quad \text{or} \quad P = 0.5$$

Case 3: $S_{T1} = S_{T2} = S_{T3} = S_{T4} = \frac{S_T}{4}$

$$\frac{(NS_{T1} + (N-1)S_{T2} + (N-2)S_{T3} + (N-3)S_{T4})}{S_T} = \frac{4N - (1 + 2 + 3)}{4} = N - \frac{3}{2}, \text{or} P = 1.5$$

Case 4:

$$S_{T1} = \left(\frac{5}{15}\right)S_T, \quad S_{T2} = \left(\frac{4}{15}\right)S_T, \quad S_{T3} = \left(\frac{3}{15}\right)S_T, \quad S_{T4} = \left(\frac{2}{15}\right)S_T, \quad S_{T5} = \left(\frac{1}{15}\right)S_T$$

$$\frac{(N_{ST1} + (N-1)S_{T2} + (N-2)S_{T3} + (N-3)S_{T4} + (N-4)S_{T5}}{S_T} = N - \frac{4}{3}, \quad \text{or} \quad P = 1.33$$

Using these formulas, the cost per application for each of a family of five systems is computed for each of the four cases (regimes). The parametric values used for the four regimes are: $S_S = 500$ KSLOC, $S_T = 450$ KSLOC, $C_{VN} = 5$ LM/KSLOC, $C_{VR} = 0.5$ LM/KSLOC, $C_{DE} = 7.5$ LM/KSLOC, and $E = 1.0$. All investment and cost figures are in LM.

In Table 9, 12,500 LM is the total cost for five application systems without reuse. The cost of money is not included. Figures 8 through 11 illustrate the data in Table 9.

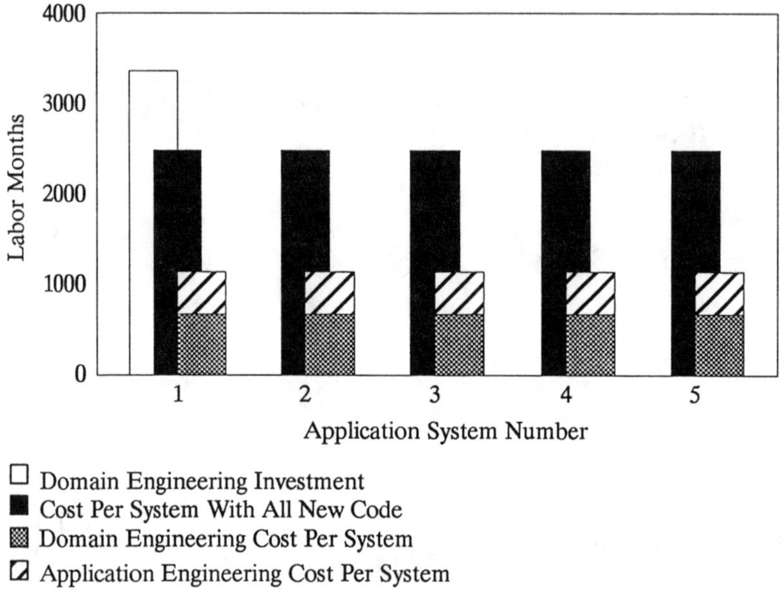


Figure 8. Case 1: Domain Engineering Invested All at Once

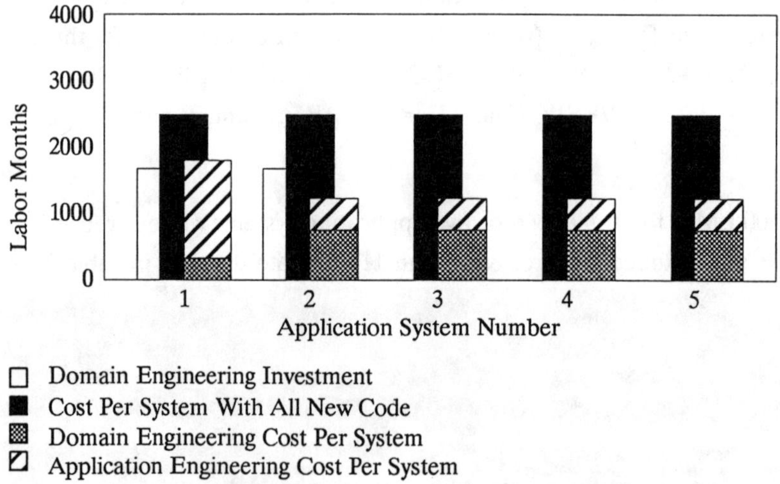


Figure 9. Case 2: Domain Engineering Spread Equally Over Two Increments

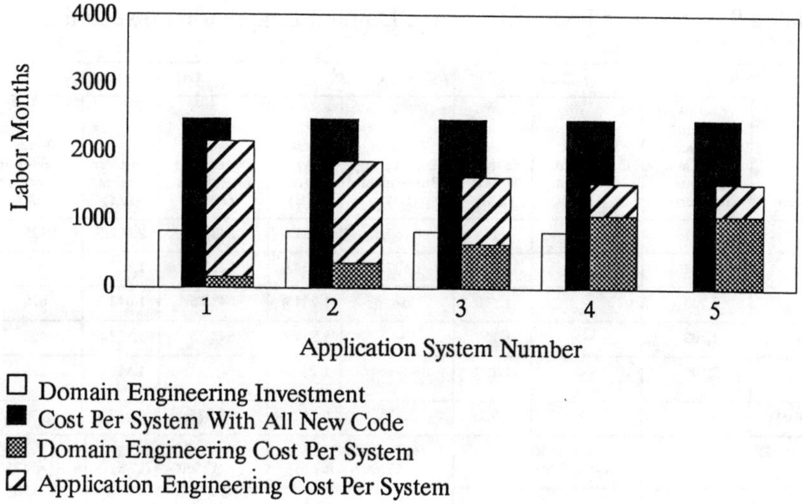


Figure 10. Case 3: Domain Engineering Invested Equally Over Four Increments

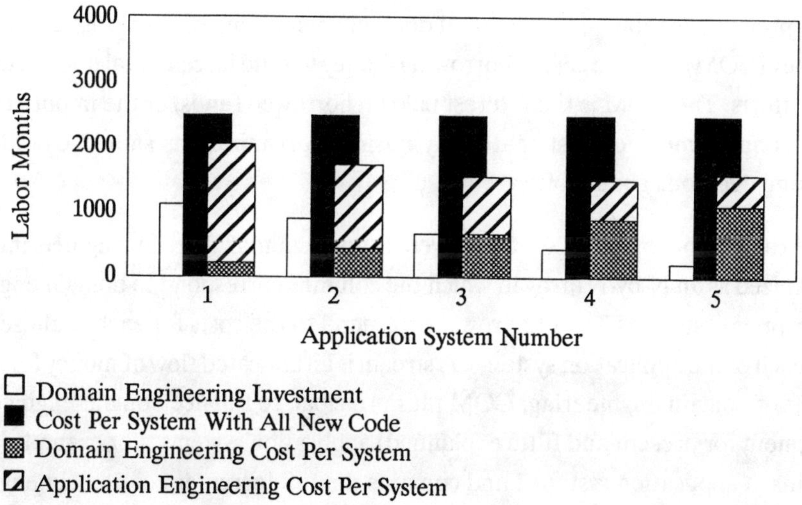


Figure 11. Case 4: Declining Domain Engineering Investment Over Five Increments

Table 9. Costs For Four Alternative Domain Engineering Investment Regimes

| | | Case 1 | | Case 2 | | Case 3 | | Case 4 | |
|---|---|---|---|---|---|---|---|---|---|
| System | Cost Per System Without Reuse and Domain Engineering | Domain Engineering Investment (LM) | Cost Per System (LM) | Domain Engineering Investment (LM) | Cost Per System (LM) | Domain Engineering Investment (LM) | Cost Per System (LM) | Domain Engineering Investment (LM) | Cost Per System (LM) |
| 1 | 2,500 | 3,375 | 1,150 | 1,687.5 | 1,825.0 | 843.75 | 2,162.5 | 1,125 | 2,050 |
| 2 | 2,500 | – | 1,150 | 1,687.5 | 1,234.4 | 843.75 | 1,867.2 | 900 | 1,735 |
| 3 | 2,500 | – | 1,150 | – | 1,234.4 | 843.75 | 1,642.2 | 675 | 1,555 |
| 4 | 2,500 | – | 1,150 | – | 1,234.4 | 843.75 | 1,557.8 | 450 | 1,510 |
| 5 | 2,500 | – | 1,150 | – | 1,234.4 | — | 1,557.8 | 225 | 1,600 |
| Totals(1) | 12,500 | 3,375 | 5,750 | 3,375 | 6,762.6 | 3,375 | 8,787.5 | 3,375 | 8,450 |
| Savings(2) | | 6750 (= 12500 - 5750) | | 5737.4 (= 12500 – 6762.6) | | 3718.5 (= 12500 – 8787.5) | | 3960 (= 12500 – 8450) | |
| Percent Return on Investment[1] = Savings/3375 | | 200 | | 170 | | 110 | | 120 | |

## Return on Investment Including the Effects of the Cost of Money

The previous section on incremental domain engineering did not consider the cost of money (COM), i.e., the cost of borrowing money to fund incremental domain engineering efforts. The COM is the interest paid on borrowed funds, or the imputed interest, and is an element of cost that many business organizations should consider when making decisions about software reuse.

The calculation of the COM involved in incremental domain engineering can be organized as an N-by-N array in which the columns correspond to domain engineering investment "streams," and the rows correspond to the costs for each of these streams for each of the application systems. A stream is an allocated flow of money for an increment of domain engineering, COM plus principal, to finance domain engineering investment for present and future (planned) application systems. For example, stream 1 begins at application system 1 and contains the full increment of domain engineering investment for application system 1 and partial increments of domain engineering investment for the future systems. Each one of the future increments has a different value since the financing for the second system is over a shorter time than the financing for the last planned system. In any cell of the N-by-N array, the COM is the product of the portion of investment borrowed for system j under investment stream i and the cost of borrowing for y years at p percent annually.

The formula for the COM in any cell in the N-by-N array (actually only the lower triangular form is used) is:

$$I_{i,j} = \left[a_i \cdot C_T - (j-i) \cdot \left(\frac{a_i \cdot C_T}{N-(i-1)}\right)\right] \cdot [1 + 0.01p)^y - 1] = F_1 \cdot F_2$$

where:

$F_1$ = Amount of domain engineering investment borrowed for a system in investment stream i.

$F_2$ = Proportion, COM. Example 0.36 means that 36 percent of $F_1$ can comprise COM (ij), or $I_{ij}$.

This formula simplifies to:

$$I_{i,j} = a_i \cdot C_T \cdot \left[1 - \frac{j-i}{N-(i-1)}\right] \cdot [1 + 0.01p)^y - 1]$$

where:

p = Annual percent interest rate.

y = Number of years to which each investment increment is applicable.

$C_T$ = Total domain engineering investment.

$a_i$ = Proportion of $C_T = C_{DE} \bullet S_T$ applied in stream i ($a_i$ is defined in the section on incremental domain engineering).

$T_j$ = Total COM for application system j, where:

$$T_j = \sum_{i=1}^{N} I_{i,j} \quad \text{and } i \le j$$

Two of the four cases, cases 1 and 4, discussed in the previous section are now used as examples of the calculation of the cost of money.

Assume a family of five application systems from the domain in question and that a system can be produced from a domain in four years. Also assume that the current interest rate is eight percent per annum. As previously, all calculations are in LM, and the same parametric values as in the section on incremental domain engineering are used: $S_S$ = 500 KSLOC, $S_T$ = 450 KSLOC, $C_{DE}$ = 7.5 LM/KSLOC, $C_{VN}$ = 5.0 LM/KSLOC, and $C_{VR}$ = 0.5 LM/KSLOC.

Case 1 uses the data in Table 9 to show that 1. 3,375 LM is borrowed for four years at eight percent to finance the up-front domain engineering effort as applied to application system 1. Since 675 LM (= 1/5 x 3,375) would be amortized by application system 1, then 2,700 LM (= 3,375 – 675) would be amortized by system 2 and would be borrowed for 4 years (the period of time required for the development of system 2). Similarly, 2025 LM would be borrowed for the next 4 years, and so on. Note that these are the entries in Table 10, which applies to case 1 for stream 1 only. This is because there is only one increment of domain engineering in this case, all up front. Thus, in this case, $S_{T1} = S_T$ and $a_1 = 1$; $a_i = 0$ and $i = 2, 3, 4, 5$.

Table 10. Cost of Money for Case 1

| Domain Engineering Investment Stream | | | | | | | | | | | |
|---|---|---|---|---|---|---|---|---|---|---|---|
| | Stream 1 | | Stream 2 | | Stream 3 | | Stream 4 | | Stream 5 | | |
| Appl. Sys. | COM | Principal | COM | Principal | COM | Principal | COM | Principal | COM | Principal | Total COM |
| 1 | 1216.65 | 675 | | | | | | | | | 1216.65 |
| 2 | 973.32 | 675 | | | | | | | | | 973.32 |
| 3 | 729.99 | 675 | | | | | | | | | 729.99 |
| 4 | 486.66 | 675 | | | | | | | | | 486.66 |
| 5 | 243.33 | 675 | | | | | | | | | 243.33 |
| Total | | 3,375 | | | | | | | | | 3,649.95 |

In case 4, there are five increments of domain engineering as shown in Table 11 and below:

$$S_{T1} = 1{,}125 = 0.333 \times 3{,}375; \quad a_1 = 0.333$$
$$S_{T2} = 900 = 0.267 \times 3{,}375; \quad a_2 = 0.267$$
$$S_{T3} = 675 = 0.200 \times 3{,}375; \quad a_3 = 0.200$$
$$S_{T4} = 450 = 0.133 \times 3{,}375; \quad a_4 = 0.133$$
$$S_{T5} = 225 = 0.067 \times 3{,}375; \quad a_5 = 0.067$$

Table 11. Cost of Money for Case 4

| Domain Engineering Investment Stream | | | | | | | | | | | |
|---|---|---|---|---|---|---|---|---|---|---|---|
| | Stream 1 | | Stream 2 | | Stream 3 | | Stream 4 | | Stream 5 | | |
| Appl. Sys. | COM | Principal | COM | Principal | COM | Principal | COM | Principal | COM | Principal | Total COM |
| 1 | 405.55 | 225 | | | | | | | | | 405.55 |
| 2 | 324.44 | 225 | 324.44 | 225 | | | | | | | 648.88 |
| 3 | 243.33 | 225 | 243.33 | 225 | 243.33 | 225 | | | | | 729.99 |
| 4 | 162.22 | 225 | 162.22 | 225 | 162.22 | 225 | 162.22 | 225 | | | 648.88 |
| 5 | 81.11 | 225 | 81.11 | 225 | 81.11 | 225 | 81.11 | 225 | 81.11 | 225 | 405.55 |
| Total | | 1,125 | | 900 | | 675 | | 450 | | 225 | 2,828.85 |

Table 12 summarizes the COM calculations. The costs have been rounded to the nearest LM.

Table 12. Summary of Cost of Money Cases

| | | Case 1 | | | | Case 4 | | | |
|---|---|---|---|---|---|---|---|---|---|
| System | Cost Per System Without Reuse and DE | Domain Engineering Investment (LM) | Domain Engineering and Application Engineering Cost Per System (LM) | Cost of Money (Interest) (LM) | Total (LM) | Domain Engineering Investment (LM) | Domain Engineering and Application Engineering Cost Per System (LM) | Cost of Money (Interest) (LM) | Total (LM) |
| 1 | 2,500 | 3,375 | 1,150 | 1,217 | 2,367 | 1,125 | 2,050 | 406 | 2,456 |
| 2 | 2,500 | — | 1,150 | 973 | 2,123 | 900 | 1,735 | 649 | 2,384 |
| 3 | 2,500 | — | 1,150 | 730 | 1,880 | 675 | 1,555 | 730 | 2,285 |
| 4 | 2,500 | — | 1,150 | 487 | 1,637 | 450 | 1,510 | 649 | 2,159 |
| 5 | 2,500 | — | 1,150 | 243 | 1,393 | 225 | 1,600 | 406 | 2,006 |
| Totals | 12,500 | 3,375 | 5,750 | 3,650 | 9,400 | 3,375 | 8,450 | 2,480 | 11,290 |
| Savings | | 3,100 (= 12,500 - 9,400) | | | | 1,210 (= 12,500 - 11,290) | | | |
| Percent Return on Investment = Savings/3,375 | | 92 | | | | 36 | | | |

Figures 12 and 13 illustrate the data in Table 12.

The least costly course of action is to borrow the entire cost of domain engineering at the beginning of the domain building effort (case 1), just as with the previous analysis of incremental domain engineering. The symmetry in the cost of money per system for case 4, with the high amount being for system 3, suggests that a concept similar to the economic lot size of manufacturing may apply.

## MODELING REUSE OF REQUIREMENTS AND DESIGN IN ADDITION TO CODE

This section explicitly considers the reuse (or multiple use, as defined earlier) of RSOs other than code. The basic reuse economics model and its variant, which covers incremental domain engineering, deal with code reuse. Recall that the factor R stands for the proportion of code reuse in an application system of size $S_S$. Reusing a unit of code includes reusing the corresponding software objects from it was derived, the requirements and design. This section addresses cases in which there is reuse of requirements and/or designs but not necessarily of code.

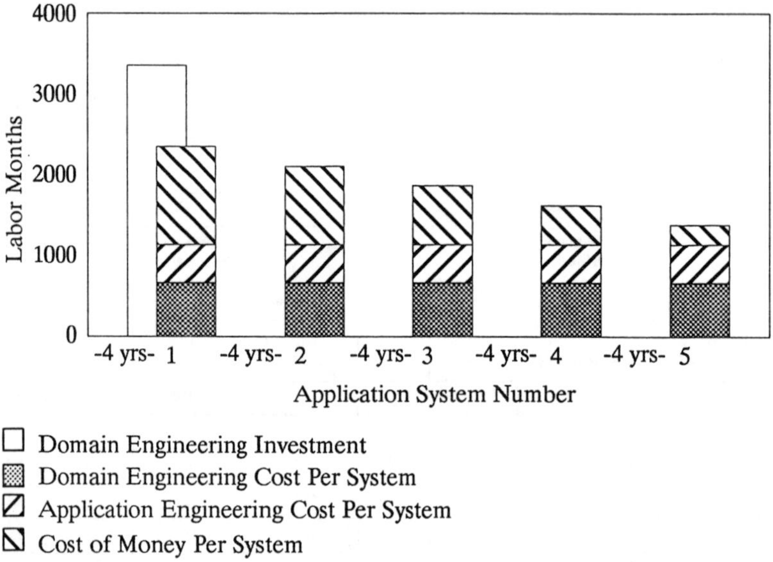


Figure 12. Cost of Money—Domain Engineering is Invested All at Once (Case 1)

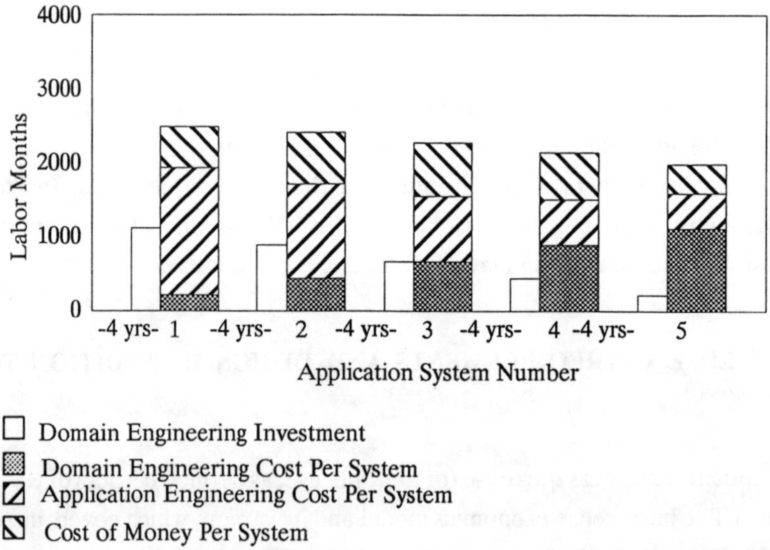


Figure 13. Cost of Money—Declining Domain Engineering Investment Over Five Increments (Case 4)

## Derivation of Cost Relationships

New code can be created from new requirements and new design, from reused requirements and new design, or from reused requirements and reused design. However, reused code cannot be derived from either new requirements or new design. This statement of simple logic underlies the development of the mathematical relations provided in this section.

The amount of reuse at later phases of development is upper-bounded by the amount of reuse at earlier phases. For example, the amount of design reuse cannot exceed the amount of requirements reuse (when both quantities are expressed in terms of equivalent SLOC or in terms of their respective proportions of total SLOC in the application software system). Now, if $S_{RR}$ is the source statement equivalent of reused requirements, $S_{RD}$ is the source statement equivalent of reused design, and $S_R$ is the source statement count of reused code, then:

$$S_{NR} + S_{RR} = S_S$$

$$S_{ND} + S_{RD} = S_S$$

$$S_N + S_R = S_S$$

Since reused code cannot be derived from either new requirements or new design, the following relationships hold:

$$S_{RR} \geq S_{RD} \geq S_R$$

$$S_N \geq S_{ND} \geq S_{NR}$$

$$R_{RR} \geq R_{RD} \geq R$$

where $R_{RR} = S_{RR}/S_S$ (the proportion of requirements reuse), $R_{RD} = S_{RD}/S_S$ (the proportion of design reuse), and $R = S_R/S_S$ (the proportion of code [and of testing] reuse).

Figure 14 graphically shows the relationships among new and reused objects in terms of size.

Let the unit costs (in LM/KSLOC, where the KSLOC represents the equivalent source statements for the reused objects) for the new and reused objects be named as shown in Table 13.

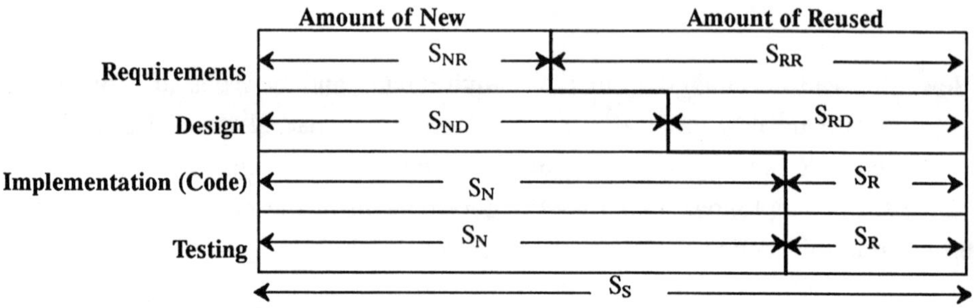


Figure 14. New and Reused Objects at Different Levels

Table 13. Unit Costs of New and Reused Objects

| Phase/Activity | Unit Costs New Objects (N) | Unit Costs Reused Objects (R) |
|---|---|---|
| Requirements (R) | $C_{VNR}$ | $C_{VRR}$ |
| Design (D) | $C_{VND}$ | $C_{VRD}$ |
| Implementation (Code) (I) | $C_{VNI}$ | $C_{VRI}$ |
| Testing (T) | $C_{VNT}$ | $C_{VRT}$ |

### Application of Cost Relationships

This section demonstrates the application of the cost relationships just developed.

Suppose that the unit cost of new code, $C_{VN}$, is 3.5 LM/KSLOC (286 SLOC/LM) and that there is equal reuse of requirements, design, code, and testing. Let the breakdown of development effort be 20 percent for requirements, 30 percent for design, 20 percent for implementation (coding), and 30 percent for testing, so that the unit cost equation for new code in this case is expressed numerically as:

$$C_{VN} = C_{VNR} + C_{VND} + C_{VNI} + C_{VNT}$$

this value of $C_{VN}$ is called $C_{VN0}$. It is the base value of $C_{VN}$.

$$3.5 = 0.7 + 1.05 + 0.7 + 1.05 \text{ LM/KSLOC.}$$

Now suppose there is unequal reuse of requirements, design, and code. Suppose that $R = 0.5$, $R_{RR} = 0.7$, and $R_{RD} = 0.7$. Then:

$$C_{VRR} = (1 - R_{RR})C_{VNR} = (0.3)(0.7) = 0.210$$

$$C_{VRD} = (1 - R_{RD})C_{VND} = (0.3)(1.05) = 0.315$$

Using the equation for $C_{VN}$ developed above:

$$C_{VN} = 1.75 + 1.05\frac{1-0.7}{1-0.5} + 0.315\frac{0.7-0.5}{1-0.5} + 0.7\frac{1-0.7}{1-0.5} + 0.210\frac{0.7-0.5}{1-0.5}$$

$$C_{VN} = 1.75 + 0.03 + 0.126 + 0.42 + 0.084 = 3.01 \text{ LM/KSLOC}$$

which is equivalent to 322 SLOC/LM. Thus by reusing some requirements and design, the new code productivity has been increased from 286 to 322 SLOC/LM.

Overall, the total cost of application engineering is (as described in the section entitled Reuse Economics Model With Up-Front Domain Engineering):

$$C_A = C_N + C_R = C_{VN}S_N + C_{VR}S_R$$

New code can be derived from reused requirements or reused design, but reused code cannot be derived from new requirements or new design. Therefore the total cost of reused code is:

$$C_R = C_{VR}S_R = (C_{VRR} + C_{VRD} + C_{VRI} + C_{VRT})S_R$$

where $C_{VR}$ is the unit cost of reusing requirements. The total cost of new code is (see Figure 14):

$$C_N = C_{VN}S_N = C_{VNR}S_{NR} + C_{VRR}(S_{RR} - S_R) + C_{VND}S_{ND} + C_{VRD}(S_{RD} - S_R) + (C_{VNI} + C_{VNT})S_N$$

Recognize that the following relationships hold (from the previous equations):

$$S_N = (1 - R)S_S; \; S_{ND} = (1 - R_{RD})S_S; \; S_{RD} - S_R = (R_{RD} - R)S_S;$$

$$S_{RR} - S_R = (R_{RR} - R)S_S; \; S_{NR} = (1 - R_{RR})S_S$$

Substituting into the previous equation for $C_N$ and dividing through by $(1 - R)$ obtains:

$$C_{VN} = (C_{VNI} + C_{VNT}) + C_{VND}\frac{1-R_{RD}}{1-R} + C_{VRD}\frac{R_{RD}-R}{1-R} + C_{VNR}\frac{1-R_{RR}}{1-r} + C_{VRR}\frac{R_{RR}-R}{1-R}$$

This is the general cost relation equation for new code under the condition of different proportions of various reused objects. Note that if $R_{RR} = R_{RD} = R$, that is, if all of the new code is derived from (corresponds to) new requirements and design, then $C_{VN} = C_{VNI} + C_{VNT} + C_{VND} + C_{VNR}$, as would be expected. That is, the general cost relation for new code reduces that for new code when all of the new code is derived from new requirements and new design.

### GENERALIZATION OF LIBRARY EFFICIENCY METRIC

This section generalizes the concept of library efficiency to cover the case in which objects other than code are reused but the code may not be. The proportion of code reuse can be less than the proportion of requirements and/or design reuse. $R_{RE}$ is the effective (overall) reuse proportion. It is a weighted sum of the reuse proportions of requirements ($R_{RR}$), design ($R_{RD}$), and code (R). Therefore, the effective (overall) reuse proportion can be defined as:

$$R_B = R_{RR} \bullet \frac{C_{VRR}}{C_{VR}} + R_{RD} \bullet \frac{C_{VRD}}{C_{VR}} + R \bullet \frac{(C_{VRI} + C_{VRT})}{C_{VR}}$$

Let $C_{VRI} + C_{VRT} = C_{VRIT}$. Then, $C_{VRR} + C_{VRD} + C_{VRIT} = C_{VR}$. Therefore:

$$\frac{C_{VRR}}{C_{VR}} + \frac{C_{VRD}}{C_{VR}} + \frac{C_{VRIT}}{C_{VR}} = 1$$

Thus, the equation for $R_{RE}$ can be written as:

$$R_B = R_{RR} \bullet \frac{C_{VRR}}{C_{VR}} + R_{RD} \bullet \frac{C_{VRD}}{C_{VR}} + R \bullet C_{VRIT}$$

When $R_{RR} = R_{RD} = R$, the case of full (code) reuse (including the reuse of requirements and design), then $R_E = R$, as it should. $R_E$ is a generalization of the proportion of reuse, R, and is used in the generalization of the basic unit cost equation as shown in the following subsections. Then $S_{RE} = R_E \bullet S_S$. If $R_{RR} = R_{RD} = R$, then $R_E = R$ and $S_{RE} = S_R$.

Now let $K = S_T/S_S$ be as originally defined, the relative library capacity. Therefore library efficiency in the case of reuse of objects other than code is:

$$E = \frac{R_E}{K} = \frac{\frac{S_{RE}}{S_S}}{\frac{S_T}{S_S}} = \frac{S_{RE}}{S_T} = \frac{R_E \bullet S_S}{S_T}$$

This definition of library efficiency represents a generalization of the original definition that takes into account the reuse of objects when code is not necessarily reused. If $R_{RR} = R_{RD} = R$, then $R_E = R$, and $E = S_R/S_T$, as originally defined.

### Generalization of N

The factor N was defined earlier as the number of application systems in the family. It was used as the number of systems over which an up-front investment in domain engineering is amortized. It presumed code reuse and reuse of the corresponding requirements and design. This section generalizes N to $N_E$, the number of equivalent application systems for amortization purposes when the amount of code reused may be less than the amount of design or requirements (as considered in the previous section).

The unit cost of domain engineering is:

$$C_{DE} = C_{DER} + C_{DED} + C_{DEIT}$$

where $C_{DER}$ is the unit cost for creating reusable requirements, $C_{DED}$ is the unit cost for creating reusable design, and $C_{DEIT}$ is the unit cost for creating reusing implementation (code) and test. The prorated unit cost is:

$$C_{DE} \cdot N_E = C_{DER} \cdot N_R + C_{DED} \cdot N_D + C_{DEIT} \cdot N$$

And therefore:

$$N_E = \frac{C_{DER}}{C_{DE}} \cdot N_R + \frac{C_{DED}}{C_{DE}} \cdot N_D + \frac{C_{DEIT}}{C_{DE}} \cdot N$$

where $N_E$ is the number of equivalent (to full) application systems considering the reuse of requirements and design objects as well as code objects, $N_R$ is the number of application systems over which the reused requirements are prorated, $N_D$ is the number of systems over which the unit cost of the reused design is amortized, and N is the number of systems over which the unit cost of implementation and testing is amortized:

$$1 \leq N \leq N_D \leq N_R$$

If $N_R = N_D = N$, then, $N_E = N$, as it should. The generalization of N and R leads to a generalization of the basic unit cost equation as shown in the next subsection.

### Generalization of Basic Unit Cost Equation

The basic unit cost equation with up-front domain engineering is generalized to take into account the reusable requirements and/or design without necessarily having corresponding code reuse. The approach is to substitute the factors $R_E$ and $N_E$ for R and N, respectively, and $C_{VN}$ is defined in its generalized form. Then:

$$C_{US} = \frac{C_{DE}}{N_E} \cdot K + C_{VN} - (C_{VN} - C_{VR})R_E$$

where $C_{VN}$ is defined in its generalized form:

$$C_{VN} = (C_{VNI} + C_{VNT}) + C_{VND}\frac{1-R_{RD}}{1-R} + C_{VRD}\frac{R_{RD}-R}{1-R} + C_{VNR}\frac{1-R_{RR}}{1-R} + C_{VRR}\frac{R_{RR}-R}{1-R}$$

## FINAL VIEW

Substantial savings can be realized in the development costs of application software systems when using a systematic reuse process as compared to either all new code development or casual reuse because of the higher development productivity that systematic reuse provides. The very nature of the systematic reuse process requires software developers to consider not only the current version of the system being composed but future versions as well. This should have a large impact on the supportability of the system with its attendant cost consequences.

Incremental funding of the domain engineering investment generally results in lower returns on investment than up-front funding but has the advantage of conserving capital until required. It recognizes that it may not be possible to fully describe a domain before any of the systems in the domain family have been constructed.

The reuse economics model not only demonstrates the economic impact of systematic reuse but also serves as a means to learn about applying a systematic reuse process. With such a model, the user can explore the costs and benefits of an investment in a domain. Such what-if explorations can help support business decisions.

## REFERENCES


Albrecht, A.J. 1989 — Personal communication.

Albrecht, A.J., and J.E. Gaffney Jr. 1983 — Software Function, Source Lines of Code, Development Effort Prediction: A Software Science Validation. *IEEE Transactions on Software Engineering SE-9.*

Campbell, G.H.
1990
*Synthesis Reference Model* Version 01.00.01. SYNTHESIS_ REF_MODEL-90047-N. Herndon, Virginia: Software Productivity Consortium.

Campbell, G.H., S.R. Faulk, and D.M. Weiss
1990
*Introduction to Synthesis.* Version 01.00.01 INTRO_ SYNTHESIS_PROCESS-90019-N. Herndon, Virginia: Software Productivity Consortium.

Gaffney, J.E. Jr.
1989
*An Economics Foundation for Software Reuse* Version 1.0, SW-REUSE-ECONOM-89040-N. Herndon, Virginia: Software Productivity Consortium. Presented at the AIAA Computers In Aerospace Conference, Monterey, California, October 1989.

Gaffney, J.E. Jr., and R.D. Cruickshank
1991a
*Code Counting Rules and Category Definitions/Relationships* Version 02.00.04, CODE_COUNT_RULES-90010-N. Herndon, Virginia: Software Productivity Consortium.

1991b
The Measurement of Software Product Size: New and Reused Code. *Third Annual Oregon Workshop on Software Metrics, Silver Falls, OR.* To be published in a forthcoming issue of *Software Engineering: Tools, Techniques, and Practice.*

Gaffney, J.E. Jr., and T. Durek
1988
*Software Reuse, Key to Enhanced Productivity: Some Quantitative Models* Version 1.0, SPC-TR-88-015. Herndon, Virginia: Software Productivity Consortium.

1991
Software Reuse—Key to Enhanced Productivity: Some Quantitative Models. *The Economics of Information Systems and Software*, pp. 204–219. Edited by R. Vergard. Oxford, England: Butterworth-Heinemann.

Parnas, D.
1976
Design of Program Families. *IEEE Transactions on Software Engineering*. 2, 1:1.

# EXPERIENCE WITH AN INCREMENTAL ADA DEVELOPMENT IN TERMS OF PROGRESS MEASUREMENT, BUILT-IN QUALITY, AND PRODUCTIVITY

Donald H ANDRES, TRW Systems Integration Group, Redondo Beach, CA
L/Col. Paul E. HEARTQUIST, USAF/Electronic Systems Center, Hanscom AFB, MA
Gerard R. LaCROIX, MITRE Corporation, Bedford, MA

29 - 30 April 1991

## EXECUTIVE SUMMARY

An incremental development and test process is being successfully used in the implementation of the Command Center Processing and Display System Replacement (CCPDS-R) Program. This program is a large U.S. Air Force Ada application comprised of several subsystems each with multiple increments of capability. The first subsystem delivery was made to the Air Force in December 1990 and consisted of over 280,000 Ada Source Lines of Code, operator display consoles, and data processing equipment.

Experience to date indicates that both the Government procuring agency (Electronic Systems Division with support from the MITRE Corporation) and the developing contractor (TRW Systems Integration Group) have had better-than-average visibility into true software development progress. This visibility is attributable to several factors discussed in this paper including prototyping, the use of design walkthroughs, formal demonstrations of functionality, early development of the architectural and system service software base, delivery of operational capability via series of tested software Builds, and the monthly application of software management metrics.

The software that has been demonstrated and delivered to date has been exceptionally reliable. Numerous failure-free demonstrations have been given to interested parties for over a year and the delivered software, although not completely tested, is being regularly used without incident by the Government for training and performance measurement purposes. Factors behind this built-in quality are addressed; namely, development of software tools to reduce error-prone coding, use of a message-based design to standardize task-to-task communications, early checkout of interfaces, and continuity of software staff.

Lastly, reasons why the program is achieving and maintaining software productivity significantly higher than industry averages are discussed. These include reuse of design and code from subsystem to subsystem; choice of a hardware architecture with virtually unlimited growth potential; and standardization of procedures for writing applications software and handling task-to-task interfaces, in addition to early integration and staff continuity.

General "lessons learned" and recommendations for the technical management of incremental Ada development projects are also provided.

## BACKGROUND

The U.S. Air Force is currently pursuing several development efforts to upgrade the tactical warning and attack assessment capabilities of the United States. The elements comprising these capabilities are commonly referred to as the Integrated Tactical Warning and Attack Assessment (ITW/AA) System.

A major component of the ITW/AA System is the Command Center Processing and Display System Replacement (CCPDS-R) Program. This component is responsible for processing data from ground and space-based radars to determine whether launches of ballistic missiles constitute a threat to U.S. interests.

CCPDS-R consists of three subsystems (see Figure 1):

a. A ballistic missile warning subsystem which makes the actual assessment of threat,

b. A missile warning display subsystem with terminals deployed worldwide, and

c. A management/survival subsystem to protect the U.S. bomber force.

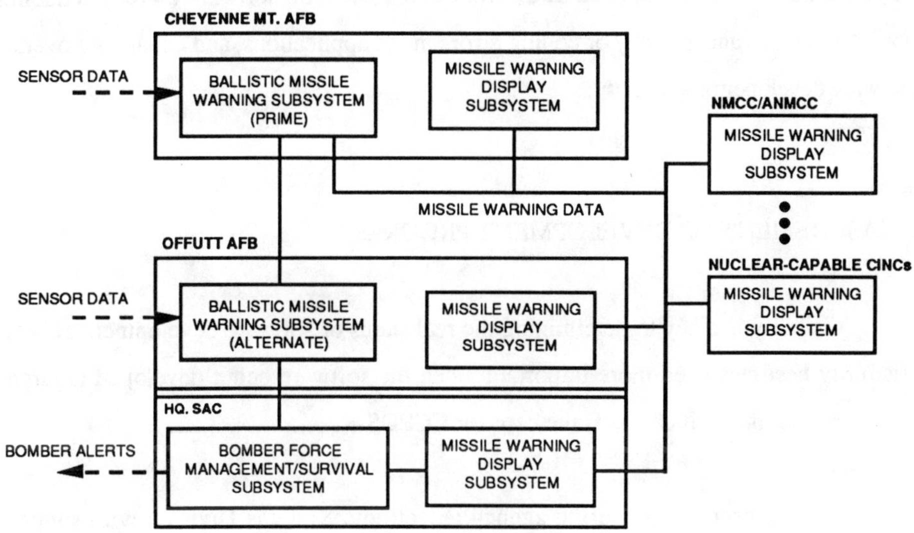


Figure 1. CCPDS-R System Overview

## SYSTEM OVERVIEW

The CCPDS-R is a large Ada software application, on the order of one million source lines of code (1M SLOC), implemented on Digital Equipment Corporation VAX computers. One of the three CCPDS-R subsystems, i.e., the Missile Warning Subsystem, consists of 340,000 SLOC installed on a VAX 6520 Mission Processor.

This processor contains the communications processing, missile warning algorithms, and databases necessary to drive operational displays located at Cheyenne Mt., CO; Offutt AFB, NE; and selected remote locations throughout the world.

The CCPDS-R hardware/software architecture employs a layered design in which hardware dependencies are confined to a small subset of the operational code. For example for the Missile Warning Subsystem, the mission processing hardware dependencies are contained in about 10,000 source lines of code (10 K SLOC) out of a total developed software size of 340 K SLOC. In addition, the more difficult Ada language constructs are isolated away from the application software thereby reducing both the number and severity of coding errors in the applications, and enhancing overall software developer productivity.

## MEASUREMENT OF DEVELOPMENT PROGRESS

Visibility is a key to determining the real status of software development efforts. Visibility becomes even more important when the software being developed is large, complex, and time-critical, as is the case for CCPDS-R.

The Government procuring agency (Electronic Systems Division with support from the MITRE Corporation) and the developing contractor (TRW Systems Integration Group) have instituted several innovative techniques for determining software development progress on CCPDS-R. These include:

a. Incorporation of working prototype code into the operational software,

b. Design walkthroughs,

c. Early development of architectural software,

d. Incremental delivery of operational capabilities via software "builds"

e. Formal demonstrations of delivered capabilities, and

f. Monthly assessment of progress via software management metrics.

The CCPDS-R Program employs a prototyping and build approach (see Figure 2) which, in essence, breaks the overall subsystem development cycle into a series of smaller, more-easily manageable, developments. This approach is characterized by three milestones:

a. A preliminary design walkthrough (PDW) for each build at which the top-level software design is reviewed along with the ability of prototype code and Ada Design Language (ADL) to compile, link, and execute.

b. A critical design walkthrough (CDW) to review the detailed design of each build and its proper operation.

c. A formal demonstration of each build which focuses on operational capability and is subject to pass/fail criteria.

Both the Government and the contractor are active participants in these three activities.

Under the prototyping and build approach, CCPDS-R software development began significantly earlier than would have been the case under a more traditional software development. By the time of Critical Design Review (CDR) of the software for the Missile Warning Subsystem, about 3/4 of the code had been designed coded, integrated, and informally tested. The earliest software developed consisted of the architectural and system service software base upon which all subsequent applications software would depend. Thus, integration, which is the most risky part of software development, has been an early and continuing effort on the CCPDS-R Program.

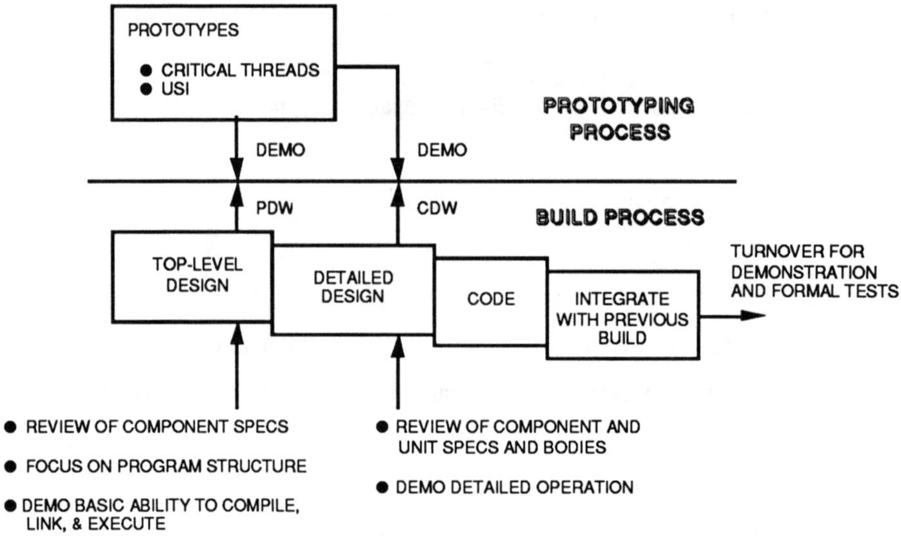


Figure 2. CCPDS-R Prototyping and Build Approach

Traditionally, integration does not begin until after CDR. As a result, integration problems tend to surface late in the development when their effects are magnified by the pressures of schedule and the contention for resources.

The CCPDS-R Program has capitalized on the numerous opportunities available to measure progress. To date, these have included about 10 formal reviews, 6 PDWs, 6 CDWs, and 7 demonstrations. In addition, the Government and TRW management receive monthly quantitative reports of progress, commonly called software management metrics. Actual vs. planned progress is tracked with regards to software staffing, software size, development progress, and test progress. Separate accounting is maintained for the % of the software which has been designed, coded, unit tested, documented, integrated, component tested, and string tested. Similar tracks are kept for test procedures completed and requirements verified. Cumulative plots of open and closed software problem reports and software documentation problem reports are generated monthly. The status of all action items resulting from formal meetings is also updated monthly along with plots of cost and schedule variances.

SOFTWARE RELIABILITY

One measure of the built-in quality of software is its reliability, i.e., mean-time between critical failures. The CCPDS-R software, even though still in the midst of development, is experiencing a reliability in excess of 10,000 hours.

This reliability is attributable to the use tools to generate code that would otherwise be labor-intensive, repetitive, and hence prone to human error; the use of a message-based design which relieves the applications developers from the burden of creating software for task-to-task communications; early integration of the architectural/system service software and applications shells which allows for the early discovery and correction of errors; and continuity of knowledgeable staff, primarily within the contractor organization but also on the Government acquisition team.

For example, the Missile Warning Subsystem uses a variety of tools to generate compilable Ada code from pseudo-English data inputs. The principal tools consist of about 22 K SLOC which are used to generate about 233 K SLOC of operational code - - an expansion factor in excess of 10 to 1. Verifying the proper operation of the tool code is easier, less time-consuming and less error-prone than manual verification of the tool-generated code. On the CCPDS-R Program, approximately 38% of the code is being generated by means of tools.

A second factor underlying CCPDS-R software reliability is the message-based design which incorporates a software architecture skeleton consisting of reusable node managers, process executives, and task executives. These permit applications developers to concentrate on the functionality associated with their respective modules without having to know the inner workings of the software infrastructure and the mechanisms by which Ada tasks communicate with other Ada tasks.

The third and fourth factors behind CCPDS-R's software reliability are the early integration of software components with resultant early identification of interface incompatibilities, and staff continuity which provides the knowledge base from which problems can be addressed. The early development of the architectural/system service software has insured its repeated use by the applications programmers and hence contributed to its inherent reliability.

## PRODUCTIVITY

The CCPDS-R Program is experiencing software productivity in the range of 4.1 to 10.6 Ada SLOC per staff-day. This range is a function of how the code is counted and is complicated by differences in the amount of effort required to produce new code, modify previously-developed code, reuse old code, and generate new code using automated tools. The computation is further obfuscated by the lack of an industry standard for counting Ada source lines of code. The approach taken on the CCPDS-R Program to compute productivity follows (see Figure 3):

a. Weight new code and modified code equally,

b. Weight reused and tool-generated code at 3/10 and 6/10 of the effort required to generate new code, respectively,

c. Compute SLOC by adding carriage returns in Ada Specifications and semi-colons in Ada Bodies; do not count "Comment" lines.

Applying this approach to the CCPDS-R code yields a weighted software productivity of 7.3 Ada SLOC per staff-day which is about 40% higher than the upper end of the usually quoted industry range of 3 to 5 Ada SLOC per staff-day.

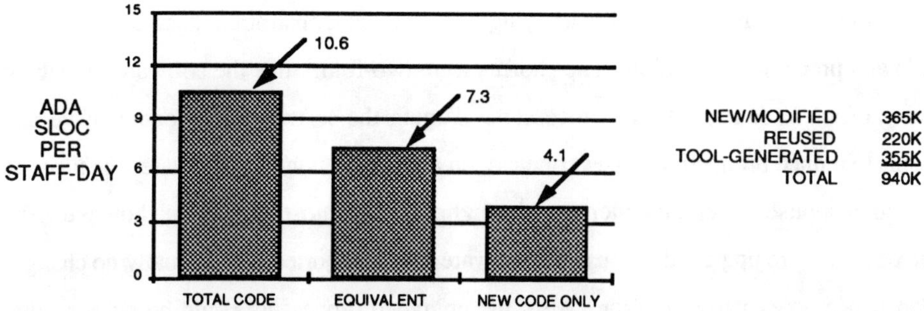


TOTAL CODE = NEW/MODIFIED + REUSED + TOOL-GENERATED
EQUIVALENT = NEW/MODIFIED + .3 * REUSED + .6 * TOOL-GENERATED
NEW CODE ONLY = NEW/MODIFIED

SLOC = SPECIFICATION CARRIAGE RETURNS + BODY SEMI-COLONS
(NO COMMENTS)

Figure 3. CCPDS-R Software Productivity

The major factors contributing to this relatively higher productivity are the reuse of design, code, and people; and the use of tools to generate code, previously discussed. In fact, on the CCPDS-R Program 23% of the code is being reused from one subsystem to the next out of the nearly 1M SLOC being developed. People reuse has taken the form of a stable, highly knowledgeable, software architect team augmented by bright applications developers organized into manageable entities. The team of software architects has been responsible for the more difficult software code, i.e., the architectural/system service software. This code effectively isolates the applications developers from the complex Ada constructs of tasking, rendezvous, time-slicing, prioritization, etc. The net result is code appropriate to the technical abilities of the individuals and hence reduced errors.

A second but less obvious contributor to productivity is the availability of a processor family that is compatible with the developed software. On several occasions during the development of the CCPDS-R System, as performance margins were reached, the Government and contractor team was faced with the decision on how to best fit the remaining software while still satisfying performance constraints, such as maximum allowed processor utilization. The choices were two-fold: tune the software to make it more efficient or upgrade the processors. Tuning the software is labor-intensive and tends to reduce productivity. Nevertheless, on a few occasions the software was tuned to speed response times and increase throughput. On most occasions, however, the processors were upgraded because the software could be ported with virtually no changes and hence no expense of labor. Also, the upgraded processors could be purchased at about the same cost as the originally planned processors. Hence, the upgrades could be made with no corresponding increases in overall CCPDS-R Program costs.

A third factor in CCPDS-R productivity has been the use by the developers of standard development procedures. These have included standard ways for developers to interface their applications modules with the reusable architectural software components, and standard ways for writing applications code using templates at both the application "process" and "task" levels. Stated another way, all of the applications developers are developing code in the same ways. This has resulted not only in fewer errors (3.5 per K SLOC vs. 5 - 12 per K SLOC industry experience) but also in high maintainability. The result is less labor to fix problems and hence higher productivity. On the CCPDS-R Program, about 2/3 of the software errors have required less than one day to fix.

The fourth and fifth factors behind CCPDS-R's productivity figures were also discussed previously as factors behind the reliability of the software. They are early integration and staff continuity. In addition to improving the quality of the software, these factors contribute to the overall efficiency of the software development process and are therefore positive influences on productivity.

## LESSONS LEARNED

When comparing the CCPDS-R Program to other programs which have had successful software developments (such as the Berlin Radar Program), certain similarities stand out. These include the quality of the documentation and test program, the close professional team relationship between the contractor and Government teams, knowledge by both of the job to be done and how to go about doing it, and continuity of key personnel. These are the characteristics of a good and well-run program. However, on the CCPDS-R Program three additional factors contribute to make it an exceptional program:

a. The existence of a Concept Definition Phase during which many of the up-front system engineering trade studies were conducted.

b. The use of a flexible architecture characterized by reusable architectural components, standard task-to-task communications, and standard applications process and task templates.

c. The use of a Software Development Process model consisting of operational code prototypes, design walkthroughs, builds, and formal demonstrations.

In conclusion, the CCPDS-R software development approach is working. Performance, schedule, and cost objectives are being met. The success enjoyed to date has been due to a combination of the capabilities provided by Ada technology and the application of previous lessons learned. This software development approach has resulted in an environment characterized by a high degree of visibility into true software development progress, high software reliability, and high software productivity. As such the CCPDS-R Program is a model for others to follow.

# Recognizing Patterns for Software Development Prediction and Evaluation*

Lionel C. Briand, Victor R. Basili and William M. Thomas
Department of Computer Science
University of Maryland
College Park, MD 20742

## 1 Introduction

Managing a large scale software development requires the use of quantitative models to provide insight and support control based upon historical data from similar projects. Basili introduces a paradigm of measurement based, improvement-oriented software development, called the *Improvement Paradigm* [1]. This paradigm provides an experimental view of the software activities with a focus on learning and improvement. This implies the need for quantitative approaches for the following uses:

- to build models of the software process, product, and other forms of experience (e.g., effort, schedule, and reliability) for the purpose of prediction.
- to recognize and quantify the influential factors (e.g. personnel capability, storage constraints) on various issues of interest (e.g. productivity and quality) for the purpose of understanding and monitoring the development.
- to evaluate software products and processes from different perspectives (e.g. productivity, fault rate) by comparing them with projects with similar characteristics.
- to understand what we can and cannot predict and control so we can monitor it more carefully.

Classical techniques for data analysis have limitations when used on software engineering data. In this paper we present a new data analysis technique, based on pattern recognition principles, designed to overcome some of these limitations.

The paper is organized as follows. In Section 2 of this paper, we discuss the needs and the constraints in building effective models for the software development

*This work was supported in part by NASA grant NSG 5123 and by AFOSR 90–0031

processes. We present a new approach for analyzing software engineering data in Section 3, called Optimized Set Reduction (OSR), that overcomes many of the problems associated with traditional techniques. In Section 4, experimental results are provided to demonstrate the effectiveness of the approach for the particular application of cost estimation modeling. Section 5 identifies major conclusions.

# 2 Requirements for an Effective Data Analysis Procedure

Based upon constraints associated with the data and the analysis procedures, we generate a set of requirements for model building approaches. In the text that follows, we will refer the variable to be assessed as the "Dependent Variable" (DV) (e.g. productivity, fault rate) and the variables explaining the phenomenon as "Independent Variables" (IVs) (e.g. personnel skills, product complexity).

## 2.1 Constraints Related to Software Engineering Data

Empirical model building in Software Engineering is faced with the following difficulties:

- $C_1$: There is no theory proven to be effective in any environment that would give a formal relationship among measured metrics in the development process. Therefore the capabilities of classical statistical approaches seem very limited.

- $C_2$: There is little evidence to support assumptions about the probability density distributions, with respect to the dependent and independent variables of interest.

- $C_3$: The sample size is usually small relative to the requirements of the classical statistical techniques, the quality of the data collected, and the number of significant independent variables. This is due to the nature of the studied objects in software engineering (e.g. software system, module, change, defect ...).

- $C_4$: "Software engineering modelers" have to deal with missing, interdependent and non-relevant independent variables: This is due to a lack of understanding of the software development process.

- $C_5$: Data defined on both continuous (i.e. ratio, interval) and discrete (i.e. nominal, ordinal) ranges have to be handled. Collecting data in a production environment is a difficult task and discrete data collection is often performed to facilitate the measurement process. Also, the nature of some of the data may be discrete.

## 2.2 Requirements to Alleviate These Constraints

Matching the constraints, we can define requirements for effective data analysis procedures:

- $R_1$ [matches $C_1, C_2$]: The data analysis procedure should avoid assumptions about the relationships between the variables regarding the probability density distribution on the IV and DV ranges.

- $R_2$ [$C_3, C_4$]: A mechanism is needed to evaluate accuracy for each performed estimation. The variations of accuracy lie in a large range depending on the object to be assessed. For example, you may want to assess a software project from the point of view of productivity.

  $C_3$ The amount of available relevant data may differ according to the characteristics of the project to be assessed. For example, you may have more data with respect to data processing business applications than with respect to real time systems. In small samples, this phenomenon can have significant consequences.

  $C_4$ The performed data collection may be more suitable to certain kinds of objects than others. For example, objectively measuring time constraints for real time systems may be difficult and therefore may introduce more uncertainty in the assessment.

- $R_3$ [$C_4$]: The data analysis procedure must be as robust as possible to missing, non-relevant, interdependent IVs and outliers. Then, some procedures should be available in order to detect and alleviate the effects related to these kinds of disturbances in the data set.

- $R_4$ [$C_5$]: The data analysis procedure must be able to easily handle both discrete and continuous metrics without biasing the obtained results.

# 3 A Pattern Recognition Approach for Analyzing Data

Due to the difficulties associated with software engineering data, new techniques have been investigated to support modeling activities. For example, Selby and Porter have advocated the use of automatically generated tree-structured classifiers as a mechanism for identifying high-risk portions of the software product [8]. A comparison of the strengths and weakness of this and regression based techniques can be found in [3]. Our goal is to develop a data analysis procedure based upon pattern recognition principles that is intended to fulfill, to a certain extent, the previously described requirements for effective data analysis. This procedure and its main supporting principles are described in the following sections.

## 3.1 Description of the Technique

The goal of the technique is the recognition of patterns in a data set. These patterns are used as a basis for understanding and assessing the development process, product and environment.

### 3.1.1 The Basic Concepts and Terminology

- A **learning sample** consists of $m$ vectors containing one dependent and $n$ independent variables: $(DV_i, IV_{i,1}, ..., IV_{i,n}), i \in (1, ..., m)$ . These vectors are defined in an Euclidian space called the "sample space". These vectors, which we will call **pattern vectors**, represent measurements taken in the environment.

- A **measurement vector** is defined as the set of independent variable values representing a particular object whose dependent variable value is to be predicted. That is, it is a pattern vector without the dependent variable.

- To be able to make predictions on the **dependent variable**, its range has to be sub-divided or grouped into what we will call **DV classes**. These classes correspond to natural situations that can be encountered in the measurement environment, with respect to the dependent variable. If the dependent variable is either "ratio," "interval," or "ordinal," the dependent variable range is sub-divided into intervals; if the dependent variable is "nominal," categories may be grouped into a smaller set of classes. They are called "states of nature" in decision theory and "pattern classes" in the pattern recognition field [9]. We have chosen the name DV classes in order to make the connection with a classical statistical approach for multivariate analysis.

- To be able to use the **independent variables** as a basis for predicting the dependent variable, they, like the dependent variables, must be mapped into **IV classes** by sub-dividing or grouping.

- A **pattern** is defined as a non-uniform distribution of probabilities across the DV classes. The further a distribution is from uniformity, the more the pattern is considered to be significant.

### 3.1.2 A Pattern Recognition Process

The problem of predicting the dependent variable for a particular project can be stated as follows: Given a particular measurement vector (MV), determine the probability that the actual dependent variable value lies in each of the DV classes. The shape of the probability density function on the DV class range associated with MV is unknown. The goal and the basic principle of this process is to find a subset of pattern vectors in the data set, whose values for the independent variable are similar to the values for the independent variables of MV, and that show a significant pattern among the DV classes.

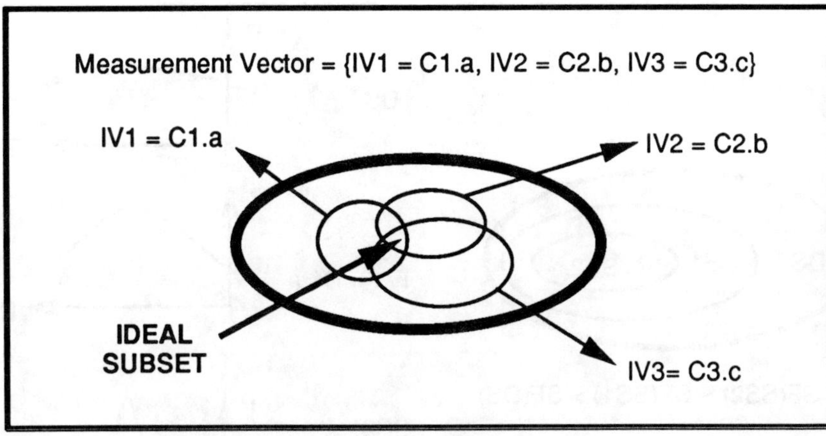


Figure 1: Ideal Approach

Taking this approach in the ideal, given a learning sample and a measurement vector, MV, we could select an ideal subset of all the pattern vectors in the learning sample having exactly the same IV instances as MV (see figure 1). However, since we are usually working with small samples and numerous independent variables, the ideal subset is typically too small to be useful, so this ideal approach is not applicable.

Alternatively, we need to find a subset of the learning sample that contains pattern vectors *similar* to MV with respect to some IVs, and that yields a significant pattern on the DV range. This subset must be large enough and contain sufficiently homogeneous pattern vectors to yield significant patterns. To extract the subset from the learning sample, we need to select a collection of IVs that will be used to determine the pattern vectors in the subset. The pattern vectors matching the MV instances with respect to the selected IVs will be extracted from learning sample.

Such a process is illustrated in figure 2. Some **selection function SF** chooses a IVs in a stepwise manner that will be used to subset the data set DS. We see that DS has a fairly uniform distribution on the DV range. SS1, a subset of DS with IV1=C1.a, shows an improvement, in that a pattern appears to be emerging. Finally, SS2, formed from SS1 with the condition that IV2=C2.b, appears to have a very clear pattern, that is, objects in this subset have the DV defined on a very narrow range. The IV selection is done so that the resulting subset has a clear pattern on the DV range, and that MV is very similar to the objects in the final subset in terms of the selected IVs (i.e. IV1=C1.a and IV2=C2.b). In other words, each subset resulting from a potential IV selection will be evaluated using SF to provide information on the degree of significance of the pattern in the extracted subset. The IV that yields the most significant pattern will be selected.

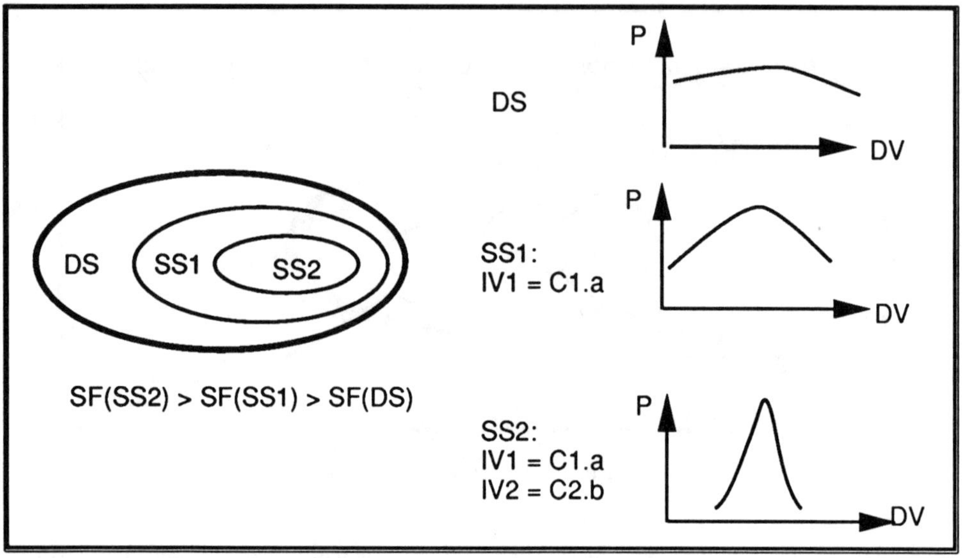


Figure 2: The Pattern Recognition Process

Two reasons justify a stepwise process:

- The number of possible IV combinations makes an exhaustive search prohibitive.
- We need to ensure a statistically significant pattern in the resulting subset, i.e. we want to ensure that all contributing IVs have a significant impact on the pattern.

A set of experiments have led us to develop the following pattern recognition process (called Optimized Set Reduction) applied for any measurement vector MV:

- Step 1: DV classes are formed either by dividing the DV range into intervals or by grouping the defined DV categories. For optimal results, a similar number of pattern vectors should be in each class. The mechanism for creating classes is described in more detail below. IV classes are formed in a similar way.
- Step 2: The learning sample is successively decomposed into subsets. At each step, an IV is selected (according to a **selection function** described below) and the objects having the same instance for the IV as the object to be assessed (MV) are extracted to form the reduced subset. This is done recursively on the reduced subsets.
- Step 3: When a predefined condition is reached, the reduction stops. This condition will be referred to as the **termination criteria** and will be discussed below. The subsets resulting from this criteria are called the **terminal subsets**.

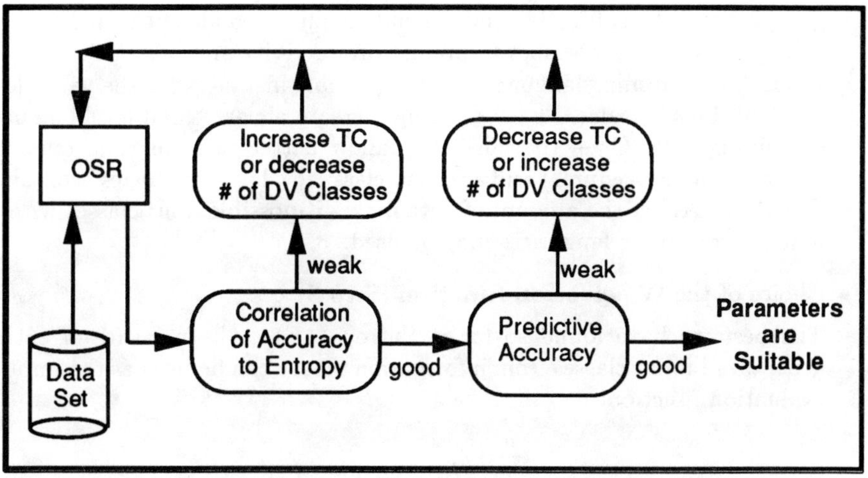


Figure 3: Tuning the OSR Parameters

- Step 4: The pattern vectors in the terminal subset(s) are then used to calculate the **probability** that the actual dependent variable value for MV lies in each of the DV classes.

The resulting probabilities (that form the obtained pattern) may be used either for **DV predictions**, **risk management** or **quality evaluation** in a way that will be described in Section 3.2.

Despite an apparent simplicity, this approach opens up a set of research questions associated with each of the steps, that need to be further investigated. The details of each of the steps, as well as some open issues are discussed here:

- Creation of suitable DV and IV classes (Step 1):

  If the variable is either continuous or ordinal, the range is divided in a fixed number of classes. This number may be determined through a trial and refinement procedure (such a tuning process is illustrated in figure 3).

  Without sufficient data, increasing the number IV classes will decrease the average number of reductions during the OSR process, because with more classes, there are fewer pattern vectors in each class, and thus smaller subsets at each step of the reduction. This may preclude certain IVs from contributing to the pattern. Also, whenever the number of DV classes increases, the number of pattern vectors per DV class decreases, and thus the calculation of the conditional probabilities may be less accurate. On the other hand, decreasing the number of DV or IV classes may make predictions more inaccurate, because real distinctions in the values of the data may be missed.

  If the variable is nominal, categories may be grouped to form IV or DV classes. With respect to DVs, the grouping will depend on the classification to be performed as well as the size of the data set, as above. For IVs, grouping may be subjective and depends upon the goals of the analysis. For example, assume one wishes to predict productivity and one of the available IVs is "programming language". If the possible instances for the variable are "C, FORTRAN, Ada, C++," one might create a class "high level language" containing Ada, C++ (because they allow better rates of code reuse and easier testing procedures) and a second class "low level languages" containing C, FORTRAN. If the amount of data makes it possible, four classes with the four programming languages may be used.

- Choice of the IV **selection function** (Step 2):

  The best we have found so far is Entropy ($F$). The measure of entropy generalized for $m$ classes from information theory can be used as the impurity evaluation function:

  $$F = \sum_{i=1}^{m} -P(C_i/x) \log_m P(C_i/x)$$

  where $P(C_i/x)$ is the conditional probability of $x$ of belonging to the DV class $C_i$, $i \in (1, ..., m)$.

  The selected IV is the one that minimizes the selection function, in this case, entropy. The lower the entropy the more likely we are to have found a significant pattern.

- Determination of the **termination criteria** (Step 3):

  The termination criteria needs to be tuned to the environment, i.e. the available data set. Logically, if measuring the significance of a pattern by calculating its entropy is reasonable, then the entropy should be strongly correlated to the observed prediction accuracy (i.e. Magnitude of Relative Error for continuous DVs and Misclassification Rate for discrete DVs). Therefore, an estimation of the prediction accuracy is possible by looking at the decomposition entropy.

  There are two bounds on the calculation. If there were no termination criteria, the reduction could decompose to a subset of a single pattern vector, trivially yielding the minimum entropy of zero. On the other hand, if we stop the reduction too soon, we have not sufficiently decomposed the data set to provide the most accurate characterization of the object to be assessed. Thus we are interested in achieving an accurate approximation of the selection function based upon some minimum number of pattern vectors in the terminal subsets. To find this minimum number, we can experiment with the learning sample by examining the correlation between the accuracy and the selection function (e.g., entropy). If this correlation becomes too weak, then the acceptable minimal number of pattern vectors in a subset should be increased. The goal is to find a compromise between a good correlation and a sufficient number of decompositions to provide a reasonable accuracy for predicting the value of the DV. This determines the number of pattern vectors used as our termination criteria. This tuning process is illustrated in figure 3. One must be concerned with both the class boundaries and the termination criteria (TC).

- Estimation of the **conditional probabilities** that the object to be assessed falls into the various DV classes (Step 4):

  A simple rule would be to calculate the probabilities as the ratios of pattern vectors falling into the various categories versus the total number of pattern vectors. This is the only solution for discrete DVs because there is no notion of distance in the range of values. A more refined approach for continuous DVs might be to sum the distances between the subset pattern vectors and the class mean for each of the DV classes. Call this $TD_n$, where $n$ represents the class index. Note that $TD_n$ is inversely proportional to the concentration of pattern vectors around the class mean for class $n$. Then calculate:

$$P(C_n/x) \approx \frac{1 - \left(\frac{TD_n}{\sum_{i=1}^{m} TD_i}\right)}{m-1}$$

  where $m$ is the number of DV classes.

  This formula assumes that the probability is inversely related to the total distance ($TD_n$) of the pattern vectors to the class mean. This approach refines the probability calculation since it takes into account the distances between the subset of pattern vectors and the class means, not just their membership in a specific class. We can further refine this probability calculation by defining $TD$ as the sum of the exponentials of the distances in order to decrease the weight of the pattern vectors furthest from some particular class mean.

## 3.2 Prediction, Risk Management and Quality Evaluation

The three processes, prediction, quality evaluation and risk assessment, can all be based on a similar quantitative approach—one based on patterns recognized from past experience. This section describes how OSR can support each of these process. Experimental results of the prediction capability are then provided in section 4.

### 3.2.1 Prediction

In this case, one is interested in estimating only one dependent variable based on the set of available independent variables. The dependent variable is a measurable object characteristic that is not known or accurately estimatable at the time it is needed. For example, one may wish to predict the error rate expected for a particular project development process in order to determine whether to apply a particular intensive code inspection process. So, one tries to estimate the error rate based on other characteristics (IVs) that may be measured, evaluated subjectively with a reasonable accuracy, or estimated through other models.

If the dependent variable is defined on a continuous range (i.e. the notion of distance between two values on the range is meaningful), the following approach may be used: by dividing the DV range into $m$ successive intervals (classes $C_i$: $i \in (1...m)$) and calculating $P(C_i/x)$ for each class $C_i$, we have in fact approximated the actual density function $P(DV/x)$ by assuming it to be uniform in each class $C_i$. Therefore, the following expected $\mu_i$ value can be calculated on $C_i$:

$$\mu_i = E[Productivity/C_i, x] = \frac{lower\_boundary\_C_i + upper\_boundary\_C_i}{2}$$

In other words, the actual density function is approximated by a histogram, where each column represents the conditional probability of a particular pattern vector $x$ that lies in a particular DV class $C_i$. No assumption has been made with respect to the form of this probability density function. The expected value on the entire DV range can be approximated as follows:

$$E[Prod/x] = \mu \approx \sum_{i=1}^{m} P(C_i/x) \times \mu_i$$

This expected value can be used as an estimate of the dependent variable. The average error interval that can be expected may be estimated by using the correlation of accuracy to entropy. This correlation will be confirmed by the experiments described in Section 5.

If the dependent variable is defined on a discrete range, then prediction becomes a classification problem: Given a set of probabilities that a particular pattern vector $x$ belongs to each DV class $C_i$, the decision maker must decide to which class to assign $x$. The class with the highest probability may not always be chosen. Rather, we may choose the class based upon the loss associated with incorrect classifications. This is the Bayesian approach. A risk (or loss) matrix $L$ has to be defined by the decision maker where $L_{ij}$ represents the loss of having chosen the strategy appropriate for $C_j$ when the DV class (or state of nature) is actually $C_i$. A Bayesian classifier [9] will try to minimize the conditional average risk or loss $R_j(x)$ ($j = 1$ ... m) considering the $m$ defined DV classes.

$$R_j(x) = \sum_{i=1}^{m} L_{ij} P(C_i/x)$$

$P(C_i/x)$ represents the probability that pattern vector $x$ comes from the pattern class $C_i$. The bayesian classifier assigns a pattern vector x to the class $j$ with the lowest $R$ value.

### 3.2.2 Risk management

Software development organizations are interested in assessing the risk associated with management and technical decisions in order to guide and improve the development processes. Referencing [6], the risk associated with an action (e.g. software development) may be described through three dimensions:

- $D1$: The various possible outcomes
- $D2$: The potential loss associated with them
- $D3$: The chance of occurrence for each outcome

Many kinds of interdependent risks may be encountered during software development (e.g. technical, schedule, cost), and this makes risk management complex. Also, the notion of risk is by definition subjective because the associated loss strongly depends upon one's point of view. Charette in [6] writes: "One individual may view a situation in one context, and another may view the exact same situation from a completely different one". According to his/her goals and responsibilities, one will define the risk in different ways, in the form of various models.

If we try to make the link between the above description of risk and OSR, the following straightforward associations may be established:

- Outcomes (i.e. dimension $D1$) and DV classes.
- Potential loss (i.e. dimension $D2$) and distance on the DV range between the DV class mean and the planned DV value.
- Chance of occurrence (i.e. dimension $D3$) and the conditional probability for each DV class.

In order to analyze risk during software development, we propose the following approach based upon OSR:

First, based on the three previously described risk dimensions, we calculate the expected difference (distance on the range) between planned and predicted values for each DV representing a potential risk (e.g. schedule, effort, ...). Let us call these distances "DV expected deviations". From a decision maker's perspective, the potential loss resulting from his/her decisions is intrinsically a function of several DV expected deviations that may be seen as a specific and subjective risk model. Therefore, a "loss function" is used as a risk analysis model and may be defined as a function that combines several DV expected deviations, parameters (e.g. reflecting management constraints) and constants (e.g. weights). The calculation details are illustrated in the example below.

Consider the following example with the two continuous DVs, productivity and fault rate. A budget and schedule have been imposed on the project manager by upper management. Therefore a specified productivity $P_r$ will be required to reach the management goals. From the point of view of the project manager, the risk of failure may be represented as a simple function calculating the Productivity Expected Deviation (PED):

$$PED = \sum_{i=1}^{m} P(C_i/x) \times (P_r - \mu_i)$$

where $\mu_i$ is the mean of $C_i$.

According to the result of this estimation, the project manager will be able assess the difficulty of the job and make a decision with respect to the development process in order to make a suitable trade-off between quality and productivity. Some analysis can be performed by the manager to see how the risk evolves according to controllable project parameters (i.e. some of the independent variables). If the project manager wants to make a risk/effort trade-off, for example, in order to improve competitiveness on a commercial proposal, he/she can calculate how the risk evolves according to the productivity required. Based on these observations, a suitable risk/effort tradeoff can be selected to maximize chances of success.

One's perspective of risk may be more complex than the previously defined function, PED. For example, assume that a contractor wishes to define risk of financial loss if the system is delivered late and/or there are effort overruns. One can define the Schedule Expected Deviation (SED) as the expected delay, i.e., the difference between the planned and predicted schedule and the Effort Expected Deviation (EED) as the expected effort overrun, i.e., the difference between the planned and predicted effort expenditures. Then

- $SED = \frac{Estimated\_Size}{PED \times Avg\_Team\_Size}$
- $EED = \frac{Estimated\_Size}{PED}$

where $Estimated\_Size$ is either a parameter, like $Avg\_Team\_Size$ (i.e. provided as an input by the manager), or another dependent variable (i.e. the result of some other estimation process). So the expected financial loss function can be defined as a function of both variables $SED$ and $EED$.

Now suppose that the cost of delay on a particular contract has an exponential relationship to the delay itself. This exponential assumption is based upon predictions with respect to the delay of other projects dependent upon the completion of this project and the resulting compensations to be given to the customer. Thus, the $SED$ needs to be weighted by some Cost per Delay Unit that is an exponential function of $SED$, call this $CDU$. Also suppose that $CEU$ is the average Cost per Effort Unit, i.e., the average cost per staff hour for the specific project development team. Then we can define

$$expected\_loss = SED \times CDU + EED \times CEU$$

### 3.2.3 Quality Evaluation

In any quality model, one needs a baseline in order to be able to make sensible comparisons. That is, to evaluate how well a particular project performed, one must be able to assess how well it ought to have performed. OSR generated predictions can provide such a baseline assessment, since they are based on past project experience. For example, let us assume that the quality perspectives of interest (i.e. quality drivers) are ***productivity*** and *fault_rate*, since management views quality as both reliable and inexpensive software.

Assume that using some project features as IVs, the OSR approach yields clear patterns (i.e. low entropy) with respect to productivity in the available data set. These patterns represent the expected productivity distributions in the current development environment for the project under study. The relationship between the actual productivity for the project under study and the expected value of the predicted patterns provides the basis for quality evaluation, from the productivity perspective.

For example, suppose the actual productivity for the project under study falls far below the expected value of the predicted patterns. This implies that the quality of the project with respect to productivity is low. Using the pattern as a basis of comparison, we may ask where the difference comes from.

Several causes may be investigated: incomplete or inadequate data collection, some possible new features or variables affecting the development process, or, of course, the process quality being quite poor.

One may want to describe quality, from the perspective of productivity, as a function of the difference between the actual productivity on the project, and the productivity that should have been achieved on the project. Actual productivity can be measured, but the notion of the productivity that should have been achieved is more difficult. One might want to determine it as the expected productivity determined from a collection of similar projects, which can be determined with OSR. Thus a quality value could be defined as a function the distance between the actual productivity and OSR generated predicted value. This distance may be defined as:

$$Prod\_deviation = AP - \sum_{i=1}^{m} P(C_i/x) \times \mu_i$$

with $AP$ the actual measured productivity.

If we include in the quality model both the *Fault_rate* and *Productivity* quality drivers and we assume an approach similar to the *Prod_deviation* evaluation for calculating a *Fault_deviation*, then a global quality evaluation may be formalized by the following quality model.

Let us define $NFD$ as *Fault_deviation* (i.e. fault rate deviation) normalized by the fault rate standard deviation in the available data set and $NPD$ as the equivalent variable for *Prod_deviation*. Based upon these unitless deviations, we define the following quality model:

- If $NFD < 0$, $NPD > 0$, the larger $|NFD \times NPD|$ is, the better the quality.
- If $NFD > 0$, $NPD < 0$, the larger $|NFD \times NPD|$ is, the worse the quality.
- If both $NFD$ and $NPD$ are negative, the larger $\frac{NFD}{NPD}$ is, the better the quality.
- If both $NFD$ and $NPD$ are positive, the smaller $\frac{NFD}{NPD}$ is, the worse the quality.
- If both $NFD$ and $NPD$ have the same sign and $\frac{NFD}{NPD}$ has a value close to 1, then quality may be assessed as average or nominal.

This particular quality model takes into account two dependent variables and illustrates that a quality model may be a subjective function of several distances on the respective dependent variable ranges. This model might be modified, according to the user perspective of quality, to change the weighting of the various factors, e.g., doubling the effect of fault rate in the evaluation of quality.

# 4 Experimental Results

In this section we demonstrate the effectiveness of the approach by applying the OSR modeling process to the problem of effort estimation and showing that OSR is able to recognize meaningful patterns on the available data sets. Although we will only be dealing with the prediction capability, this experiment also provides an indication of the effectiveness of the risk assessment and quality evaluation capabilities, since the three processes are all based on the conditional probabilities estimated on the dependent variable range. Therefore the accuracy of the three formulas are all dependent on the significance of the recognized patterns.

## 4.1 Description of the Experiment

The largest part of our data set comes from the COCOMO database, consisting of 63 projects [5]. A second source of data is provided by Kemerer (15 projects), collected in a COCOMO format and used in an evaluation of a collection of cost models [7].

The COCOMO projects are a mix of business, system, control, high level interface and scientific applications. A significant percentage of these projects has been developed in FORTRAN (38%) and a very small number in Cobol (8%). The other projects include a variety of data processing applications, primarily developed in Cobol (87%). The following sections describe an experimental evaluation of the OSR technique as applied to effort estimation based upon these two data sets. Results obtained with the OSR approach are compared to results from other standard approaches in order to provide some basis for comparison.

In what follows, we will use the term data set to refer to the combined COCOMO and Kemerer data sets, test sample to refer to the Kemerer data set (the sample on which we are going to assess the OSR capabilities), and learning sample (for each optimized set reduction) to refer to the data set minus the project that is being assessed. Thus, 15 optimized set reductions will be performed, one for each of the test sample pattern vectors. Each time, the pattern vector to be assessed will be removed from the complete data set to form the learning sample (77 projects).

However, one must consider that various subsets of the 78 projects have been developed in various environments, at different points in time and collected by different people according to different procedures, in different organizational structures. The difficulties in tailoring the COCOMO cost drivers to various environments causes a loss of consistency in the data collection regardless of the analysis technique. Moreover, it is important to notice that the project productivities lie over a very large range (i.e. from 20 to 2491 LOC/MM). The 78 pattern vector data set is small enough to assess the capability of the approach to deal with small samples. The number of independent variables used (15) compared to the available data set and the nature of these IVs (i.e. ordinal, nominal) make any pure regression analysis based approach difficult to apply.

Kemerer found that all the models investigated showed a large relative error in predicting effort, ranging from 772% for SLIM and 583% for intermediate COCOMO, to 103% for function points and 85% for ESTIMACS [7]. According to the author, one of the reasons for which the last two models yielded substantially better results is that they are built on business data processing application projects. Since the data used to develop the function point and ESTIMACS models were either not available or not provided in a COCOMO format, we cannot include them in our data set even though they may be more suitable as a learning sample for the fifteen projects of the test sample.

In the following sections, we first summarize the results obtained from the use of OSR to predict effort for the fifteen projects in the test sample based on their COCOMO cost drivers, and then compare these predictions with those obtained using two more traditional approaches:

- a calibrated intermediate COCOMO model,
- a stepwise regression approach.

## 4.2 Predicting Development Effort Using OSR

As the dependent variable, we use project productivity (i.e. size/effort). The size metric used is the "Adjusted Delivered Source Instruction" (ADSI) as defined in [5], and the effort unit is staff-months. The independent variables are the COCOMO cost drivers. The ranges for the IVs have been divided into two intervals

| Project | Act. Prod. | Pred. Prod. | Act. Effort | Pred. Effort | MRE | Entropy |
|---|---|---|---|---|---|---|
| 1 | 884 | 299 | 287 | 846 | 1.94 | 0.63 |
| 2 | 491 | 935 | 82 | 44 | 0.46 | 0.24 |
| 3 | 580 | 674 | 1107 | 668 | 0.40 | 0.45 |
| 4 | 2467 | 643 | 87 | 333 | 2.83 | 0.06 |
| 5 | 1338 | 952 | 336 | 473 | 0.41 | 0.27 |
| 6 | 595 | 1196 | 84 | 42 | 0.50 | 0.47 |
| 7 | 1853 | 1016 | 23 | 42 | 0.83 | 0.47 |
| 8 | 1535 | 1006 | 130 | 199 | 0.53 | 0.52 |
| 9 | 2491 | 431 | 116 | 670 | 4.78 | 0.56 |
| 10 | 542 | 1028 | 72 | 38 | 0.47 | 0.06 |
| 11 | 983 | 1028 | 258 | 247 | 0.04 | 0.06 |
| 12 | 557 | 1025 | 231 | 125 | 0.46 | 0.06 |
| 13 | 1028 | 1035 | 157 | 155 | 0.01 | 0.06 |
| 14 | 667 | 1070 | 247 | 154 | 0.38 | 0.27 |
| 15 | 881 | 964 | 70 | 62 | 0.11 | 0.06 |

Table 1: Experimental Results

(i.e. the boundary being located either just below or above nominal depending on the IV), and the DV (productivity) range into five intervals, each containing an equivalent number of pattern vectors, to the extent possible. The termination criterion was set to 8 projects, after being tuned based upon the learning sample. No more sophisticated decomposition heuristic was used. OSR was used to predict productivity, and effort was estimated as size (ADSI) divided by the predicted productivity.

Table 1 gives the results for each of the fifteen data points of the test sample. The columns contain the project number, the actual productivity, the predicted productivity, the actual effort, the predicted effort, the MRE of the predicted effort, and the entropy yielded by the OSR process.

Overall, we see a positive relationship between entropy and the predictive error, MRE. When entropy is low, the error is low, and when entropy is high, the error is high. The three most accurate predictions, for projects 11,13 and 15, occurred when entropy was at it lowest value.

One problem that may affect the analysis is that the estimation accuracy can be significantly disturbed when the actual productivities of projects are close to the extreme boundaries of the productivity ranges. This is because the density of projects in these parts of the range may be much lower than projects found in the middle of interval ranges. Only intuition based upon understanding the particular situation can help the manager detect an unusual, extremely low/high productivity so the effort estimate may be increased/decreased. Obviously, something that has never or rarely occurred is difficult to predict.

Despite an encouraging predictive accuracy, the two data points with highest productivity (projects 4 and 9 in Table 1) yield large effort overestimation. These projects have a productivity far above the other projects of the learning sample. More information on these particular projects would be necessary to understand why the productivities were so high. It appears clear that something occurred that was not captured by the ADSI and the COCOMO cost drivers. However, in order to keep these projects from introducing noise in our analysis, we will analyze the results obtained both with and without them in the learning sample.

Discounting the projects with the extreme productivities, the worst predictions occurred on projects 1, 7, and 8. However, these predictions also had the highest associated entropies, supporting our belief that entropy can serve as an indicator of predictive accuracy.

Overall, the mean MRE of the OSR predictions was 94%. However, if the projects with the extreme productivities are not considered, the mean MRE becomes 50%, an improvement over what was cited in [7].

## 4.3 An Evaluation of the OSR Technique

To allow for an evaluation of the use of OSR technique for the prediction of productivity and effort, a comparison with more conventional techniques is provided. A calibrated intermediate COCOMO model was built (for each project in the test sample) by recalculating the nominal equations based on the learning sample, as recommended in [5]. A second model was built using a stepwise regression procedure to select the significant productivity drivers, and dividing size (ADSI) by this predicted productivity to obtain an effort prediction. Again, this was done once for each project in the test sample.

Table 2 summarizes the results by giving, for three entropy intervals, the mean Magnitude of Relative Error of the effort estimation for each modeling technique, (columns MRE–OSR, MRE–CC for calibrated COCOMO and MRE–SR for stepwise regression), and the percent of the test sample falling in that interval, (column %TS). This provides some insight into the correlation between the accuracy of the effort estimation and the entropy. The results are provided both with and without projects 4 and 9. It should be noted that all three techniques performed poorly on these projects.

Comparing the results of the OSR and regression based techniques leads to several observations. First, for this data set, the OSR technique provides a significantly better prediction than either a tailored COCOMO or a stepwise regression. For 10 of the 15 projects, the prediction of the OSR model was more accurate than that of both regression models. If outliers are not removed, the two regression based models had an average MRE of 206% and 115% respectively, while the OSR model had an average MRE of 94%. If the projects that showed extremely high productivities are not considered, the MRE for the regression models becomes 104% and 72% respectively, while the OSR model is 50%. The results for OSR are much better that the regression techniques in the two lower entropy categories (37% vs. 109% and 66%, respectively, for the calibrated COCOMO and the step-

| Data Set | Entropy Interval | MRE–OSR | MRE–CC | MRE–SR | % TS |
|---|---|---|---|---|---|
| all projects | $F \leq 0.06$ | 0.65 | 0.34 | 0.78 | 40 |
| | $0.06 < F \leq 0.47$ | 0.49 | 1.71 | 0.80 | 40 |
| | $F > 0.47$ | 2.46 | 6.22 | 2.61 | 20 |
| | any | 0.94 | 2.06 | 1.15 | 100 |
| 4,9 removed | $F \leq 0.06$ | 0.22 | 0.33 | 0.48 | 38 |
| | $0.06 < F \leq 0.47$ | 0.49 | 1.71 | 0.80 | 46 |
| | $F > 0.47$ | 1.24 | 0.77 | 1.03 | 15 |
| | any | 0.50 | 1.04 | 0.72 | 100 |

Table 2: Comparison of the Three Techniques

wise regression models). However, in the highest entropy class, all techniques fare poorly. For OSR, this result should have been expected, since poor entropy implies that no significant pattern has been found, and thus OSR is not expected to give a very accurate result. Consequently, in the highest entropy category, regression based techniques may perform better.

For the OSR method, the predictions are clearly more accurate when the associated entropy is low. If, using the reduced data set, we test the null hypothesis that the MRE means of the three categories are equal against the hypothesis that they are not equal, we can conclude that there is a difference among the mean MREs at the 0.03 level of significance. Therefore, whenever one makes an estimate, the entropy of the pattern on which the estimate is based can be used to provide an assessment of the accuracy of the estimate. For example, in this environment, if the obtained entropy is around 0.06, the expected accuracy should be around 22%, according to the results presented in table 2.

One clear benefit of the OSR technique is this ability to provide an indication of the expected accuracy of the prediction, as demonstrated by the clear correlation of MRE to entropy. Projects with characteristics that have previously shown widely varying productivities (i.e. no clear patterns) are flagged with high entropies, allowing the manager to recognize that the prediction may be suspect. The regression based models provide no such indication of the accuracy for an individual prediction.

For example, the tailored COCOMO model provided relatively accurate predictions for projects of the semi-detached mode (an average MRE of 32%), except for a poor prediction for project 8, with an MRE of 133%. The prediction for project 8 using the OSR model was better (MRE of 53%), but still not very accurate. However this prediction was flagged with a high entropy, indicating an unstable prediction. The regression based models provide no indication of the potential of the inaccurate prediction, while the OSR technique indicates that no significant pattern has been recognized in the available data set.

One interesting observation in the performance of the regression based techniques is that the OSR produced entropy also appears to provide an indication as to the quality of these predictions. Both the calibrated COCOMO and stepwise regression based models have a better accuracy when the associated entropy is low than when it is high. Thus it appears that the two approaches may be very complimentary. The regression techniques may fare better when a high entropy was generated (i.e. no pattern was found). In any case, the entropy can serve as an indicator of the expected accuracy of the prediction, and help to determine the most appropriate prediction method.

# 5 Conclusions

Optimized Set Reduction (OSR) has been developed in order to address data analysis issues within the software development process. The procedure has the following positive characteristics:

- It makes no assumptions with respect to probability density functions on the dependent and independent variable ranges. It does not attempt to fit data to predefined distributions, rather it uses the data to approximate the actual distribution (i.e. patterns). No particular mathematical relationship between the DV and IVs needs to be assumed. Thus OSR seems to fulfill $R_1$. Also, it handles discrete and continuous IVs in a natural and consistent way, and therefore meets $R_4$.

- It allows an estimation of accuracy for each prediction so we can answer the question: Is *this* estimate usable? This fulfills $R_2$. When relevant IVs are not available at the time of the prediction, OSR still allows a prediction to be made; however, OSR will provide a warning if the prediction is expected to be poor. While other techniques provide model-level warnings (such as a low R-squared for regression techniques), OSR will also report on the predictions where it is still expected to be accurate. In these circumstances, OSR may be more useful to the manager than the other techniques. This satisfies in part $R_3$ (i.e. missing information). The issue of outliers is still under investigation.

- It provides an automated refinement of the model as new data is incorporated into the data set. The process for selecting the most relevant IVs from those available in the data set can be automated. Thus, the prediction process may automated and supported by a tool in an effective way.

The results of the preliminary experiments have been encouraging, since the predictions obtained with OSR typically were more accurate than those of other modeling techniques, and the entropy of the extracted subset was found to have a strong correlation with the MRE of the prediction.

The technique has been applied to other problems of the software development process, such as classifying components as likely to be error prone or difficult to maintain based on their structural characteristics. The preliminary results from these experiments are reported in [2, 4]. Also under investigation are techniques to support interpretation of the patterns, to better facilitate improvement–orineted software development. A prototype tool supporting the OSR approach has been developed at the University of Maryland as a part of the TAME project [1].

# References


[1] V. R. Basili and H. D. Rombach. "The TAME Project: Towards Improvement-Oriented Software Environments," *IEEE Trans. Software Eng.*, 14 (6), June, 1988.

[2] L. Briand, V. Basili and C. Hetmanski. "Providing an Empirical Basis for Optimizing the Verification and Testing Phases of Software Development," *IEEE International Symposium on Software Reliability Engineering*, North Carolina, October 1992.

[3] L. Briand, V. Basili and W. Thomas. "A Pattern Recognition Approach for Software Engineering Data Analysis," *IEEE Trans. Software Eng.*, November, 1992.

[4] L. Briand and A. Porter. "An Alternative Modeling Approach for Predicting Error Profiles in Ada Systems," *EUROMETRICS '92: European Conference on Quantitative Evaluation of Software and Systems*, Brussels, April, 1992.

[5] B. Boehm. *Software Engineering Economics*, Prentice-Hall, 1981.

[6] R. Charette. *Software Engineering Risk Analysis and Management*, McGraw-Hill, 1989.

[7] C. Kemerer. "An Empirical Validation of Software Cost Estimation Models," *Communications of the ACM*, 30 (5), May, 1987.

[8] R. W. Selby and A. A. Porter. "Learning from Examples: Generation and Evaluation of Decision Trees for Software Resource Analysis," *IEEE Trans. Software Eng.* 14 (12), December, 1988.

[9] J. Tou and R. Gonzalez. *Pattern Recognition Principles*, 1974.

# CALIBRATION OF SOFTWARE COST MODELS TO DOD ACQUISITIONS

**Audrey E. Taub**
**The MITRE Corporation**
**Bedford, Massachusetts 01730**

## INTRODUCTION

During a 1987 model recalibration study [1], the MITRE Cost Analysis Technical Center (CATC) showed that COCOMO [2] models significantly underestimated USAF Electronic Systems Division (ESD) software project efforts and schedules. Subsequently, new CATC models were calibrated based on a regression analysis of historical ESD and related programs. Our current research has focused on two goals: (1) to expand our software database of typical ESD software developments, and (2) to develop statistically-based software models that improved upon our ability to estimate the effort and schedule of ESD software developments. The recent database effort involved the validation and updating of the existing CATC database and the addition of four new data points. The statistical analysis was aimed at improving effort and schedule predictive models through the use of various regression methodologies such as linear and nonlinear regression, correlation analysis, and error analysis. The purpose of this paper is to discuss the results of this research, which include the development of six new effort models, one new schedule model, and an uncertainty methodology for determining confidence limits around effort and schedule point estimates.

During this discussion, we will make reference to various model "types" such as basic embedded and nominal semidetached, which correspond to the definitions provided by B. W. Boehm [2]. Familiarity with Boehm's work is assumed on the part of the reader.

## DATA ANALYSIS

In this section we present the effort and schedule equations resulting from our research along with the criteria we used for model selection. A brief description of our database is also included. It is very important to understand the type of data on which these models are based if the models are to be used on projects outside the ESD environment.

The effort data are analyzed in terms of what we have defined as subsystems. A subsystem can be a single Computer Software Configuration Item (CSCI) or an aggregation of CSCIs where each cannot be developed in isolation from the other(s). The subsystems themselves are defined as being relatively independent of each other, in the sense that the people developing different subsystems do not need to communicate extensively with each other and the software of one subsystem does not require extensive integration testing with another subsystem. For example, a data reduction CSCI (subsystem) can often be developed in relative isolation from the applications software, since it is only dependent upon receiving files of specified format, from which it will extract the data and perform specific analyses. Or, a signal processing subsystem for a radar system can be developed in isolation from the applications that perform detection, tracking, correlation, and identification of objects.

Schedule data, on the other hand, are analyzed at the project level. While individual CSCI or subsystem development efforts may be independent of each other, the overall schedule of the project is dependent upon the completion of every CSCI or subsystem. In addition, numerous resource constraints (technical personnel, computers, support staff) limit the number of software development tasks that can be performed in parallel. As a consequence, we believe the overall schedule is more closely correlated with total effort expended on all subsystems than with the effort expended on any single CSCI or subsystem.

## The CATC Database

The CATC software calibration database contains descriptive data on 35 ESD software subsystems whose sizes range from 6 to 264 KEDSI[1]. The applications are varied and include command and control, radar, simulation, and training.

Table 1 contains a summary of the CATC software development data used during this study. The table is divided into two sections, one for embedded mode subsystems and one for semidetached mode subsystems. For each subsystem we present KEDSI, actual effort measured in staff months (SM), nominal effort[2] in SM, the higher order language (HOL) in which the program was written, and the productivity (Prod) given in equivalent delivered source instructions (EDSI) per SM. Table 2 contains project level schedule data and includes KEDSI, effort, and schedule (or project duration) measured in months.

## New Effort and Schedule Equations: A Summary

The principle method of analysis throughout this study was regression analysis, which included the use of linear least squares and nonlinear regression techniques. These techniques were applied to our entire data set as well as subsets of the data. The subsets were generated by subdividing the data by size (lines of code), application (e.g., radar, command and control), and language (e.g., FORTRAN, Jovial). A number of regression analyses were performed until we determined a set of equations whose standard errors were lower than those of our previously calibrated models. Table 3 contains a summary of our recalibrated effort and schedule equations. We found that subdividing the embedded

---

[1] KEDSI is the number, in thousands, of equivalent delivered source instructions as defined by B. W. Boehm [2].

[2] Nominal effort is computed by dividing actual effort by the effort adjustment factor (EAF) [2].

**Table 1. CATC Software Database Summary Statistics Embedded Data**

| Sub-system # | KEDSI | Actual Effort (SM) | Nominal Effort (SM/EAF) | HOL Language | Prod (EDSI/SM) |
|---|---|---|---|---|---|
| 1 | 6.1 | 150 | 142 | Assembler | 40 |
| 2 | 6.1 | 85.8 | 51.7 | C | 71 |
| 3 | 9.1 | 13.1 | 18.5 | Jovial | 693 |
| 4 | 10.4 | 691 | 601 | Jovial | 15 |
| 5 | 11.5 | 169 | 91.5 | Assembler | 68 |
| 6 | 16.0 | 61.3 | 51.1 | FORTRAN | 261 |
| 7 | 16.9 | 56.0 | 72.7 | Assembler | 302 |
| 8 | 20.3 | 241 | 119 | CMS-2 | 84 |
| 9 | 25.6 | 72.4 | 94.0 | Assembler | 353 |
| 10 | 25.8 | 161 | 31.6 | Jovial | 160 |
| 11 | 26.2 | 289 | 85.1 | EDL | 91 |
| 12 | 37.5 | 157 | 123 | FORTRAN | 239 |
| 13 | 45.0 | 469 | 539 | FORTRAN | 96 |
| 14 | 55.7 | 341 | 182 | Assembler | 164 |
| 15 | 63.1 | 430 | 229 | Jovial | 147 |
| 16 | 75.1 | 1678 | 1459 | Jovial | 45 |
| 17 | 103 | 1222 | N/A | FORTRAN | 84 |
| 18 | 106 | 479 | 417 | Jovial | 221 |
| 19 | 106 | 1474 | 780 | FORTRAN | 72 |
| 20 | 144 | 415 | 256 | C | 346 |
| 21 | 157 | 2043 | 1310 | Jovial | 77 |
| 22 | 162 | 3499 | 1871 | FORTRAN | 46 |
| 23 | 232 | 5103 | 2700 | CMS-2 | 45 |
| 24 | 264 | 6496 | 2980 | FORTRAN | 41 |

**Table 1. (Concluded)**
**Semidetached**

| Sub-system # | KEDSI | Actual Effort (SM) | Nominal Effort (SM/EAF) | HOL Language | Prod (EDSI/SM) |
|---|---|---|---|---|---|
| 25 | 5.40 | 52.2 | 25.0 | Jovial | 103 |
| 26 | 7.41 | 28.0 | 8.7 | Jovial | 265 |
| 27 | 8.70 | 115 | 61.3 | Jovial | 75 |
| 28 | 8.78 | 94.0 | 79.7 | Jovial | 93 |
| 29 | 9.00 | 59.1 | 44.4 | FORTRAN | 152 |
| 30 | 9.05 | 53.0 | 70.7 | Jovial | 171 |
| 31 | 12.9 | 132 | 66.8 | Jovial | 98 |
| 32 | 46.4 | 158 | 180 | C | 294 |
| 33 | 73.1 | 385 | 196 | Jovial | 190 |
| 34 | 139 | 586 | 814 | FORTRAN | 237 |
| 35 | 165 | 704 | 1006 | Assembler | 235 |

mode data by size (in terms of lines of code) was the most effective means of reducing modeling error. Thus, embedded mode subsystems have models designated as small and large, where small represents models based on subsystems whose size fell between 6 and 63 KEDSI and where large represents models based on data whose size fell between 75 and 264 KEDSI. Semidetached data were originally subdivided into small (seven points) and large (4 points) subsets. Although a small improvement was made in terms of reducing the standard error, it was not substantial. Therefore, we decided not to adopt two separate models on the basis of such limited data. The selected nominal embedded mode effort models were based on ordinary least squares methodologies [3], whereas the selected basic embedded mode effort models for small and large subsystems, basic semidetached models, and the new schedule model were based on nonlinear regression methodologies [4].

**Table 2. Project Level Schedule Data**

| Project Designator | KEDSI | Effort (SM) | Schedule (Months) |
|---|---|---|---|
| A | 16 | 61 | 26 |
| B | 20 | 157 | 18 |
| C | 26 | 241 | 33 |
| D | 38 | 289 | 29 |
| E | 45 | 469 | 13 |
| F | 47 | 335 | 26 |
| G | 139 | 586 | 26 |
| H | 169 | 1231 | 33 |
| I | 193 | 623 | 31 |
| J | 200 | 2862 | 35 |
| K | 222 | 5103 | 75 |
| L | 233 | 2350 | 40 |
| M | 250 | 6496 | 43 |

Although it may seem unusual to have obtained linear nominal models from data that is typically associated with a nonlinear model, the phenomenon can be explained as follows. Consider the equation for productivity implied by the nominal effort equation,

$$E = a(EAF)(KEDSI)^{b}$$

$$\text{Productivity} = \frac{EDSI}{E} = \left(\frac{1000}{a}\right)\left(\frac{1}{EAF}\right)(KEDSI)^{(1-b)}.$$

**Table 3. New Calibrated Effort and Schedule Equations**

| Model # | Model Type | Prediction Equations |
|---|---|---|
| 1 | Basic Embedded/Small[1] | $E = 91.0 + 0.66\,(KEDSI)^{1.52}$ |
| 2 | Basic Embedded/Large[2] | $E = 425 + 0.09\,(KEDSI)^{2.00}$ |
| 3 | Nominal Embedded/Small | $E/EAF = 46.0 + 2.31\,(KEDSI)$ |
| 4 | Nominal Embedded/Large[3] | $E/EAF = -462 + 12.4\,(KEDSI)$ |
| 5 | Basic Semidetached | $E = 10.7\,(KEDSI)^{0.82}$ |
| 6 | Nominal Semidetached | $E/EAF = 45.0 + 0.09\,(KEDSI)^{1.82}$ |
| 7 | Schedule | $S = 5.90\,(E)^{0.25}$ |

1. Small refers to subsystems that are > 6 and < 75 KEDSI.
2. Large refers to subsystems that are ≥ 75 KEDSI and ≤ 264 KEDSI.
3. Although this model has a negative intercept, negative effort is never predicted because KEDSI ≥75.

This expression implies the following:

if $b = 1$, productivity does not vary with size

if $b > 1$, productivity decreases with an increase in size

if $b < 1$, productivity increases with an increase in size.

However, it is possible that the EAF multiplier is correlated with size. In our embedded mode data we found that productivity is correlated with the inverse of the EAF, i.e.,

$$\text{Productivity} \approx \frac{C}{EAF},$$

where C is a proportionality factor. This expression is comparable to the previous expression for productivity when b = 1. Thus, when the variable EAF is introduced into the nominal effort equation, the parameter b may be one, and the effort linear with respect to size. The EAF may, in effect, be capturing any relationship that exists between productivity and size.

The basic semidetached model (model 5) has an exponent less than one, a phenomenon often interpreted in the literature as representing an economy of scale. That is, it implies that the greater the number of lines of code to be developed, the smaller the dollars per line of code. However, we are not ready to make this generalization based on such a limited data set. Figure 1 illustrates the basic semidetached data and corresponding prediction equation.

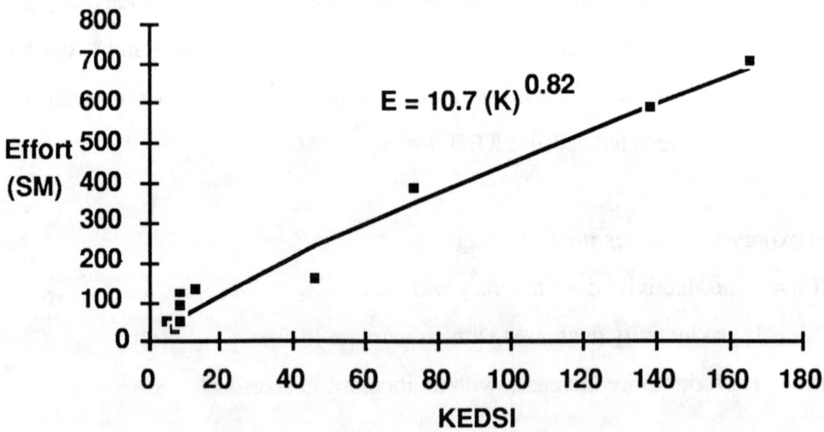


Figure 1. Basic Semidetached Data with Prediction Equation

The nominal semidetached model (model 6), unlike the nominal embedded models, is nonlinear. Figure 2 illustrates the data along with the three-parameter prediction model. In this case, the EAF values are large (2.1, 3.2, 1.9) for several of the smaller subsystems

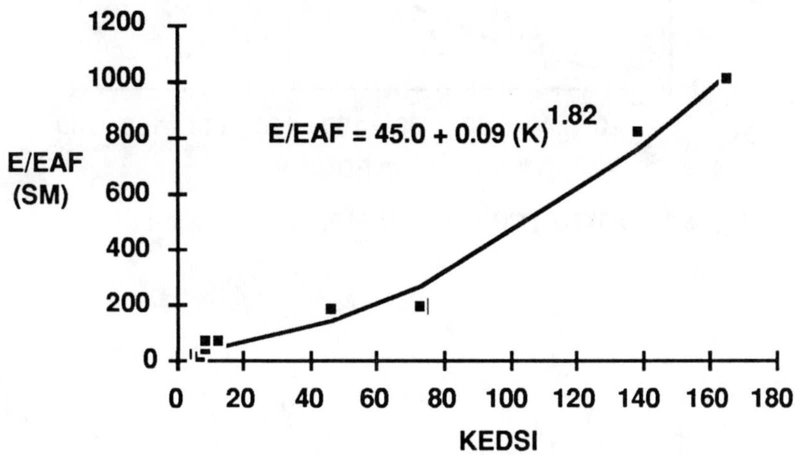


Figure 2. Nominal Semidetached Data with Prediction Equation

and small (0.72, 0.70) for the two largest subsystems. Since actual effort is divided by EAF to obtain the nominal data, we experience a relative decrease in the small subsystem effort and a relative increase in the large subsystem effort. This results in a concave up data set, best represented by a near-quadratic model.

## Model Determination

We first recognized the inadequacies of the COCOMO models for the ESD environment in our 1987 model calibration study [1]. In particular, COCOMO underestimated effort for most large ESD subsystems and schedule for all but one project. These findings are illustrated in figures 3 and 4. Our recalibrated equations represent the best fit to the data we have obtained to date. Figure 3 illustrates the embedded mode data along with the new CATC models for small and large subsystems compared with the

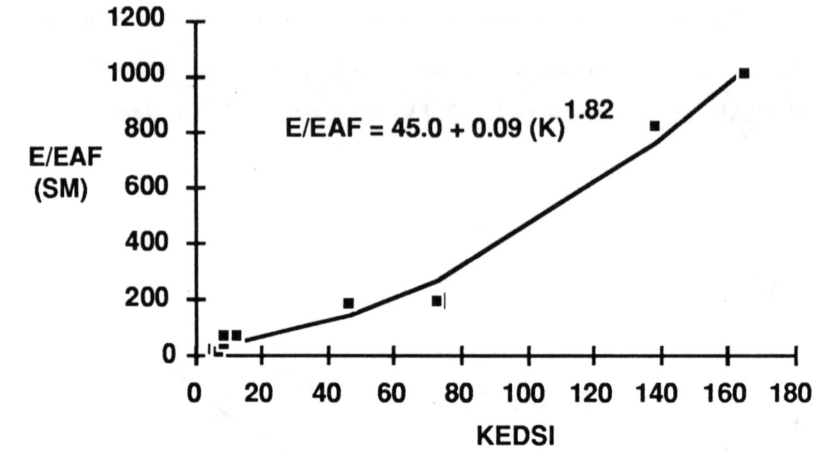


Figure 3. CATC and COCOMO Basic Embedded Models

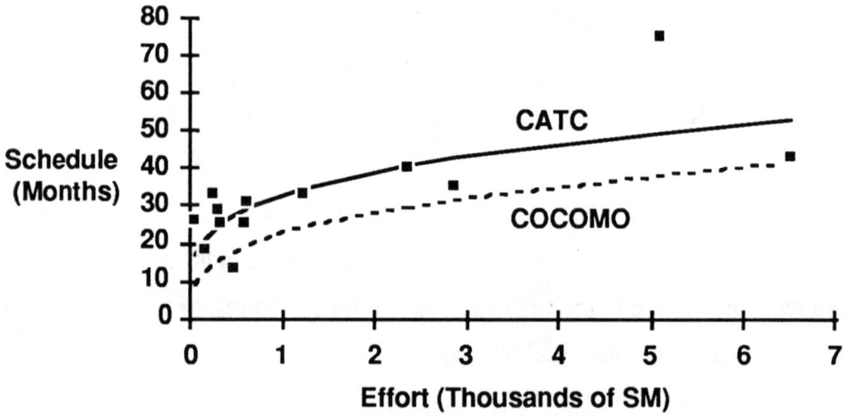


Figure 4. Schedule Data with CATC and COCOMO Models

COCOMO basic effort model. Figure 4 illustrates the schedule data along with the new CATC and COCOMO schedule models.

In addition to the differences between the models, figures 3 and 4 illustrate the high degree of variability among the data. Unlike textbook data sets, these data do not lend themselves to straightforward model characterization. Nevertheless, we have attempted to develop models whose modeling errors are smaller than those of our previous models.

Error reduction was measured in terms of standard error (SE). When effort (E) is the variable of interest, SE is mathematically defined as

$$SE = \sqrt{\frac{\sum_{i=1}^{n}(E_i - \hat{E}_i)^2}{(n-p)}}$$

where $E_i$ is the actual effort for the ith data point, $\hat{E}_i$ is the effort estimated from one of our models, n is the number of data points used to calibrate the model, and p is the number of parameters in the model. Although effort is used in this definition, the same definition applies to schedule or any other variable of interest. The term

$$e_i = E_i - \hat{E}_i$$

is called the residual (or error) term and (n - p) is the degrees of freedom [3]. Figure 5 illustrates the residuals for the COCOMO model applied to our large subsystem data. Figure 6 illustrates the same for the CATC model. The SE for the COCOMO model is 1935 staff months while the SE for the CATC model is 990 staff months, a 49 percent reduction.

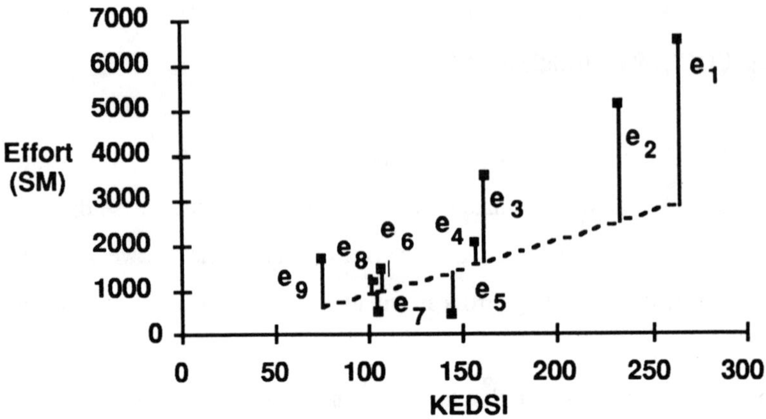


Figure 5. COCOMO Model Residuals for Large Subsystems

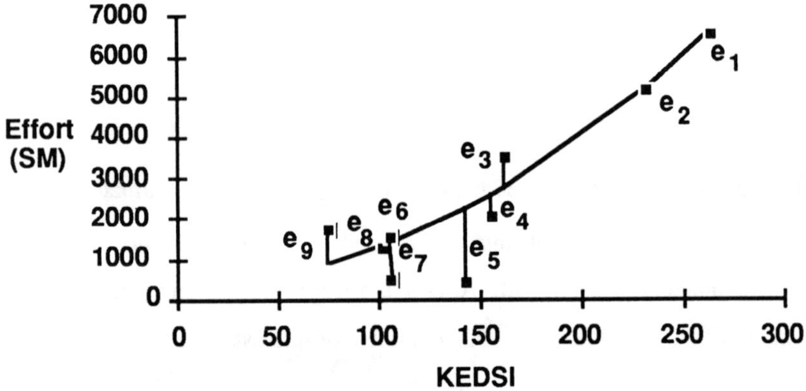


Figure 6. CATC Model Residual for Large Subsystems

Improvement over the COCOMO models was achieved by considering alternative model forms. COCOMO-like effort and schedule models are of the form [3]

$$Y = a\,(X)^b.$$

That is, they can be expressed, by a suitable transformation of the variables, in a linear model form.

For example, a two-parameter nonlinear model of the form

$$Y = a(X)^b.$$

can be linearized using a natural logarithm transformation that puts the model in the form

$$\ln Y = \ln(a) + b(\ln X).$$

A significant drawback to this model form is that it underestimates effort for our large subsystems. Therefore, we decided not to limit ourselves by the regression technique and considered a more general, three-parameter model of the form

$$Y = a + b\,(X)^c.$$

The parameters a, b, and c were estimated using nonlinear regression techniques.

Table 4 displays the SE for both the 1990 recalibrated CATC models and the COCOMO models. Without exception, significant improvements in prediction accuracy are achieved when using the recalibrated models. Figures 2 and 3 illustrate this point.

**Table 4. Standard Errors (SE) for Calibrated CATC Models**

| Model # | Model | SE (SM) COCOMO | SE (SM) (1990) | % Change |
|---|---|---|---|---|
| 1 | Basic Embedded/Small | 107 | 95 | -11 |
| 2 | Basic Embedded/Large | 1935 | 990 | -49 |
| 3 | Nominal Embedded/Small | 101 | 41 | -59 |
| 4 | Nominal Embedded/Large | 734 | 650 | -11 |
| 5 | Basic Semidetached | 103 | 40 | -61 |
| 6 | Nominal Semidetached | 73 | 40 | -45 |
| 7 | Schedule | 15.5 | 2.8 | -82 |

## UNCERTAINTY ANALYSIS METHODOLOGY

To realistically capture the error associated with each of the prediction models, we have developed a methodology for imposing uncertainty bounds on an estimate. This method involves generating a cumulative distribution function about the ratio of the actual and estimated effort. We have generated uncertainty distributions for each of our seven models, but will limit our discussion to selected models. While this discussion will use effort as our variable of interest, the same arguments hold for schedule.

### Uncertainty Distribution Generation

For ease of computation, we would like the lower and upper bounds of our uncertainty interval to be a multiplicative function of our point estimate. That is, we would like to multiply our estimate by factors to obtain the lower and upper uncertainty bounds. In this discussion, we will refer to these multiplicative factors, generically, as $r_e$ (for effort ratio). In addition to these factors, we would also like to have a probability associated with each interval such that we can say there is a probability of p that the actual effort (or schedule) falls within the computed interval.

We begin by computing our effort ratio. If E represents the actual effort, and $\hat{E}$ the effort estimate computed from one of our parametric models, define $r_e$ as

$$r_e = \frac{E}{\hat{E}}$$

where

$$0 < r_e < \infty.$$

Our ESD software database provides us with values of E for each of our subsystems, and $\hat{E}$ is computed for each subsystem using one of our parametric models. We assume that the ratio of actual effort to estimated effort on future developments (within the size range of our data) will behave in a similar fashion.

We know that if our models could predict without error, then $E = \hat{E}$, or,

$$r_e = \frac{E}{\hat{E}} = 1.$$

In this most <u>un</u>likely case, there would be no uncertainty about our point estimate (i.e., $r_e$ would equal one for the upper and lower bounds). In reality, $r_e$ is distributed about one. Therefore, we want to generate the cumulative distribution function (CDF) of $r_e$ for each of our seven models. An example of such a distribution is given in figure 7, which illustrates the CDF for small embedded subsystems.

Table 5 contains the effort ratio distribution for the basic embedded small subsystems. In this table we have computed (interpolated from the CDF column) the 10th, 20th, 80th,

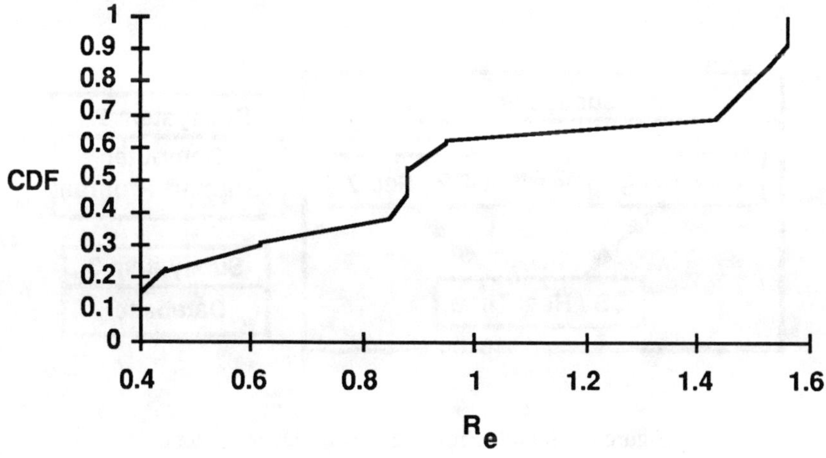


Figure 7. Relative Error CDF for Small Basic Embedded Subsystems

and 90th percentiles for the distribution of effort ratios. An 80 percent uncertainty interval for the effort ratio may be computed using the bounds associated with the 10th and 90th percentiles (i.e., 0.40 and 1.55). To compute 80 percent uncertainty bounds on an effort estimate, we simply compute the lower and upper bounds as

$$0.40(\hat{E}) \text{ and } 1.55(\hat{E}), \text{ respectively.}$$

We say that there is an 80 percent chance that the true effort falls within these bounds. In general, we are not restricted to capturing the middle p percent of the uncertainty distribution. For example, we may want just an upper bound such that there is an 80 percent chance that the estimate is less than or equal to that upper bound. From table 5, we see that the upper bound is 1.50 times the estimated effort.

**An Effort Estimation Example**

As an example, let us consider the proposed development of a system containing three subsystems. Figure 8 illustrates the system configuration. Subsystem 1 contains

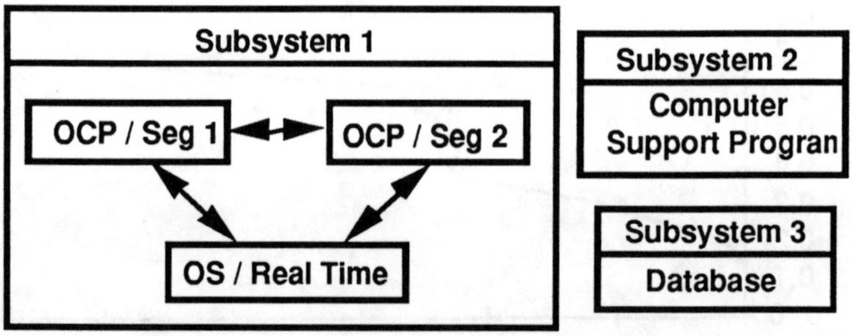


Figure 8. Sample Project Software Development

**Table 5. Basic Embedded Small Subsystem Uncertainty Factors**

| Sub-system # | KEDSI | Basic Effort (SM) | Estimated Effort (SM) | Effort Ratio ($r_e$) | CDF | %tile | Uncertainty Factors |
|---|---|---|---|---|---|---|---|
| 11 | 26 | 289 | 185 | 1.56 | 1.00 | | |
| 8 | 20 | 241 | 155 | 1.56 | 0.92 | | |
| | | | | | | 90 | 1.55 |
| 13 | 45 | 468 | 306 | 1.53 | 0.85 | | |
| | | | | | | 80 | 1.50 |
| 1 | 6 | 150 | 101 | 1.48 | 0.77 | | |
| 5 | 12 | 169 | 118 | 1.43 | 0.69 | | |
| 15 | 63 | 430 | 450 | 0.95 | 0.62 | | |
| 10 | 26 | 161 | 183 | 0.88 | 0.54 | | |
| 14 | 56 | 341 | 388 | 0.88 | 0.46 | | |
| 2 | 6 | 86 | 101 | 0.85 | 0.38 | | |
| 12 | 38 | 157 | 254 | 0.62 | 0.31 | | |
| 6 | 16 | 61 | 136 | 0.45 | 0.23 | | |
| | | | | | | 20 | 0.43 |
| 7 | 17 | 56 | 140 | 0.40 | 0.15 | | |
| | | | | | | 10 | 0.40 |
| 9 | 26 | 72 | 182 | 0.40 | 0.08 | | |

three CSCIs: an Operational Control Processor/Segment 1 (OCP/Seg 1), an Operational Control Processor/ Segment 2 (OCP/ Seg 2), and a real time operating system (OS/Real Time). Subsystem 2 consists of a single Computer Support Program CSCI, and subsystem 3 consists of a database CSCI. Table 6 contains the KEDSI estimates for each CSCI along with the estimated development effort. All of the CSCIs are required

**Table 6. Line of Code Estimates**

| CSCI | KEDSI | Effort Estimate |
|---|---|---|
| OCP / Seg 1 | 17 | |
| OCP / Seg 2 | 35 | |
| OS / Real Time | 25 | |
| *Subtotal (Subsystem 1)* | 77 | 958 |
| Computer Support Program (Subsystem 2) | 32 | 219 |
| Database (Subsystem 3) | 50 | 343 |
| TOTAL | 159 | 1,520 |

to operate within a strongly coupled complex of hardware, software, and operational procedures. We know from this description of the system's operational environment that these are embedded developments. We see that subsystem 1 falls into the large subsystem (≥ 75 KEDSI) category, while subsystems 2 and 3 are in the small subsystem (< 75 KEDSI) category. Thus, we need to use the large, basic embedded prediction equation,

$$\hat{E} = 425 + 0.09(\text{KEDSI})^{2.00}$$

for subsystem 1, and the small, basic embedded prediction equation,

$$\hat{E} = 91.0 + 0.66(\text{KEDSI})^{1.52}$$

for subsystems 2 and 3.

Our effort point estimate is 958 staff months for subsystem 1; 219 staff months for subsystem 2; and 343 staff months for subsystem 3. This gives us a total project estimate of 1,520 staff months. Eighty percent uncertainty bounds for subsystems 2 and 3 can be computed by determining the multiplicative factors (given in the ratio column) associated with 0.10 and 0.90 in the CDF column of table 5. Since 0.10 and 0.90 are not explicitly listed in the CDF column, we linearly interpolate and find the associated effort ratio values of 0.40 and 1.55. For subsystem 2, the lower uncertainty effort bound is 0.40(219) = 88 staff months and the upper bound is 1.55(219) = 340 staff months. For subsystem 3, the lower uncertainty effort bound is 0.40(343) = 137 staff months and the upper bound is 1.55(343) = 532 staff months. To estimate the uncertainty interval for subsystem 1, we need table 7. In this case, the 10th percentile is 0.18 and the 90th percentile is 1.30. Thus, the lower uncertainty effort bound for subsystem 1 is 0.18(958) = 172 staff months and the upper uncertainty bound is 1.30(958) = 1245 staff months. In summary, our 80 percent intervals for each subsystem are given by

Subsystem 1: (172, 1245) SM
Subsystem 2: (88, 340) SM
Subsystem 3: (137, 532) SM.

To obtain a distribution for total project effort, we need to combine the information we have for each of the three subsystems. One method for accomplishing this is Monte Carlo simulation. For each subsystem, one would generate a random variate from the appropriate error ratio distribution (small embedded for subsystems 2 and 3, and large embedded for subsystem 1), multiply by the respective point estimate for each subsystem, and sum the generated effort values for each of the three subsystems. This procedure would be replicated a suitable number of times (at least 1000) and a distribution of total effort could be generated. The resulting total project CDF may then be used to determine an uncertainty interval for total project effort (using the same method discussed for individual subsystems.)

**Table 7. Basic Embedded Large Subsystem Uncertainty Factors**

| Sub-system # | KEDSI | Basic Effort (SM) | Estimated Effort (SM) | Effort Ratio ($r_e$) | CDF | %tile | Uncertainty Factors |
|---|---|---|---|---|---|---|---|
| 16 | 75 | 1678 | 933 | 1.80 | 1.00 | | |
| | | | | | | 90 | 1.30 |
| 22 | 162 | 3499 | 2801 | 1.25 | 0.89 | | |
| | | | | | | 80 | 1.07 |
| 19 | 106 | 1474 | 1443 | 1.02 | 0.78 | | |
| 24 | 264 | 6496 | 6697 | 0.97 | 0.67 | | |
| 23 | 232 | 5103 | 5264 | 0.97 | 0.56 | | |
| 17 | 103 | 1222 | 1376 | 0.89 | 0.44 | | |
| 21 | 157 | 2043 | 2632 | 0.78 | 0.33 | | |
| 18 | 106 | 479 | 1433 | 0.33 | 0.22 | | |
| | | | | | | 20 | 0.30 |
| 20 | 144 | 415 | 2286 | 0.18 | 0.11 | | |
| | | | | | | 10 | 0.18 |

## CONCLUSIONS

It is clear from this analysis that the considerable variability in our database makes the development of a single software effort or schedule prediction model with a small error difficult. However, subdividing the data by size and mode and implementing the uncertainty methodology provides the analyst with a structured and reasonable approach to bounding an effort (or schedule) estimate at a quantifiable probability level. However, if we want major improvements in our software predicting capability, we need to break away from the basic line-of-code model and turn to models that better capture the software development process. One suggestion is to utilize a System Dynamics model [5], which attempts to reflect the dynamic interactions among software development activities. Its parametric inputs allow the user to perform sensitivity analyses that aid in strategic planning.

## REFERENCES

1. Funch, P. G., "Recalibration of Basic and Nominal COCOMO Equations to Recent Air Force Acquisitions," Third Annual COCOMO Users' Group Meeting, Software Engineering Institute, Carnegie Mellon University, Pittsburgh, PA, 1987.

2. Boehm, B. W., *Software Engineering Economics,* Prentice Hall, Inc., Englewood Cliffs, NJ, 1981.

3. Draper, N. R. and Smith, H., *Applied Regression Analysis,* John Wiley and Sons, Inc., New York, NY, 1981.

4. Ratkowsky, D. A., *Nonlinear Regression Modeling*, Marcel Dekker, Inc., New York, NY, 1983.

5. Cho, C. C., "A System Dynamics Model of the Software Development Process," Fifth Annual COCOMO Users' Group Meeting, Software Engineering Institute, Carnegie Mellon University, Pittsburgh, PA, 1989.

# ESTIMATING SOFTWARE SIZE FROM COUNTS OF EXTERNALS, A GENERALIZATION OF FUNCTION POINTS

by

John E. Gaffney, Jr. and Richard Werling
Software Productivity Consortium
2214 Rock Hill Road
Herndon, Virginia 22070

## I. OVERVIEW

Estimating the size of a new software system is key to estimating the amount of labor required to develop it. The error in the estimate of the size of a prospective software system often exceeds the estimation error for the amount of labor required for development and for productivity of its creation. Hence, the development of a method to better estimate software size, especially one that can be applied relatively early in the development cycle, should be of considerable interest to the software development community. All of the parametric software development cost estimating tools/methods on the market, such as COCOMO, require as a primary input the size of the intended system, typically denominated in either source statements or function points. The values of other parameters input to these models, such as the type of platform on which the proposed system is intended to operate, generally relate to the estimation of productivity.

This paper demonstrates how to estimate the size of a software system in source statements from the unweighted counts of four measurables of the intended system's requirements. These unweighted counts are often available very early in the development cycle. These measurables are: external inputs, external outputs, external inquiries, and external interfaces (with other programs). The standard function point measure is based on counts of these same four measurables, plus the count of internal logical files. The sum of the counts of the first three items (that is, excluding external interfaces) is also relatively strongly related to the software size. Thus, one can develop a relationship between this count and software size that can be employed to estimate software size. This paper presents some analyses of function point data on some commercial software systems (Albrecht 1983; Kemerer 1987; Kemerer 1990). They suggest that the unweighted sum of the counts of the externals (the primitives from which the function point value is determined) correlates about as well with the source statement count as does function points. Since the calculation of function points involves a subjective estimation of some additional factors, including the appropriate weighting to apply to the counts of each of the primitives, use of the "raw" sum of the primitives could prove advantageous. Not doing the weighting and other processing of the raw counts would be simpler and might result in a reduced degree of error in the source statement estimate determined from it.

Experience with MIS (management information systems) and commercial software using function points shows that an early estimate of size can be made, generally quite successfully, for those classes of software. However, function point advocates typically use the counts of the five items cited above to calculate function points, and not an estimate of the count of source statements.

Two empirically derived relations, between the sums of the counts of three and of four externals and the size of the system in KSLOC (thousands of source statements), are provided for nineteen non–MIS aerospace software systems. The three count relationship explains 86.8 percent of the variation in KSLOC, while the four count relationship explains 89 percent of the variation in KSLOC. Data on two sets of business systems also were analyzed (Albrecht 1983; Kemerer 1987; Kemerer 1990). The analysis indicates that the unweighted count of inputs and outputs is correlated about as well as with program size as was function points. This observation suggests that weighting these counts as well as calculating a "value adjustment factor" by which the weighted sum would be multiplied, per standard function point methodology, would often add minimal incremental accuracy to the size estimate. The analysis suggests that estimates of the counts of the three or of the four externals cited above can be used in a parametric algorithm to estimate the size of a system in source statements. The analysis further suggests it is likely that this can be done for embedded systems as well as for MIS and commercial (business oriented) systems.

## II. DEFINITION OF FUNCTION POINTS AND HOW TO COUNT THEM

This section briefly describes the nature of the function point measure and its origin, and summarizes how it is calculated. The function point measure was created by Allan J. Albrecht of IBM as a means to quantify the size of certain customer applications (pertaining to business operations) that would be programmed by IBM on a contract basis. The measure was created as an ingenious response to a classical problem in software development, the often–found difficulty for customers to convey what they want an intended software system to do. The function point measure also embodies the idea of creating a measure of software size independent of the language in which it is coded, indicating the amount of function it provides rather than the number of source statements the programmer writes. Indeed, as tallied by Capers Jones (Jones 1986), various coding languages (e.g., assembly, Ada, Jovial, COBOL, etc.) differ considerably with respect to the amount of function they convey on average in each statement written using them.

One begins calculating the function point measure of a system by counting the numbers of each of four categories of externals of the system cited above, plus the count of internal logical files. Good practice for developing software system requirements says that the statement of requirements should deal only with the externally visible behavior of the intended system; the four types of externals are just such items. The four externals are:

- External inputs (e.g., transaction types), items that enter the boundary of the system that cause processing to take place.

- External inquiries (e.g., types of on-line inquiries processable by the system), unique inquiries that require an immediate response.

- External outputs (e.g., types of reports), items that leave the system boundary after processing has occurred.

- External interfaces (e.g., interfaces to other systems, including files accessed by the system but not modified by it, basically external sources of information required for its processing).

The complexity of each of the four types of externals and internal logical file(s) are estimated as low, medium, or high. Their counts are weighted correspondingly and then summed to determine the "function count." The next step in the calculation of function points is to determine the "value adjustment factor" which involves assessing the impact of 14 factors relating to the operation of the system (likely, or actual in the case of an existent system). Finally, the function point count is calculated by multiplying the "function count" by the "value adjustment factor," As pointed out in (Albrecht 1983), it is reasonable to expect that the size of a program (in terms of the number of source statements composing it) should be a function of the number of high level inputs and outputs to it. Indeed, this is a generalization of Halstead's (Halstead 1977) concept of "program volume" (which he applied only at the algorithm level).

## III. ANALYSIS USING AEROSPACE SOFTWARE DATA

The possibility was investigated of generalizing the concept of the function point measure and of applying it to aerospace software. Function points are currently used primarily for commercial or business and MIS, not for aerospace systems. The concept was to try to develop an algorithm for estimating software size from items available very early in the development cycle, preferably at the requirements stage. That is, the objective was to develop an empirical relationship between counts of measures of the "externals" of a program and its size in source statements. The prime motivation was to determine if the counts of the externals of these programs were sufficiently associated with the actual size of these systems so that a parametric estimating algorithm could be developed to estimate the size of such systems from this data.

Data for 19 aerospace (non–MIS) software systems, ranging in size from 2,000 to 235,000 source statements was studied. Table 1 presents the data used; it includes the counts of three externals (A), the counts of four externals (E), and the size in KSLOC for each of the 19 cases.

First, an equation was developed relating the sum of three of the externals—-inputs, outputs, and inquiries—-to the size of the system in KSLOC. The sample correlation between the unweighted sum of these variables and the size of the system in KSLOC was found to be 0.9315. This means that 86.8% ($.9315^2$) of the variation of KSLOC was "explained" by the variation of the sum of the input/output variables (see Table 2). Similarly, an equation was developed relating the sum of four externals, the three cited above plus interfaces, and the KSLOC count for each program. The sample correlation was 0.9434; 89 percent of the variation was explained (see Table 3). Figure 1 shows a plot of the the empirical data and the equation fitting it using the sum of the four externals (E).

Three different fits were made to the data for A (the sum of four externals) and E (the sum of four externals) in Table 1. The three fits were based on:

- Using all 19 points (with the four externals ranging from 29 to 6822).
- Using points 1 through 13 (ranging from 29 to 99).
- Using points 13 through 19 (ranging from 99 to 6822).

Table 1. Actual KSLOC vs. A and vs. E

| Point Number | A, Sum of three externals | E, Sum of four externals | Actual Size, KSLOC |
|---|---|---|---|
| 1 | 29 | 29 | 2.00 |
| 2 | 28 | 32 | 6.00 |
| 3 | 36 | 36 | 17.35 |
| 4 | 35 | 36 | 13.21 |
| 5 | 35 | 36 | 11.14 |
| 6 | 30 | 36 | 13.66 |
| 7 | 40 | 40 | 5.20 |
| 8 | 41 | 42 | 9.86 |
| 9 | 49 | 49 | 1.47 |
| 10 | 50 | 50 | 18.00 |
| 11 | 50 | 65 | 20.00 |
| 12 | 58 | 59 | 36.20 |
| 13 | 67 | 99 | 75.85 |
| 14 | 180 | 188 | 11.83 |
| 15 | 653 | 653 | 22.15 |
| 16 | 9 | 920 | 41.00 |
| 17 | 1463 | 1464 | 13.98 |
| 18 | 4019 | 4519 | 147.00 |
| 19 | 6072 | 6822 | 235.00 |

Table 2 provides the equations of fit, the sample correlation ( r ) values for KSLOC and A, the percent variation in KSLOC explained by A, and $r^2$ times 100. In all three cases, a linear equation in A provides a reasonably good fit to the observed values of

KSLOC. This is supported by the high values of $r^2$, an indication of the degree of fit in the sense that $r^2$ times 100 is the percentage of variation in the one variable explained by the other. Table 3 provides information similar to that in Table 2 but for the sum of four externals (E). Thus, the relatively good fits obtained were not due just to either the very large or to the very small values of A or E, whichever data set was employed. The experience with this data set should suggest the utility of considering a piece–wise fit to his data as an empirical size-estimating using equation counts of the program externals.

Figure 1 shows a plot of the KSLOC values versus the sum of the four externals (E), as well as the linear fit to that data which appears curved because the horizontal axis of the plot is a log scale. A log scale was used because of the wide range of the values of E and because they are grouped.

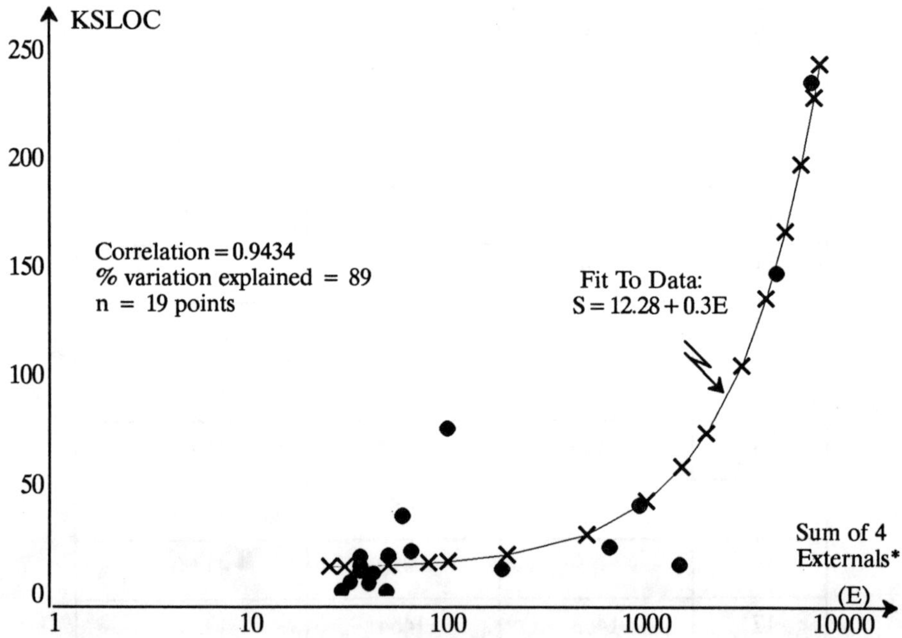


* = External Inputs, External Outputs, External Inquiries, External Interfaces.
** = Horizontal Axis Proportional to Log E

Figure 1. KSLOC as a Function of Count of Program Externals*

Table 2. Data Fits Using Sum Of Three Externals (A)

| Case | Equation Of Fit | Sample Correlation of A and KSLOC, r | Percent Variation explained, $r^2$*100 |
|---|---|---|---|
| Points 1–19 | S = 13.94 + 0.034A | 0.9315 | 86.77 |
| Points 1–13 | S = -36.33 + 1.28A | 0.7741 | 59.93 |
| Points 13–19 | S = 20.87 + 0.032A | 0.9139 | 83.52 |

Table 3. Data Fits Using Sum Of Four Externals (E)

| Case | Equation Of Fit | Sample Correlation of E and KSLOC, r | Percent Variation explained, $r^2$*100 |
|---|---|---|---|
| Points 1–19 | S = 12.28 + 0.03E | 0.9434 | 89.00 |
| Points 1–13 | S = -26.09 + 0.93E | 0.8955 | 80.19 |
| Points 13–19 | S = 14.56 + 0.03E | 0.9284 | 86.20 |

## IV. ANALYSIS USING COMMERCIAL SOFTWARE DATA

An investigation similar to that described above was then conducted using data on commercial software. Two sets of data were considered. The first set was that from (Albrecht 1983). The second was from (Kemerer 1987; Kemerer 1990).

Data from the three externals (inputs, outputs, and external inquiries) was considered for a data set of 24 systems (Albrecht 1983). The data set did not include the counts of external interfaces, so such data could not be employed in the evaluation. The simple sum of the three externals defined above, as well as the value of function points for the 24 programs, was related to KSLOC. The three variable sum provided a somewhat better relationship for estimating KSLOC than did function points. The results of the analyses of this data are summarized in Table 4.

Table 4. KSLOC As A Function of Sum Of Counts Of Program Externals, Albrecht and Gaffney Data

| Size Measure | Sample Correlation With KSLOC, r | Percent Variation explained, $r^2*100$ |
|---|---|---|
| Three Externals: Inputs, Outputs, Inquiries | 0.8896 | 79.1 |
| Function Points | 0.8199 | 67.2 |

Testing the values of the sample correlation coefficients in Table 4 shows both of them to be significant at better than the one percent level. Further, the hypothesis that the correlation coefficients, of which these samples are estimates, are equal was accepted at the one percent level using procedures in (Graybill 1961; Quenouille 1952). That is, it is a virtual certainty that the two sample correlation coefficients are estimates of the same correlation coefficient. This suggests that using the more complex function point measure may provide no advantage over the simpler sum of three externals as the basis for estimating KSLOC.

The results of analyzing the Kemerer data on 15 systems are summarized in Table 5. In this case, the function point measure provides a better basis for estimating KSLOC than does either the sum of three or the sum of four externals, unlike the Albrecht data set. However, the "function count" measure has a somewhat better sample correlation with KSLOC than does the "function point" measure. That is, the intro–

Table 5. KSLOC As A Function Of Sum Of Counts Of Program Externals, Kemerer Data

| Size Measure | Sample Correlation With KSLOC, r | Percent Variation explained, $r^2*100$ |
|---|---|---|
| Three Externals: Inputs, Outputs, Inquiries | 0.6974 | 48.6 |
| Four Externals: Inputs, Outputs, Inquiries, Interfaces | 0.7944 | 63.1 |
| Function Counts | 0.8782 | 77.1 |
| Function Points | 0.8350 | 69.7 |

duction of the "value adjustment factor" (see the earlier section on how to count function points) adds noise. This confirms Kemerer's observation that his "unmodified Function Counts have a higher correlation than the modified Function Points. This suggests that....the 14 'complexity adjustment' factors are not adding any information for this particular sample." (Kemerer 1987)

Testing the values of the sample correlation coefficients in Table 5 shows that each of them is significant at better than the one percent level. Further, the hypothesis that the correlation coefficients, of which the samples are estimates, are equal was accepted at the one percent level. That is, it is a virtual certainty that the four sample correlation coefficients are estimates of the same correlation coefficient. This suggests that using function counts or function points may provide no advantage relative to the simple sum of either three or four externals for the purpose of estimating KSLOC.

Analysis of the computation of function points for the two commercial system data sets suggests that the function point measure may be, at least in some cases, more noisy than the basic data from which it is calculated. That is, weighting the counts of the five items to compute the function count, and weighting that figure by the value adjustment factor may contribute relatively little to the accuracy of the estimate. Estimates of KSLOC may be made, based on the unweighted sums of the number of top level externals of the program at issue, that are about as good as those based on function points. This suggests that any given item of the five may contribute no more or less, on average, than any other to the amount of function in the software system. The analyses of the two sets of data for the commercial systems suggest that the counts (or estimates of the counts) of these variables might be used in a parametric size estimating algorithm.

## V. CONCLUSIONS

The analyses summarized here suggest that an empirical software size estimating model based on program externals may be developed for embedded software systems as well as for business systems . The parameters of such a model would be best developed by the organization intending to use it based on data from the experience of that organization, not that provided in this paper. A prime purpose of this paper is to present the concept, not the particular data employed to support its utility. The data to be used in such a model can be obtained and used to develop an estimate of software size for a project at requirements time. This would enable a more accurate estimate of development costs to be made earlier in the project.. The estimate so obtained can be pooled with size estimates developed using other techniques. Such a technique is that suggested by (Gaffney 1984) in which counts of CSCIs and CSCs would be used as the basis for estimating the ultimate size of a software system, given that data is available on the sizes of these major software system units from previous projects.

Analysis of the computation of function points for some commercial systems suggests that the function point measure may be, at least in some cases, more noisy than the basic data from which it is calculated. This confirms Kemerer's observation (Kemerer 1987, p.425). That is, weighting the counts of the items to compute the function count, and weighting that figure by the value adjustment factor, may contribute relatively little to the accuracy of the estimate and may add noise to it. Estimates of the size, in KSLOC, of business systems may be made based on the unweighted sums of the number of top level externals of the program at issue, that are about as good as those based on function points. Very importantly, analysis of some data on non–MIS aerospace systems suggests that the sum of the counts of the externals of aerospace programs may be reasonably well correlated with the size of these programs, measured in KSLOC. Thus, a software organization which develops such systems should be able to develop an empirical system useful for estimating software size that is a function of the number of externals of the program.

## VI. REFERENCES


Albrecht, A. J., and J.E. Gaffney, 1983 — Software Function, Source Lines of Code, and Development Effort Prediction: A Software Science Validation, *IEEE Transactions on Software Engineering,* Vol. SE–9.

Gaffney, J. E., 1984 — Estimation of Software Code Size Based on Quantitative Aspects of Function (With Application of Expert System Technology), *Journal of Parametrics*, Vol. 4, No.3.

Graybill, F.A. 1961 — *An Introduction to Linear Statistical Models. Vol. 1.* McGraw–Hill.

Halstead, M. H. 1977 — *Elements of Software Science*, Elsevier.

Jones, C. 1986 — *Programming Productivity*, McGraw Hill.

Kemerer, C.H., 1987 — An Empirical Validation of Software Cost Estimation Models., *Communications of the ACM.*

Kemerer, C.H, 1990. — Private communication.

Quenouille,M.H. 1952 — *Associated Measurements*. Butterworth's Scientific Publications.

# CECOM's Approach for Developing Definitions for Software Size and Software Personnel - Two Important Software Economic Metrics

**Stewart Fenick, Project Leader, Software Process Metrics Program**
**US Army Communications-Electronics Command (CECOM)**
**Research, Development & Engineering Center (RDEC)**
**Software Engineering Directorate (SED)**
**AMSEL-RD-SE-ST-SE**
**Fort Monmouth, New Jersey 07703 USA**

## Introduction

This paper addresses a study by U.S. Army Communications-Electronics Command (CECOM) into aspects of two management metrics with great impact on software economics - software size and software personnel. The common denominator between them being software productivity.

**Problem.** Currently, there does not exist firm definitions of meaningful measures for assessing software size and software personnel. As a result, these two metrics are being applied inconsistently across the defense software industry with no commonality of understanding or usage.

**Impact.** The proliferation of metrics terminology and of application methodologies hampers achievement of the primary purposes for using metrics. Those are:

- to derive trend and deviation indicators and problem pointers to aid management control and direction of ongoing projects through early awareness and insight;
- to leverage lessons learned in order to promote global improvement of organizational ways-of-doing-business, and of software acquisition, development and support processes;
- to provide historical data for tracking and assessing gains in software process productivity and efficiency;
- to identify desirable characteristics of software system processes and products for translation into definitive quality requirements;
- to enable estimates based on quantitative information in order to assure economic stability through smart resource planning;
- to provide an objective management mechanism to help produce supportable, quality software products on schedule, within cost.

**Towards A Solution.** The defense software community has at least taken a first step to solve the problem - realization and identification of that problem. This has led to attempts across the industry to derive solutions. But solution alternatives are also proliferating and include, among others:

- Software Reporting Metrics and Software Management Metrics developed by the Air Force System Command (AFSC) Engineering System Division (ESD) and MITRE Corporation;
- AFSC and Army Materiel Command (AMC) Software Management and Quality Indicators;
- Software Management and Quality Indicators of Project Manager Field Artillery Tactical Data Systems (PM FATDS);
- Software Development Status Indicators of the US Army Missile Command (MICOM);
- The Software Quality Framework of the USAF Rome Labs;
- The Applied Metrics Program of the Naval Undersea Warfare Center (NUWC);
- Software Development Measures of NASA Software Engineering Lab (SEL);
- Software Support Qualitative Measures of the US Army Information Systems Engineering Command (USAISEC);
- U. S. Air Force Operational Test & Evaluation Center (USAFOTEC) Life-Cycle Support Metrics;
- DoD core set of Acquisition Metrics developed under the metrics initiative of the Software Engineering Institute (SEI) of Carnegie Mellon University (CMU);
- US Army Software Test & Evaluation Panel (STEP) T&E Metrics;
- Institute of Electrical and Electronics Engineers (IEEE) terminology standardization efforts;
- Many private sector measurement programs - usually proprietary.

Further proliferation occurs as each set is "handed-off" to a user because the sets are modified as each user organization then follows an independent validation and upgrade path. This is true even if organizations initially adopt the same set, unless they join to follow the same path.

CECOM is also attempting a solution, but with a difference - rather than champion a single set of metrics, we hope to coordinate and integrate with other investigations so as to hasten the development of a global metrics methodology. In fact, the CECOM baseline draws from a number of state-of-the-practice programs, and from information exchange at a number of defense software community working groups and other forums.

Further, rather than a "hand-off", a dynamic, follow-on support program is proposed that includes technology transfer (training and seminars, guidance, awareness briefings), services (system-specific customization, application teams, real-time problem solving), and upgrade (validation efforts, gathering feedback and lessons learned, advanced issues workshops, guidance updates).

**Local/Global Coexistence.** Note the prior reference to a global metrics methodology. This does not necessarily mean **adoption of** a singular, common metrics set and application process, but can also refer to **adapting to, and inclusion of,** local implementations, methods and techniques that satisfy management needs and priorities. This then is a **flexible global methodology**. As it turns out, many concerns (e.g., cost, schedule, personnel) are common across systems anyway.

The need for a local/global methodology is driven by the fact that most organizations have ingrained ways of building software. This includes the way that productivity and size measurements, and personnel assignments, are addressed and managed. These system-specific considerations manifest themselves as obstacles to doing software measurement in the first place, and to developing a singular metrics methodology in the second place. These obstacles include:

- resource shortfalls;
- natural resistance to change;
- fear of intrusion and of being critiqued;
- lack of on-board expertise
  - and thus the need for more staff, training, learning curve adjustments;
- not-on-my-watch syndrome;
- too costly to change for perceived added value;
- lack of a track record for the new methodology
  - no validation, no earned credibility, no confidence).

Therefore, the existence of these local implementations, issues and obstacles, may preclude development of a "superset" of common or standard measures. Instead, both *local and global versions may need to coexist* and, in fact, to be integrated. Thus there will be a need to develop normalization or conversion analysis techniques so local measures can be made compatible within the global setting - primarily for entry of data and information into, and retrieval of lessons learned from, a global database.

Compatibility of data, data formats, terminology and metrics criteria is also important for promoting good communications among all the players, which is essential to the success of any measurement program.

**Objectives.** As for specific metrics for size and personnel, there is concern about the current situation, and the need to address the issues surrounding these two important, and basic, management and economic factors. The goal of the CECOM study is analytical derivation of informative and useful definitions based on criteria related to the significance of their impact on the evaluative, predictive and corrective functions of program management oversight. This should lead to new, refined or modified algorithms available for utilization in existing resource estimating models and in management metrics application process models.

Several alternatives exist and will be investigated: various physical and logical measures for size; and personnel measures by technical area, mission domain, abilities and skills, and so on. In addition, the notion of value - of a line of code; of a man-hour - will be addressed.

These investigations will span all life-cycle activities and may result in derivation of multiple metrics. For instance, in addition to code measures, size metrics algorithms can be derived based on numbers of requirements, on design structures related to functional complexity and modularity, or on numbers of tested units. The choice of which to use would depend on the particular data point of interest, and where in the life-cycle it occurred.

**Software "Value".** This paper considers a **quality perspective** on software size and personnel and their relationship to software productivity. The perspective is that of **software value** - that simple counts (of lines of code, of people, of man-hours) are not sufficient for defining size, staff and productivity for meaningful utilization in estimating, measuring, assessing, evaluating and predicting those areas of software acquisition, development and support, that are of primary interest to managers.

Knowledge beyond line count, people count and man-hour count is required. There is need to know the effort (to develop, to utilize) represented by lines - the notion that a line of code has value (complex and critical software costs more than routine software). There is need to know the quality of an individual's effort (to analyze, to produce) as represented by a man-hour - the notion that an individual's output has value (proficient people produce more and better than inexperienced people). Productivity is not linearly related to numbers of people, but is dependent on abilities of people.

Value can be used to:

- compare producibility of modules;
- compare application of capabilities to similar projects by different organizations;
- make timely trade-off decisions based on early awareness of significant economic implications.

The study will attempt to quantify software "value" components of algorithms for software size, manpower and productivity.

Is it farfetched to aim to be able to answer contractor productivity questions like:

• If a software task of value **V** is assigned to a software engineer of proficiency **P**, how many lines of useful code per day can be expected to be produced?

Or to aim to be able to make government estimation statements like the following?

• This is a Value_Type_3_System and thus requires a Maturity Level 2 contractor, 38 man-months, 10 senior people with 8.5 average proficiency, and $6.6 million. If only 6 seniors are proposed, then expect 52 man-months and $8.3 million. If only Level 1, increase estimates 42%. Where Type_3 might be: tactical mission, Ada, complexity level B, size range C, and so on.

**CEMSM and the CCDM.** As noted, CECOM RDEC, through its Software Engineering Directorate (SED), has started a program for development of a metrics set and methodology for use by high level managers - CECOM Executive Management Software Metrics (CEMSM) and the CEMSM Criteria-Driven Methodology (CCDM), an issue-driven, process-oriented approach to measurement. As a general statement, the larger the project, the greater the value of a measurement program. As defense industry software systems continue to grow in size and complexity, an approach like CCDM takes on added importance.

Although there are a number of factors not fully resolved (such as the size and personnel concerns discussed in this paper), there is a need to take an initial stand based on existing knowledge, and get measurement into practice. Thus CEMSM and CCDM are being made available to managers of SED-supported systems. This will allow the technology to evolve out of the R&D phase in a structured way, be applied to actual systems, and mature through iterative growth based on real-world feedback. But research into basic issues must go on in parallel.

The initial CEMSM set[1] consists of the metrics shown in the table on the next page (please note that size and personnel R&D issues considered in this paper are not yet reflected in this set - an upgrade, incorporating advanced material and guidance for application of a full measurement process, is scheduled for a 1993 release).

---

1 CEMSM Guidebook, SPS-EMSM-00391, 31 October 1991, Revised

---

**<u>CECOM Executive Management Software Metrics (CEMSM)</u>**

1. Cost/Schedule Performance
2. CSU Development Progress
3. Test Progress
4. Incremental Release
5. Software Size
6. Software Development Personnel
7. Staff Experience
8. Target Computer Resource Utilization
9. Host Computer Resource Utilization
10. Requirements and Design Stability
11. Design Structure
12. Software Fault Profile

---

The CCDM incorporates consideration of:

- leveraging defense industry state-of-the-practice / influencing the state-of-the-art;
- variety of audiences;
- system status (new, in-process, deployed);
- use of CEMSM as a default, if a viable and compatible local adaptation can not be found;
- tailoring of data, metrics and metrics criteria based on managers' primary life-cycle issues, priorities, risk assessments and resource constraints;
- need for full application and acquisition guidance;
- need for full guidance for analysis including inter-metric correlations;
- assimilation of quantified metrics data with data from other sources of system information;
- a give-and-take, non-adversarial, government-contractor "negotiated" process;
- promoting organizational improvements of software engineering, software management and software measurement processes;
- promoting improvement of the acquisition life-cycle software development and support processes;
- "lead-in" guidance for issues better left to local implementation;
- incorporation of local lessons learned into a global project database;
- technology insertion, transfer and stabilization;
- developing metrics expertise among project personnel;
- full-service support aimed at a customer hand-off;
- user-friendly implementation and problem-solving;
- automation - to better facilitate data collection and analysis, reduce costs, and reduce delay between collection data points and corrective action injection points;
- periodic CEMSM upgrade based on pilot project validation and user feedback.

**Impact of Value on Life-Cycle Activities.** Size and staff measures play important roles, in determining if contemplated software system concepts (especially for unprecedented systems) will lead to beneficial results, by helping to answer:

- what it costs to produce the software;
- what the software is worth to the customer.

Each of these roles influences the other. When customer requirements are for a complex and critical software system, then the developer must propose and provide first-rate capabilities including proficient staff. Towards this end, SEI Contractor Capability Assessments are starting to play into the pre-award process. Of course, the customer must be prepared to provide sufficient funding and commitment to enable stated requirements to come to fruition in a quality way. Conversely, when the customer is estimating a budget and other resources, then the developer's current capabilities (staff, processes, automation) for building the desired product must be factored in. It is important to capture the specifics of a development on both sides - government requirements and developer capabilities. As evidence of the realization of this, defense industry Request For Proposals (RFP) and contractual language is maturing all the time from abstract and general statements to more definitive quantifications and descriptions of quality software requirements and of the processes and facilities needed to produce them.

It is also becoming accepted practice to require bidders to provide a description of their measurement methodologies as part of their proposal. Thus the government can leverage industry practices for measuring and tracking size, staff and productivity issues.

These economic roles depend on the value of the software and on the quality of the effort to produce the software. Costing software accurately requires consideration of:

- its producibility
    - is this the best design (most efficient, most suitable) for this development? can it be developed productively? are government-imposed standards (DOD-STD-2167A documentation and reviews, ANSI/MIL-STD-1815A for Ada, etc.) a barrier or catalyst? can it be implemented cost-effectively (e.g., is it too complex an application)? is it documented well for purposes of repeatability and maintainability? and so forth;
- its usefulness
    - what it does and how well (is it a critical application?); what the customer's benefits are; if it has a user-friendly human interface; how it handles faults and errors; how it recovers from a crash; what the operational life expectancy is, and the maintenance requirements over its lifetime; etc.;
- its physical attributes
    - size; complexity; host requirements; limits and constraints under which the software must operate; etc..

During initial applications of the CEMSM set, lessons learned will be sought to determine important components of the size value and personnel value equations. In other words, the study will look at the "value of value" for purposes of controlling and managing (planning, estimating, assessing, redirecting) a number of software life-cycle activities, of interest to both government and developers, including:

- pre-award activities
  - RFP preparation;
  - proposal preparation;
  - proposal evaluation;
  - generation of statement-of-work (SOW) requirements;
- developing formal budgets, milestone schedules and resource allocation plans;
- estimating and assessing progress;
- estimating and assessing resource utilization needed to complete acquisition, development and support activities;
- determining staffing levels and distribution of those levels over the life-cycle; and, making personnel assignment decisions;
- pricing deliverables;
- determining impact on schedule of software complexity and the need for qualified personnel with the expertise and experience to address that complexity
  - in general, complexity grows with size, personnel proficiency addresses the ability to deal with that complexity;
- striving for quality
  - both size and personnel directly impact on the *risk of achieving quality*;
- evaluating productivity for making programmatic decisions related to:
  - learning curve mitigation;
  - training;
  - reassignments and corresponding loss of corporate memory;
  - management structure and communications;
- assessing near-term risk and long-term impact
  - benefits vs. cost, i.e., the value of investing in process improvements in order to obtain improved products;
  - ripple effects, good and bad;
  - by-products, e.g., organizational improvements in efficiency, productivity;
  - improvements to the management function for better control and direction of the acquisition, development and support of software systems;
  - ability to express quality requirements in implementable terms;
  - side effects, e.g., improving the metrics application process itself.

# Software Size

Size is not a simple concept involving just count. Qualifiers, weightings or modifiers are needed to fully understand exactly what the count is counting. A thousand lines of information system software does not hold the same economic implications as a thousand lines of embedded, tactical software.

Measuring size of a software system is only partially addressed by the notion of physical space as usually associated with lines of code, semicolons, etc.. Nor is it fully addressed by the notion of logical partitions - requirements, function points, mental discriminations, etc.. What's missing is knowledge of the complexity of the lines, of the requirements, and, knowledge of the depth and breadth of their use. Also, criticality and usefulness, of the function performed by the software, should be considered.

To provide this missing dimension, size measures need to address issues of **effort** - effort for production, for implementation, for utilization. The driver for determining a suitable size measurement is its impact on primary management concerns - cost; productivity; human and computer resources; schedule; functionality; usability, etc.. A simplistic line count does not provide the right kind of information. A <u>value component</u> addressing the effort behind the lines must be added in.

Additionally, there are issues of language (e.g., an Ada program with a percentage of Assembly; recoding a FORTRAN system in Ada); of code type (new, modified, reused, replicated, delivered, support, etc.); of software work breakdown structure (WBS) granularity (CSCI, CSU, subsystem, etc.); and, of development configuration (distributed hosts, prime-subcontractor, etc.).

In a local setting, measures must be defined for each system or class of systems, and then *applied consistently over the life-cycle*. Multi-language systems should <u>count compatibly</u> across those languages - e.g., don't use line counts of one with statement counts of another (unless a cross-language weighting scheme is developed and validated).

**Physical, Functional, Virtual.** Purely physical size deals with line counts; bits, bytes, and blocks; semicolons, executable statements; and so forth. Logical measures deal with numbers of requirements (shalls); procedures; functions; etc.. Virtual size deals with issues of effort where the apparent effort (as judged by just a few lines of code, or by re-use of many lines) is not the true effort that went into building those lines as, for instance:

examples where effort is greater than evidenced by the line count

- coding a very complex function requiring many hours of "conceptualizing", research, communication with peers, or trial-and-error;
- modifying a module or reworking a module in development, but where only a small percentage of code is touched after many hours of analysis and redesign;
- maintenance activity where magnitude of effort (analysis, rework and more rework) does not equate to the few lines of software produced or altered;

example where effort is less than evidenced by the line count

- use of code generators;
- repeated use of already developed code (reuse by library; by reference; by replication).

As an example of a virtual measure, a simplistic way to assess the amount of rework is to weight the size of the module (in which the code being reworked resides) with the amount of time expended on the problem. As an option, the manager can choose to separate the time into "bins" for junior staff, for senior staff, for support personnel such as QA folks, and so forth. This accounts for the "kinds" of time being expended. But doing that does not fully factor in the proficiency of the personnel assigned to the problem, and, therefore, does not address the issue of the quality of the time spent on the problem. That proficiency must be included in order to produce a true rework measurement. Proficiency is addressed later in this paper.

Therefore, virtual size is not a count, but a weighted count dependent on expended effort. And, effort is gauged not only by elapsed man-hours, but by the technical depth applied during those hours - i.e., the proficiency of the man in man-hours.

Physical count gives credit for writing code down; logical count gives credit for functional partitioning (what it does / how efficiently); virtual count gives credit for not re-inventing the wheel (by taking into account reuse and re-thinking).

**A Comment.** An ongoing issue is whether to include comments in line counts. Comments can be regarded as quality indicators, inasmuch as they affect understandability, evaluation and rework, traceability, and, maintainability. This would lead one to classify comments under documentation rather than software.

Another issue concerns documentation itself as a side issue of the size problem. If documentation measures are employed, there is risk of a development being document-driven. However, if documentation is not assessed for size, completeness, etc., then the risk is of poor documentation and its impact on supportability and usability.

Both these issues will be addressed by the CECOM study.

**Comparative vs. Absolute.**

**Different Size, Same Technicals.** Measuring by pure physical count has its most value when it comes to appreciating the relative size of software programs, especially when there are orders of magnitude involved. In other words, a reasonable picture or understanding of what your dealing with (and have to plan and prepare for) can be obtained when comparing the ten thousand line program you've just completed with a one-hundred thousand line program you're thinking of undertaking.

However, the picture becomes cloudy unless mission domain, functional complexity, selected development process, and implementation language, are roughly equivalent.

**Same Size, Different Technicals.** But what if programs are similar in size? What does it mean to develop ten thousand lines of Ada code vs. ten thousand lines of FORTRAN? The differences have impact on planning, resource utilization, productivity and implementation requirements. Lines of code, by themselves, do not fully cover the situation. Language vs. language considerations involve staff skills, training, automated capabilities, company standards, and specific company experience with the language.

As an example, one obvious economic impact for a defense contractor wishing to stay competitive, is the retraining or restaffing needed to bring a DoD-mandated Ada capability in-house, and then building on that initial capability to develop a corporate, Ada project experience-base.

Again, the same cautions apply when there are differences in mission domain, design methodologies, development process models, and so on.

**A Matter of Perspective.** A dozen apples sounds simple enough until your wife fusses that the Red Delicious you brought home aren't as good as Yellow; or she needs larger apples for baking.

Size can have simple interpretations targeted for certain audiences. But it must be adaptable so as to be discernible and describable in more detail for other types of audiences. There are particular concerns for which different perspectives on size is important. One thousand boxes of apples may be enough information for a shipper, but others involved in the process of production and delivery (growers, marketers, auditors, buyers, for instance) need to know what kind, from what State, if treated with pesticide, what size, picked how long ago, and so forth. For instance, the supermarket manager needs to know all these things about a product before determining a price, and whether to put an item on sale or not. The premise here is that size without a full description of what that size relates to, is not very useful.

• *A full description is the equivalent of a "valued count".* •

Consider manufacture and delivery of cereal by ABC Company. ABC produces several kinds of cereal in packages of various shapes and sizes - bran cereal, corn cereal, and software cereal. Some packages have three hundred flakes of cold cereal (or is that code cereal), some have three thousand. ABC's operation includes the production and shipping processes needed to handle all their different cereals and sizes, and to get those products from the host manufacturing facilities and host development computers to the target cereal bowls of consumers and to the target serial computers of soldiers in the field.

Again, size has different views for different audiences: how many crates for a shipper; cases for a store manager; boxes for a shelf clerk; how many bowls in a box, and what kind of cereal, for a consumer. Size must be presented in differing and various formats in order to be useful in a variety of contexts. This is exactly the case for software.

• *The software business is no different than any other business when considered from an economic perspective.* •

**Software Size Submetrics.** Based on the study described in this paper, the current CEMSM Software Size Metric may evolve to an advanced Software Size Index Metric that will include components of two submetrics, Software Size Count and Software Size Value. The count submetric relates most to application. The value submetric accounts for technical quality aspects of the building, implementation and maintenance of the software.

There are numerous studies dealing with all the various counting alternatives. This paper will not address the specifics to any great detail, but, rather, will cover various issues and approaches. An objective of the study is to settle on some initial common counting algorithms, promote their use in actual practice, and iteratively evolve and upgrade based on user feedback.

This multidimensional size measure (Software Size Index Metric) involves the following components of its submetrics:

**Submetric: Software Size Count**

- *Count*: as expressed by physical or logical measures;
- *Repeat_Count*: a virtual count
  - a weighted count that takes into account reuse of previously developed code, and rework that may not result in any code at all;
- *Variants* of these two components include deliverable code, support software, new code, replicated code, reused code, modified code, etc..

<u>Submetric: Software Size Value</u>

- *Producibility* includes:
  - effort and capabilities of the software developer;
  - reliability and maintainability (R&M) aspects of the selected development processes, design methodology and implementation (e.g., the practices that lead to historically proven reliable software);
  - complexity of software design (code and structure);
  - note that reusable components have different value to different applications;
- *Usefulness* involves:
  - criticality of function (mission value);
  - understandability;
  - simplicity and ease of use;
  - demand on the target environment to give it a "home";
  - dependency on computer and human resources to make it work beneficially;
- *Language Weighting* considers:
  - language A does in 5 lines what language B does in 8;
  - multiple language usage, e.g., an Ada system with some Assembly;
  - the impact of language-specific implementation requirements for software interfaces, system integration and portability issues.

**Software Size Algorithm.** To completely describe a software package so that the description is useful to a wide audience, it may be necessary to include:

- a *counting measure* (SLOC is in vogue but others need to be considered);
- *value modifiers* to discern level of difficulty (such as a complexity measure score that addresses Producibility and Usefulness);

combined with -

- a *weighting scheme* to account for the specifics of a project (mission-area, HOL(s), process model, design methodology, SEI Contractor Capability Maturity Level, etc.).

To develop an algorithm, the various value components will have to be quantified to some degree. For instance, formulating and assigning relative scores for complexity and effort to describe FORTRAN vs. Ada vs. Assembly. The same for mission domains and functional requirements. They have to be classified and weighted based on required complexity, reliability and performance. Difficulty of hosting on a particular target computer and operating system has to be considered. Skill level of intended users in the field is a factor - well-engineered software has no value if it is too sophisticated to be used and maintained by the intended customer or audience. Cost of producing software will also be impacted by resources available to the developer including staff skill level, and this is another item to be factored into the algorithm. For instance, what is the value to a customer of a module produced by inexperienced personnel vs. a like-function module produced by senior people. SEI Contractor Capability Maturity Levels could be a starting point for quantifying available resources and capabilities. An Algorithm Component Table, as proposed later in this paper, will be employed to help develop the algorithm.

There are a number of side issues. For instance, a complex radar module may contain some routine routines such as writing to a file or sorting a list. In such a case, either the module could be treated entirely as a complex unit, or the size algorithm could allow for partial complexity. Criteria for defining complex units could provide a fuzzy classification scheme (very complex, complex, difficult, average, . . .), or a scheme using definitive classifications based on percentages of complex vs. routine (complexity level A, B, C . . .). As another alternative, all modules would be regarded either as complex or as non-complex based on the software function, where, either:

- "complex" is formally defined by system-specific attributes; or,
- "complex" is informally established primarily based on judgement and evaluation of technical management in conjunction with the technical staff and software system architect.

A similar side issue concerns modules containing both newly developed and reused code. A scheme is needed to deal with all new vs. part new/part reused, and so forth.

Side issues such as these may represent *unreasonable fine tuning*. This investigation will evaluate if these are major components of the algorithm or not.

Another issue. Earlier it was noted that use of multiple metrics may be appropriate to deal with different life-cycle activities that need to be measured. But during any one activity, there are also different aspects of that activity that need to be measured and managed. So, perhaps simultaneous use of multiple size measures, depending on specific management concerns of the moment, is also appropriate.

For instance, for cost estimating, line counts are what the defense software industry has the most experience with, and what many cost estimating models utilize as an input. But logical counts may be more useful for determining where and when to assign senior vs. junior staff. And for planning milestone schedules, tracking numbers of completed modules may be most helpful.

Thus, we see a possibility for use of various types or sets of metrics, such as system-based, activity-based, issue-based and problem-based. Each comes into play, as appropriate, for different purposes.

## Software Personnel

Software Personnel measures determine: (1) adherence to staffing plans or replans; (2) if the planned staffing levels are adequate and remain so as the project progresses; and, (3) if proposed qualifications are adequate and continue to be adequate during the project.

This metric deals, across the life-cycle, with personnel levels and proficiencies of all organizations: acquisition office; developer; life-cycle center for software engineering and post-deployment support services; and support functions such as QA, IV&V, CM and Tech Writing. However, this paper concentrates on the area with the most economic impact - the development phase or activity including support provided during the development. A poorly implemented development will lead to extensive post-deployment support costs.

**Software Development Personnel.** A primary program manager area of concern is the adequacy of the development team's **in-place** resources and abilities. Key resources and abilities cover: personnel capability; management architecture (structure, procedures, communications, reporting practices); and, software development methodology (processes and standards) and facilities (primarily automated capability).

*• Pre-award evaluation and on-the-job re-evaluation of capabilities are essential because they measure ability to do the job at all, let alone doing it well or on time. •*

Of these, the most critical area is personnel capability. Assessment begins with the proposal stage where a proposed staff's level and proficiency is evaluated against RFP requirements. The concern continues into the development phase as the government Contracting Officer's Representative (COR) continually assesses programmatic and technical risks by evaluating adequacy of contractor-initiated personnel changes for maintaining schedule and for completing the project with required product functionality, performance and quality. An example of a monitoring concern would be assessment of the contractor's strategy for mitigating turnover, especially of key individuals.

**Software Development Personnel Submetrics.** The CEMSM Software Development Personnel and Staff Experience Metrics may evolve to an advanced version of a single Software Development Personnel Metric that includes both major and minor components of two submetrics, Software Development Staff Profile and Software Development Personnel Qualification. These would be applied to each category of interest - junior staff, senior staff, management, QA, CM, IV&V, Life-Cycle Center, total system, prime, subcontractor, distributed developments, and so forth. This metric will also be an upgrade based on results of the study described in this paper. It is planned to combine the two current CEMSM metrics, and to then factor in personnel proficiency, in order to enable a manager to get a total picture of staff capability. Further advances contemplated will add metrics for personnel management of acquisition and support phases and activities, as well as for development.

The major-minor division is made along the lines of two principles: the 80/20 rule and KIS (keep it simple). Minor components are basically omitted, but not forgotten, from the algorithm. They can surface and be utilized for specific situations and at the discretion of management. The 80/20 rule, as applied to a metrics algorithm, states that: "for the value-added or cost-benefit expected, it is not worth the effort to capture the least significant 20% of components in the algorithm. Even if those components are available for the collecting, they do not have sufficient impact on the overall algorithm to justify the cost of analysis." KIS dictates that **other-than-very-significant** components requiring data that is hard to collect or not readily available, be designated as minor components. In other words, the difficulty of the effort involved in adding those components to the aggregation of the algorithm, does not justify that they be included.

This highly complex personnel measure (Software Development Personnel Measure) must be scaled back to where it is a manageable entity. This study will attempt to do this by investigating and then defining reasonable algorithms for the following components of the submetrics:

**Submetric: Software Development Staff Profile - major components**

- *Staff Level* relates to numbers of people and their distribution over time (the life-cycle). Part-timers are counted in the true, for instance, two half-timers are equivalent to one full-time person. For Staff Level calculations, members of a category are considered equivalent to other members of the same category, i.e., a senior = a senior. Differences in skills, such as one senior engineer/scientist being Ada trained and the other not, are accounted for under the Software Development Personnel Qualification submetric.

- *Staff Availability* relates to maintaining developer capabilities, including the prime-subcontractor relationship, during the entire development. Lack of available personnel (staff spread thin over other contracts for instance) is an indicator of future requests for schedule adjustments, learning curve training or subcontracting. "Double staffing" is a particular concern during the proposal stage where a contractor may be bidding on several RFPs. With no way of predicting an outcome, they may very well propose the same key personnel assets on more than one offer.

- *Company Retention Rate* statistics relate to corporate stability.

• *Staff Variation*: *Turnover* relates to **planned and unplanned** movement on and off a project, which results in creating a number of problems. Two such are learning curve impact and loss of corporate memory, for the current project.

- There is a *learning curve impact* whenever there is a turnover or any other staffing change resulting in a new individual coming on board. Such individuals need to become familiar with: the work environment; project requirements; normal way-of-doing-business; standards; job ethics and protocols; and, the management climate including proper response procedures, chain of command and other communications issues.

- If planned downsizing includes key players, then *loss of corporate memory* and of job-specific rationale can impact on rework, Reviews and walkthroughs. The same is true of unplanned turnover, even more so. This is a critical factor because a replacement, even if of a higher proficiency, will require learning curve adjustments. In fact, an unplanned loss often times represents an *unrecoverable corporate and job memory loss*. Replacing an individual with another (even of higher proficiency) may not recover (immediately, or at all) the specific project knowledge held by the lost staff member.

- *Unplanned changes* such as excessive surges of manpower growth may indicate a problem with meeting project schedule because of: requirements or design instability; unavailability of full development capability (automated tools, workstations, networks, distributed databases, etc.); lack of full project understanding by the developer; and so on. Replacing junior staff with senior staff may indicate the developer is having software complexity problems. In general, adding staff will not help a project in trouble unless the cause of the trouble is identified and dealt with. In fact, added staff will probably make matters worse because "unenlightened input" can create other problems that also must be dealt with.

- If reassignments occur, the phenomenon of a *ramp-up period* surfaces. That is, even though an individual is now, or had previously been, engaged on a project, being reassigned, (for instance, from design to test; or to code/recode the next module) will require a certain period of time to re-acclimate to the work climate and environment, and to project requirements. Even with familiarity with a department or specific task, a ramp-up period is required for any returning individual no matter what the reason for having left the project previously. Ramp-up periods can range from minor to significant and therefore should be factored into the algorithm. Note that, the number of times an **individual** is reassigned on a project is considered a minor component (see Staff Allocation below), while the **overall** staff profile of total number of reassignments, and, the individual types of reassignments (using designers to do testing for instance), are considered major at this point in time in the study.

• *Staff Variation: Plan/RePlan* relates to the baseline against which actuals are compared to identify trends and deviations. Plan updating is an extremely important function. Updates result either when a plan's deficiencies surface during project implementation, or when a plan is revised as a result of government-contractor action. The plan (or replan) in-place at the current time during a project represents the **baseline**. Each plan revision should be uniquely identified such as: **Plan, RePlan$_1$ . . . RePlan$_n$**. To reduce chance of confusion, such formalization should occur only at those points in time when significant changes have accumulated.

- If the schedule is being maintained, but the current staff level is *not* the baseline level, then the current level *may* be the correct level - i.e., the planned estimates, comprising the current baseline, missed the mark. At this point, consideration should be given to updating the staffing Plan or RePlan that is currently in-place. The magnitude and number of plan-to-plan changes and baseline modifications are an indicator of program understanding and stability (or lack thereof).

• *Inaccuracies and deficiencies of the original plan become lessons learned for conceptualizing and planning the next project.* •

**Submetric: Software Development Staff Profile - minor components**

• *Staff Mix* relates to staff distribution by activity (design, code, test, etc.).

• *Staff Allocation* relates to staff movement within a project (e.g., **number** of individual reassignments - note that **type** of reassignment, and **total staff** reassignments, are covered as major components under Staff Variation: Turnover). Capturing data on numbers of reassignments is cumbersome for there are many situations where individuals are "borrowed" on a daily basis to put out a fire in real-time, then return to the primary task to which they are formally assigned. Therefore, tallying of **individual** reassignments may be meaningless, while counting **total staff** reassignments is necessary as a critique of project stability (but may need to be calculated through an averaging function to include borrowed personnel because counting only the total formal reassignments does not give the full picture).

• *Manager:Engineer Ratio*[2] refers to assuring an efficient supervisory structure. This is a major component for evaluating RFP responses to assure reasonable levels-of-effort are proposed, but overall is considered a minor component because it is not needed

---

[2] **Note that a number of terms in this paper (such as Repeat_Count, Double-Staffing, and Manager:Engineer Ratio, among others) will not be familiar to the reader as the author has used "description labels" to try to capture particular new ideas and approaches for future use. Some, such as RePlan, are currently included in the work at CECOM.**

past the RFP stage. This is because, after award, all key personnel changes need government approval anyway, and thus the Manager:Engineer Ratio would be a redundant check. By evaluating contractor-proposed levels-of-effort at the proposal stage, the government can determine if an excessive number of high-priced management man-hours have been included and can request a proposal change as appropriate. During development, the government representative can assure the final proposed level is maintained.

**Software Development Staff Profile Algorithm.** Development of the algorithm will have to proceed in a very orderly manner due to the many issues and components involved. The Algorithm Component Table will also be used for this part of the study.

Staff profile data should be readily available. Important program decisions are tied to frequency of collection, and of reporting, of staff data. Understanding of contractor internal labor practices is critical for aggregating this submetric. Note that, as for any deliverable, metrics data items should be verified through periodic or random auditing to assure integrity (that the right data item is reported, and reported correctly).

**Submetric: Software Development Personnel Qualification - major components**

• *Proficiency Level (major)* relates to the total of individual proficiencies and assurance that the baseline average staff level of proficiency is maintained, and includes:

- advanced education level/type of degree;
- years with company which relates to firsthand knowledge of, and involvement with, company standards (e.g., Ada Programming Standard) and established way of doing software business; also relates to corporate memory on similar projects; and, provides added value because loyalty, dedication and high morale translate to productivity and a "*caring for quality*";
- years of software development experience;
- years of experience in the mission domain (tactical, communications, etc.);
- years of experience on similar projects ("similar" can refer, either singly or combined, to complexity, size, HOL, development process and environment, functionality, etc.);
- depth of relevant specialty training (design, test, reuse, Ada, SQL, etc.);
- years of relevant specialty experience.

• *Senior Gate* refers to developing the right combination of senior qualifications for the current project. An interesting scenario concerns an employee who is, let's say, 30% less productive than another, and would be expected to produce complex software in 3/10 more time. But the lower productivity person might be a junior engineer not able to produce the complex software at all.

Senior person qualifications must be defined for the job at hand. A 20 year software veteran without adequate Ada training is, at best, a junior on an Ada project - or, at worst, not acceptable at all for the project at this time. This again points up how important it is, for reasons of staff allocation and technical progress, to define "senior" accurately, and to assure a very definite dividing line (gate) between the junior and senior labels - because junior people can have high proficiency scores, but in the wrong areas or for the wrong factors.

• *Junior:Senior Ratio* relates to creating an efficient technical atmosphere and balance of experienced and inexperienced people (does not apply to management category).

• *Management Experience* relates to years of software project management experience (only applies to management category). It is preferred that the types of projects, on which the experience was gained, be similar. Therefore, two tallies - total years of experience and years of similar experience - should be kept.

• *Project Commitment* refers to the amount of time (by percentage) an individual is assigned to a project. Commitment level should be tracked by activity - requirements analysis, design, code, etc.. Staff level figures should be weighted not just counted, because whether its senior or junior staffers that are being counted impacts on staff proficiency rating averages. The proficiency of an individual with a partial commitment to the current project also should be weighted to obtain a true proficiency measure. Rather than refer to a "halftime person", refer to a "halftime person with a 3.1 proficiency rating", or a "halftime Level B senior engineer" (proficiency categories are discussed later).

**Submetric: Software Development Personnel Qualification - minor components**

• *Proficiency Level (minor)* relates to items not deemed to have an affect on the algorithm significant enough to pay for their collection and analysis, and includes:

- basic education level/type of degree;
- quality of education ("A" student vs. "C" student; school credentials);
- professional licenses;
- total years of software engineering experience (as contrasted with experience specifically on software developments);
- other specialty training (in technologies not relevant to the current project);
- on-the-job-training overlaps a bit with experience and is hard to quantify or collect;
- personal attitude/commitment is important but hard to quantify - it can be reasonably assumed that most people want to do a good job but a caution is necessary because there are a few that can negatively impact a job - a specific

situation that must be avoided is where a manager is, or is perceived as, a poor leader, and an undermining negative atmosphere pervades throughout an otherwise competent and reliable staff - in such situation, communications suffer;

- depth and breadth of experience can be a revealing set of measures but it is difficult to collect data with a sufficient level of completeness - this component can be characterized as follows:

  depth and breadth relate to

  -- experience working on complex vs. routine assignments;

  -- experience working on a variety of tasks vs. limited exposure;

  -- having responsibilities vs. being an assembly-line employee;

  some possible measures in this category (: = divided by)

  -- *job ratio* = years of experience : number of assignments or projects;

  -- *tech area ratio* = years of experience : number of assignment types (test, Ada, etc.);

  -- *mission ratio* = years of experience : number of project types (tactical, radar, etc.)

  -- a further weighting is required to account for long-term vs. short-term assignments;

  -- each of these ratios can be further decomposed to account for difficulty of the assignment, and level of assigned responsibility;

  interpretation

  -- high scores indicate stability;

  -- medium scores indicate stability plus diversification;

  -- low scores can indicate a lack of focus and career direction.

**Using Proficiency.** Individual proficiency measures can be used:

- during the Source Selection process:
  - to "certify" proposed personnel;
  - to help with the Contractor Capability Assessment process;

- during development:
  - to critique if personnel changes are equivalent;
  - to accomplish on-the-job evaluation of developers to determine if total staff capabilities are living up to pre-award assessments.

**Loss Of Identity.** The ultimate use of proficiency measurements is **not** to critique individual personnel. Rather it is to aggregate a cumulative staff proficiency from **impersonal** individual proficiencies (i.e., no names attached).

First though, an organization would have to define junior and senior category criteria, and use those criteria to partition the staff proposed for a project. The criteria would also be used during the job to determine personnel assignments and reassignments, both, for personnel newly assigned, and for junior staff attaining senior status.

As mentioned before, the junior-senior partition is extremely important because there are a number of ways an individual could attain a specific proficiency rating - i.e., several combinations of various education and experience levels could aggregate up to the same score but would actually represent different capabilities available to the project. For instance, a high-scoring COBOL programmer may be a junior engineer on an Ada project until some actual (and substantial) Ada experience is acquired.

But once categorized, proposed staff bring individual proficiencies to the project, which add to, and are considered an integral part of, a total staffing capability available to the project - i.e., as part of the whole, individual proficiencies then lose their identity. Collected data then refers to movement of individuals by type (e.g., senior computer scientist), not by name. When movement of specific individuals (by name) is indicated as a corrective action, that action belongs to immediate supervisors or department heads, not to the higher program or system management levels.

Thus, proficiency measures are used to track that the *baseline level of total staff proficiency is maintained throughout the project regardless of movement of individuals from assignment to assignment or project to project.*

**Acquired Capability, Innate Ability and Adapt-ability.** Total proficiency includes *individual smarts plus an ability to get smarter* - to cope with the next challenge. Thus proficiency consists of:

- *acquired capability:*
  - basics acquired through formal education and training; and through self-development in an inherited environment (such as a local education system);
  - expertise acquired through experience and on-the-job-training in selected environments (such as employment with a defense contractor or a government agency);
- *innate ability*, its growth and use for adapting to new technological situations.

How would one assess value, to a development effort, of one employee with specialty training in, let's say, Ada and OOD, compared to another employee trained in Ada, SQL and 4GLs. Are we comparing software apples with software oranges? The answer is yes if considering just the current snapshot. Yes, they are different combinations of acquired capabilities for specific areas. One may be applicable, one not. But diversification of skills is an indication of being able to tackle, or adapt to, new assignments.

To know if individuals can be "counted on" for the job ahead, both *current capabilities*, and *ability-to-adapt* to what comes along, must be gauged. Personnel need to be assessed as to their ability to adapt to new technology, new projects, new kinds of assignments - i.e., an overall personnel software engineering capability assessment. Knowing the extent to which employees can expand their skills-base becomes important.

Proficiency is a measure of both of these - acquired capability plus adapt-ability. Capability depends on the software proficiency acquired year after year - i.e., the quality and depth of each year's new knowledge, experience and training. Adapt-ability is based on innate ability, and the rate of development or use of that ability by the individual. Normally, both these factors grow and so a person's proficiency will increase as years go by. Thus there may be project management value in assessing proficiency of all assigned personnel at least once a year, and also whenever there is key personnel turnover, and then rolling those assessments up to new total staff proficiency figures.

**The Pre-School Concept.** Let's look at two new employees, one a former "C" student, the other an "A". If the "C" employee is a true "C", then his annual productivity rate will be less than the "A's". If he's just a school "slacker" but has "A" capabilities, then he'll start off slower but eventually reach parity with the "A". It seems that slow starters tend to catch up in short order if they possess innate ability. An individual's innate ability is an overriding element of the formal education process and resultant on-the-job productivity.

This concept has been validated in the public school system where non-preschool children tend to catch up, to those who have attended a preschool, by fourth grade. It appears that this principle also applies to the mission-critical defense system (MCDS) world or to any technical field.

There is an underlying assumption to all this - that an individual possess a positive, want-to-produce, attitude or commitment - we find that most do.

**Adapting to Technology.** Without adapt-ability, personnel would have to be assigned to the same type of job over and over, if such jobs are available. More often than not, the next assignment is dissimilar in many respects than the last assignment. Technology and project requirements' changes over the years mean new system concepts are being developed, along with new methods and techniques for implementing them. Therefore, new and diverse personnel capabilities are constantly needed.

Thus, proficiency level measures have added value when used to assess whether skill-levels are adapting to an ever evolving and ever advancing defense industry technology-base.

**Software Development Personnel Qualification Algorithm.** A point system algorithm might do very nicely. There are some components of proficiency that may easily be quantified. Initial quantifications would then mature along with the algorithm development and metrics validation processes. For instance, a "C" grade is about a 70%. So why not use .7 as a start. A "B" would be .8, etc.. This level of granularity should prove sufficient - i.e., .73 or .86 would not be necessary.

A Bachelor's Degree is about a four year effort, so let's assign a .4; with .8 for a Masters; and 1.2 for a Doctorate. Similarly, post-degree years of study could be figured as .1 per year. A PE could earn an extra .2. An alternative scoring might be to consider a Bachelors' as equivalent to a year's experience (= .1), a Masters = .2, and a Doctorate = .4.

Another consideration concerns overlapping of qualifications. Does ten years of software engineering experience, where two of them are MCDS-related, mean credit should be given for eight years of software engineering + two years of MCDS, or ten + two? Overlapping specialty experience on top of general experience amounts to extra credit for the special expertise and may be warranted. But such extra credit may only be deserved if, for instance in this example, the MCDS experience was meaningful, not routine. And, if it was continuous. Two years of piecemeal MCDS tasking spread over four or five years may not produce a qualified MCDS software engineer. An investigation of weighting schemes will address these issues.

An alternative is to categorize personnel by proficiency levels. Such a scheme would first sort on junior-senior. Then, rather than carry an individual score, each staff member would be placed in a proficiency category (say A, B, C) dependent on meeting predetermined criteria derived from system qualification requirements. The resulting metrics report presented to a manager would address the adequacy of numbers of individuals in each category, rather than tracking every individual proficiency (and annual proficiency delta) in order to arrive at an overall score averaged for the full staff. Whether tracked for total staff or by activity or skill, staff category levels, verified on an annual basis, may have more meaning, to the management function, than staff scoring.

As previously noted, accurate determination of staff proficiency is a complex subject and R&D results will not be achieved easily. However, the result, down the road - i.e., being able to easily quantify staff qualification measurements in a structured way so as to quickly determine capability on a project (and therefore help determine the feasibility of the project's success) - would provide a benefit to future government software procurements for large, complex systems. As for all algorithm development in this study, use will be made of the Algorithm Component Table.

## Software Productivity

The size and value of a software project, and the size and proficiency of the staff assigned to the project, determine the average productivity being applied to the project. The average productivity is a weighted composite of individual productiveness.

There are three aspects of individual productivity that are of interest to a software manager:

- a person's *relative productivity* (compared to another person) **[current capability]**;
- a person's *complexity-weighted productivity* (where the complexity/criticality of the project impacts on both the quality and the rate of an individual's output) **[actual contribution]**.
- a person's *productivity increase* **[growth potential]** over time;

Care should be taken to assess productivity within the context of the current technical area of interest. A productive database designer may be unproductive on a radar algorithm package development. But assessment should be on an annual basis because individuals will increase their capabilities rapidly through experience, and through formal, and on-the-job, training.

**Productivity Limits.** Productivity eventually reaches a saturation point sometime during the career of a professional. There is a trade-off on new-skills-for-old which stabilizes productivity. Even as very senior employees pick up new specialty skills and capabilities, productivity is not likely to increase proportionally because either:

- they become "rusty" or lose productivity in the older specialties from lack of use of those skills, or from obsolescence of the technology; or,
- the older specialties are not applicable to current projects; or,
- technical advances are so profuse that individuals find it hard to find the time to keep up; or,
- its just simply a matter of how much a person can accomplish in a day's work.

As a result of this "trade-off" of skills, average productivity eventually stabilizes some years into a career, although its technical character will change. An average is used because, even years into a career, productivity dips slightly at those times when new skills are being learned, only to rise slightly subsequently.

Another consideration is potential decrease of productivity due to loss of motivation usually related to job environment and morale problems. A company can make a big difference by constantly upgrading facilities and conditions, or by simply paying attention to the "factory atmosphere" so as to prevent "stagnation".

**Man-hour Depth.** Man-hour counts should consider value of the effort expended. Different individuals produce differently during a fixed time period. The "count" aspect must be taken one step further to address value, to where it is understood that **man-hours have depth.** Depth is comprised of a number of facets that make up an individual's time:

- *analysis time* for understanding and evaluation;
- *creativity time* for formulation of ideas and innovations;
- *production time* for writing it down or recording results;
- *assurance time* for verifying both the ideas and their implementation;
- overhead time related to organizational and administrative activities.

**Competent Man-hours.** If a program is orders of magnitude larger than another program, then of course, you would expect to see a great difference in the number of man-hours needed to produce the two packages. But, the difference is not linearly proportional to the size difference. Rather, it is very dependent on:

- the abstractness of the functional and performance requirements;
- the complexity of the software implementation of those requirements;,
- the modularity of that implementation;
- the qualifications of the organization for building that implementation.

For software systems with similar line counts, the "value" of the software is a greater factor than physical size for determining the number of required man-hours, and those man-hours must have corresponding value or man-hour depth (very productive vs. limited-productivity personnel performance - it is futile to assign relatively inexperienced people to a complex task, no matter how much time you give them to accomplish it). The equivalent "competent man-hours" affect a number of important economic areas:

- level of staff qualifications needed to produce the software;
- level of resources required to apply the product and maintain it over an extended period;
- benefits of the results to the user.

• The point is that man-hours relate to sheer line count, but *competent man-hours* relate to producing "value-able", or cost-beneficial and usable software. •

An example of how to use this concept is illustrated with the following scenario. Say senior people with a proficiency "score" of 1.0 provide one man-hour's worth of effort per hour. Individuals with a score of 2.0 provide 1.2 man-hours of effort each hour. A contractor has to assign senior capability to a task estimated to be a 1,000 man-hour effort. Competent man-hours scoring would enable assignment of either: five senior people with 1.0 scores at 200 hours each; or four seniors with 2.0 scores at 208 hours each.

So various combinations of proficiencies could result in a contractor needing less staff. This is important considering the shortage of qualified software engineers in the field today. Also, the salary outlay for the staff with fewer but higher qualified people would be roughly equivalent to the staff with more individuals of less proficiency. But, the savings on employee benefits packages and administrative costs would be reflected in lower bids for defense contracts. And the quality of the required products would not be compromised.

**"Countless" Hours.** Here is an interesting scenario. Employee A produces 100 lines of code in a week, but they fail testing. The unit comes back to coding and A spends another week in finding a small, but key, missing or erroneous portion of code. So A has produced 95% of the unit in one week and 5% in another week. What is A's productivity? One-hundred lines in two weeks? Well, what if the unit came back and A was busy or reassigned to another task so the rework went to employee B, who arrives at the same solution. Now A has produced unusable code and B has produced almost no code. But the package works. Can we even determine B's productivity? Does A have <u>any</u> productivity under this circumstance?

Are lines of code a measure of productivity? It seems the lines must be assigned a value reflecting usefulness and efficiency. And, complexity and criticality of the function being coded must also be factored into the determination of how much productivity was achieved? If the 95% usable software produced by A in the above example was all the routine code, and B produced the solution with only 5% of the code, but that 5% was complex code, then isn't B's productivity greater? And even more so if A had spent time on the problem but couldn't solve it. Which effort had greater impact (was more productive) in producing a usable package?

This points up the concern for being able to measure **rework turnaround-time and rework effort** where few lines may be created or changed during many man-hours of analysis. In fact, many productive efforts actually result in lines being deleted. This is another example where simple line counts and man-hour counts are not very good measures of productivity - aspects of value must be considered. What is needed are virtual counts of productive time that measure value of the effort involved.

This scenario plays frequently during maintenance activity where many hours of troubleshooting and rework may result in just a few line changes. This is also true when, during development, as a software system progresses toward qualification and acceptance, modules are sent back for rework as errors and omissions are found. Note that the principles of measuring productivity value apply across all activities of the life-cycle, not just coding.

**Software Productivity Increase.** Let's look at individual productivity growth. As a reasonable, but hypothetical, starting point, let's say a technical person's normal software engineering productivity jumps sharply every year for the first few years out of school, but then the annual productivity increases start to flatten out and finally stabilize (with a + or - delta) at some point in a person's career.

Following is a Productivity Increase Table for an employee starting with an arbitrary initial productivity rating of 1.000. The increases reflect, through some TBD algorithm, the employees annually acquired new knowledge, experience and formal training.

---

<u>Productivity Increase Table</u>

| YEAR | ANNUAL SW ENG PRODUCTIVITY RATING | ANNUAL SW ENG PRODUCTIVITY INCREASE |
|---|---|---|
| 01 | 1.000 | 20 % |
| 02 | 1.200 | 20 |
| 03 | 1.440 | 20 |
| 04 | 1.728 | 15 |
| 05 | 1.987 | 15 |
| 06 | 2.285 | 10 |
| 07 | 2.514 | 10 |
| 08 | 2.765 | 05 |
| 09 | 2.903 | 05 |
| 10 | 3.049 | 05 |
| 11 | 3.201 | 05 |
| 12 | 3.361 | 05 |
| 13 | 3.529 | 00 |
| 14 | " | 00 |
| I | " | 00 |
| I | " | 00 |
| V | | |

---

If this represents close to a real-world scenario, it means technical productivity over a long career can be expected to grow to 3-4 times greater than a person's initial capability.

This is within the ballpark of the results of a NASA study[3] on similar factors. That study showed (Table 3-3, reproduced below) that 2.3 times more effort was needed when personnel had to deal with new application domains and new capabilities (software engineering environments). To put it another way, 2.3 times more productivity can be expected when application and development environments are familiar entities.

Table 3-3. Complexity Guideline

| PROJECT TYPE[a] | ENVIRONMENT TYPE[b] | EFFORT MULTIPLIER |
|---|---|---|
| old | old | 1.0 |
| old | new | 1.4 |
| new | old | 1.4 |
| new | new | 2.3 |

[a] Application, e.g., orbit determination, simulator. The project (or portion of the project) type is old when the organization has more than 2 years experience with it.

[b] Computing environment, e.g., IBM 4341, VAX 8810. The environment type is old when the organization has more than 2 years of experience with it on average.

Also, when personnel had ten years of experience in an application domain, then 5.2 times more productivity could be expected (see Table 3-4, reproduced below).

Table 3-4. Development Team Experience Guideline

| TEAM YEARS OF APPLICATION EXPERIENCE[a] | EFFORT MULTIPLIER |
|---|---|
| 10 | 0.5 |
| 8 | 0.6 |
| 6 | 0.8 |
| 4 | 1.0 |
| 2 | 1.4 |
| 1 | 2.6 |

[a] Average of team member's years of application experience weighted by member's participation on the team. Application experience is defined as prior work on similar applications, e.g., attitude and orbit determination. Member's participation is defined as time spent working on the project as a proportion of total project effort.

3 NASA SEL Manager's Handbook for Software Development, SEL-84-101, Revision 1, Nov 90

**Productivity Value.** But what about the quality of productivity? Does A do as good a job as B? Can A even do the job? Again, this is where the notion of "value" comes in. The value of the software being produced (its complexity, utilization, functionality, criticality, etc.) must be weighed in any determination of the real productivity of an employee. What has it cost in man-hours? Productive output of more experienced employees will make up for the extra cost represented by their higher salaries. Either they'll produce the same product with fewer people, or produce the same product in less time, or produce more in the same amount of time. *And the product will be of higher quality.*

An added benefit to a private sector defense contractor is that a highly efficient and productive staff qualifies the company for more lucrative competitive awards.

A further application of the ideas of value as discussed in relation to size and staff extends naturally to productivity. One employee produces 1000 lines of complex software, another produces a 1500 line module of routine software in the same period of time. To know the relative productivity, one must determine how much more complex one module is than the other. To compare value, one must determine how much more useful one module is than the other. This can present a dilemma since the package implementing the less complex function may be used in a more critical application. The first job is important but the second may be critical and the bottom line is that you certainly would want to see more proficient personnel working that second problem.

## Algorithm Development

Use of "living" Algorithm Component Tables is contemplated for this study (see next page). The intent is to keep tables as representations of algorithms which mature as table contents are upgraded periodically. It is anticipated that ample size, staff, proficiency and productivity data is available on completed projects, so that initial algorithm formulas can be developed, and then early validation efforts can be implemented. Sensitivity analyses can then be performed. For instance, by comparing projects of similar size and complexity, the affect that staff proficiency had on productivity can be evaluated. Initial identification of major and minor algorithm components can then be achieved.

## ALGORITHM COMPONENT TABLE

| Components | | Weight | A | B | C | D | E | F | G | H |
|---|---|---|---|---|---|---|---|---|---|---|
| **Majors** | X | | | | | | | | | |
| | Y | | | | | | | | | |
| | Z | | | | | | | | | |
| **Minors** | 1. | | | | | | | | | |
| | 2. | | | | | | | | | |

**A.** Is this component important?
**B.** Is this component important but a minor part of the equation?
**C.** Is this component trivial?
**D.** Is this component hard to collect?
**E.** Does this component give added benefit and/or information worth the cost to collect it (80/20 rule)?
**F.** Does this component need feedback or further analysis in order to determine its importance?
**G.** Is this component weighted correctly/reasonably as determined by previous analysis/trial/use? Or is it an estimate/guess?
**H.** Provide narrative rationale for current weighting, or with new suggested weightings (narratives for A thru F may also be provided).

## Conclusion

There is great need to derive an initial set of commonly understood and utilized measures to address the issues of size and staff. Measurement of various aspects of these two entities is extremely important to managers for planning, estimating, tracking and evaluating large, complex software systems. Besides productivity, managers are also greatly interested in progress, stability, supportability, quality, resource utilization, and so on. Size and staff metrics provide insight into these various areas of software acquisition, development and support. The benefits will accrue both to current projects and future efforts. It would be beneficial if this problem were tackled in a coordinated manner by researchers from both the government and private sectors of the defense software industry. The stress should be on simplicity, cost-effectiveness, and timely insight.

# AN ECONOMIC ANALYSIS MODEL FOR DETERMINING THE CUSTOM VERSUS COMMERCIAL SOFTWARE TRADEOFF


Michael F. Karpowich
Thomas R. Sanders
Robert E. Verge
Science Applications International Corporation (SAIC)
3045 Technology Parkway
Orlando, Florida 32826-3299


## INTRODUCTION

Recent cuts in defense spending have prompted managers to seek to conserve resources in many innovative ways. Whereas historically a program development effort would make only marginal efforts to borrow techniques and take advantage of technology transfers from mature programs, today's programs are attempting to minimize the "reinventing the wheel" behavior. Along those lines, the modern program manager has additional decisions to make concerning how to satisfy his application software requirements. Before deciding in which software language and environment his program will be developed, he should determine just how much software he must develop, and how much may have already been developed for him; i.e. he must determine whether a commercially available software package would satisfy some of his requirements. Today's competitive environment has led to the creation of several commercial off-the-shelf (COTS) software products that are capable of satisfying very large software system requirements, often at a fraction of the cost of newly-developed software projects. Subsequently, each program manager owes it to himself to investigate these products for use in his program. More recently, government customers are requiring an economic analysis to help choose the preferred software alternative.

The cost analysis model presented here has been developed by SAIC to assist in the custom versus commercial software tradeoff decision. The Lotus-based model offers a disciplined method of assessing relative life-cycle costs by incorporating a comprehensive SAIC-developed Work Breakdown Structure (WBS), an embedded software development parametric estimating model (REVIC), and the concept of net present value in a user-friendly format. In addition, the model is self-documenting and auditable, allowing for quicker "what-if" exercises to be performed. The model truly is a necessary tool for our changing times.

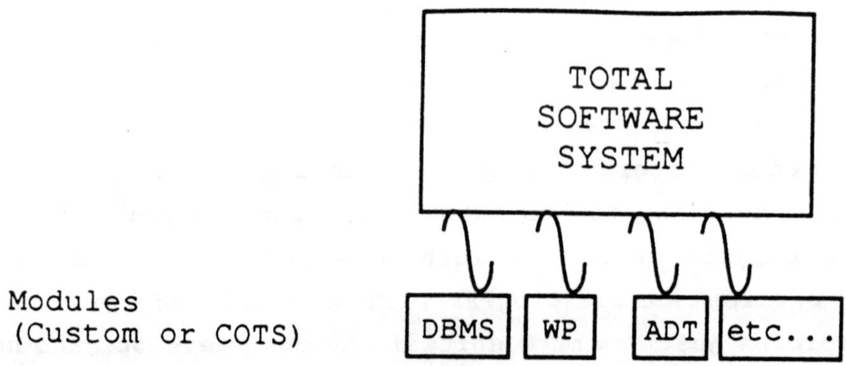


**Figure 1**

Figure 1 describes the software tradeoff as assessing "modules" of a total system software effort. That is, while the top-level portions of the software system must be uniquely developed for the specific program, the software modules (Word processor, Database Management System, Spreadsheet, etc.) can be either purchased or developed, depending upon which is more cost-effective.

The tradeoff process insists that the analyst assess functionally-equivalent custom and COTS software products. To assure this functional equivalence, the COTS software may require some custom software "hooks" to allow the COTS package to link with the rest of the software system. The model's Work Breakdown Structure (WBS) explaining these intricacies is described in more detail later in this paper.

## BACKGROUND

SAIC has performed a series of software tradeoff studies in the past ten years for programs ranging from simulators to major weapon systems. As a result, the authors have assessed numerous COTS software packages as well as several development software parametric estimating models such as COCOMO, PRICE S, and REVIC. While each parametric model and COTS software package contributes part of the picture, SAIC recognized that a single tool that provides a thorough, comprehensive analysis addressing all the life-cycle cost impacts of the custom versus commercial software cost tradeoff was lacking.

## THE MODEL

The primary purpose of SAIC's Software Cost Tradeoff Model is to compare costs of a custom software module to those of a chosen functionally equivalent COTS alternative. The model is logically laid out in three parts. Part One assesses the COTS software alternative using vendor inputs, factors, and engineering assessments as to hardware and interface software to estimate costs. Part Two employs the REVIC parametric software estimating model to estimate the costs of the custom software. Finally, Part Three compares a chosen COTS alternative to the custom software from a life-cycle cost viewpoint, incorporating the concepts of time-phasing and net present value.

The Model is written in Lotus version 2.1 and requires an IBM-PC 286 or compatible machine running at 16 mHz for optimal operation.

## Work Breakdown Structure

To guarantee a thorough cost analysis, SAIC developed and embedded in the model a comprehensive WBS. This WBS is used as an accounting checklist to insure all conceivable costs are addressed. While functionally similar, many COTS software packages require unique interfaces (hardware and/or software) that the model must consider. Similarly, performing a cost tradeoff between commercial and custom products is not as easy as "swapping" the cost of a COTS software package for that of the developed software, and vice versa. Seldom is a commercial software product alone "functionally equivalent" to a custom product; some amount of interface hardware or software is almost always required. The WBS's for both commercial and custom software are listed in Figure 2.

While the WBS is intended to be rather generic, some elements may seem uncommon. Development Kits are those

| Commercial | Custom |
| --- | --- |
| Acquisition | Acquisition |
| Development Kits/Licenses | Systems Engineering |
| Run-Time Kits/Licenses | Preliminary Design |
| Interface Design | Critical Design |
| Hardware | Code & Debug |
| Software | Integration & Test |
| Training | Development Test |
| | Documentation |
| | Training |
| Maintenance | Maintenance |
| Software Service Agreements | Code Updates |
| Development Systems | Debugging |
| Run-Time Systems | System Design Updates |
| Interface Software Maintenance (identical to custom software maintenance) | Training |
| Training | |

Figure 2

COTS software packages purchased for use during a program's development testing phase. They are generally more robust and are supported by a greater level of maintenance than the Run Time Kits which are purchased for a program's production phase. Interface design software represents the "hooks" required to allow COTS software to operate with the rest of the system. These hooks may be required to allow the COTS software package to operate with the system software, the system hardware, or both. The other WBS elements are fairly common and straight-forward.

The WBS should insure that all cost elements are addressed. While this may be relatively easy in the case of custom software, the large number of different vendors providing commercial software often provide peculiar licensing, service, or interface hardware and software options to consider. The analyst must make sure to define functionally equivalent, "apples-to-apples" COTS and custom products.

## Ground Rules and Assumptions

Although the model is designed to accommodate many different types of alternatives, a small set of model assumptions do apply. These assumptions include:

1) Custom software will be written in the Ada development environment.

2) Candidate commercial software will operate on the available hardware, even if some custom software "hooks" must be developed to facilitate operation.

3) All required interfaces to create functional equivalence of tradeoff alternatives are identified.

4) Enough information is known about the custom software such that accurate software sizing estimates can be made.

5) An expenditure profile for each WBS can be created.

## Model Construction

The Software Cost Tradeoff Model is designed to operate in both an automated and manual mode. As such, it is laid out in five discreet areas in the Lotus spreadsheet. Those areas include:

1) Automated Screen Display - That spreadsheet section where data entry screens are displayed in the automated mode.

2) Automated Mode Program Code - The spreadsheet section containing the automated entry program macro codes.

3) Database - The spreadsheet section where input data is stored and cost computations made.

4) Output Form - The spreadsheet section containing the model output form.

5) Net Present Value - The spreadsheet section where net present value computations are made.

Figure 3 describes these spreadsheet ranges.

| AUTOMATED SCREEN | PROGRAM CODE | DATABASE FORM | OUTPUT DISPLAY | NPV CODE |
|---|---|---|---|---|
| (a1..g113) | (ba1..bi285) | (bz1..ct84) | (aa1..ak78) | (db1..dn162) |

Figure 3

Table 1

| WBS | COST MODEL EXPRESSION |
|---|---|
| Commercial (COTS) Software | |
| Acquisition | |
| Development Kits/Licenses | V * S * B |
| Run-Time Kits/Licenses | V * S * B |
| Interface Design | $6.8\ (KDSI)^{.941} * 1.34 * DMOD * DLR * HMM$ |
| Hardware | |
| Software | |
| Training | P * F * C |
| Maintenance | |
| Software Service Agreements | V * S * Y * B |
| Development Systems | |
| Run-Time Systems | |
| Interface Software Maintenance | $MM^{NOM} * MMOD * ACT * MLR * HMM * Y$ |
| Training | P * F * C |
| Custom Software | |
| Acquisition | $6.8\ (KDSI)^{.941} * 1.34 * DMOD * DLR * HMM$ |
| Maintenance | $MM^{NOM} * MMOD * ACT * MLR * HMM * Y$ |

Variables

V = Vendor quote (unit cost)
S = Qty. of Systems
B = Contractor Burden
P = # of students in training class
F = # of training sessions
C = Training session cost/student
Y = # of years
$MM^{NOM}$ = Nominal manmonths
DMOD = Development environmental modifier
MMOD = Maintenance environmental modifier
ACT = Annual change traffic
(DMOD, MMOD, ACT: See Env. Modifier Screen)
DLR = Development phase composite labor rate
MLR = Maintenance phase composite labor rate
HMM = Hours per manmonth

## Model Operation

The model computes costs using WBS Cost Model Expressions. Cost Model Expressions are formulas for estimating the cost of each WBS element; applicable expressions are illustrated in Table 1.

Variable inputs are provided by the user by selecting either the automated or manual input method from a main menu screen. Selecting the automated mode will display a series of user friendly screens (See Figures 4 through 8) requesting cost model expression input variables and a calendar-year expenditure profile. Upon entering these inputs, the model transfers them to the database and displays the next WBS element for data entry. (Note that Figs. 4 - 8 represent Data Entry Screens for the custom software "hooks" required for the COTS to be functionally equivalent to custom software.)

```
PHASE:            COTS ACQUISITION                LEGEND

COST'                                             [ ]= DEFAULT
CATEGORY:         TRAINING                        { }= CALCULATED
                                                       INTERNALLY
COST                                              ( )= INPUT FORMAT
EXPRESSION:       P * F * C

NON-REVIC         VAR TITLE                                VALUE
    1              V  VENDOR QUOTE PER UNIT ($)
    2              S  # SYSTEMS
    3              B  CONT BURDEN [1.46]
    4              Y  # OF YEARS
    5              P  # OF PEOPLE IN EACH TNG CLASS
    6              F  # TNG SESSIONS
    7              C  TNG SESSION COST PER PERSON
```

Figure 4

The alternative manual input method takes the user directly to the database, where inputs are made by scrolling through each WBS element. Cost calculations are automatically made in the database using the provided

PHASE: COTS ACQUISITION

COST CATEGORY: SOFTWARE INTERFACE

COST EXPRESSION: $(6.8*(KDSI)^{.941})DMOD*DLR*HMM*1.34$

| REVIC | VAR | TITLE | VALUE |
|---|---|---|---|
| 8 | KL | KDSI LOW ESTIMATE | |
| 9 | KMP | KDSI MOST PROBABLE ESTIMATE | |
| 10 | KH | KDSI HIGH ESTIMATE | |
| 11 | DLR | DEV LABOR RATE [$67/HOUR] | |
| 12 | HMM | HOURS PER MANMONTH [152] | |
| 13 | ACT | ANNUAL CHANGE TRAFFIC FACTOR (.xx) | |
| 14 | MLR | MAINT LABOR RATE [$42/HOUR] | |

Figure 5

PHASE: COTS ACQUISITION COMPOSITE MULTIPLIER: 1.00

COST CATEGORY: SOFTWARE INTERFACE

COST EXPRESSION: $(6.8*(KDSI)^{.941})DMOD*DLR*HMM*1.34$

| ENVIRONMENTAL FACTORS | VL | L | N | H | VH | XH | SELECTED |
|---|---|---|---|---|---|---|---|
| Analyst Capability? | 1.46 | 1.19 | 1.00 | .86 | .71 | .71 | |
| Programmer Capability? | 1.42 | 1.17 | 1.00 | .86 | .70 | .70 | |
| Applications Experience? | 1.29 | 1.13 | 1.00 | .91 | .82 | .82 | |
| Virtual Machine Experience? | 1.21 | 1.10 | 1.00 | .90 | .90 | .90 | |
| Program Lang Experience? | 1.14 | 1.07 | 1.00 | .95 | .95 | .95 | |
| Execution Time Constraints? | 1.00 | 1.00 | 1.00 | 1.11 | 1.30 | 1.66 | |
| Main Memory Constraints? | 1.00 | 1.00 | 1.00 | 1.06 | 1.21 | 1.56 | |
| Virtual Machine Volatility? | .87 | .87 | 1.00 | 1.15 | 1.30 | 1.49 | |
| Computer Turnaround Time? | .79 | .87 | 1.00 | 1.07 | 1.15 | 1.15 | |
| Requirements Volatility? | .91 | .91 | 1.00 | 1.19 | 1.38 | 1.62 | |

Figure 6

input data. Once all desired WBS Cost Model Expression inputs are provided, the model automatically completes an output form displaying the custom versus COTS software cost tradeoff.

PHASE: COTS ACQUISITION COMPOSITE MULTIPLIER: 1.00

COST CATEGORY: SOFTWARE INTERFACE

COST EXPRESSION: $(6.8*(KDSI)^{.941})DMOD*DLR*HMM*1.34$

| ENVIRONMENTAL FACTORS | VL | L | N | H | VH | XH | SELECTED |
|---|---|---|---|---|---|---|---|
| Required Reliability? | .75 | .88 | 1.00 | 1.15 | 1.40 | 1.40 | |
| Database Size? | .94 | .94 | 1.00 | 1.08 | 1.16 | 1.16 | |
| Complexity of the Code? | .70 | .85 | 1.00 | 1.15 | 1.30 | 1.65 | |
| Is It Written for Re-Use? | 1.00 | 1.00 | 1.00 | 1.10 | 1.30 | 1.50 | |
| Modern Programming Pract? | 1.24 | 1.10 | 1.00 | .91 | .82 | .82 | |
| Use of Software Tools? | 1.24 | 1.10 | 1.00 | .91 | .83 | .73 | |
| Management Reserve? | 1.00 | 1.20 | 1.40 | 1.60 | 1.80 | 2.00 | |

| | CLASSIFIED | UNCLASSIFIED |
|---|---|---|
| Security Required? | 1.10 | 1.00 |

Figure 7

PHASE: COTS ACQUISITION

COST CATEGORY: SOFTWARE INTERFACE

| CY | AMOUNT (%) | CY | AMOUNT (%) | CY | AMOUNT (%) |
|---|---|---|---|---|---|
| YR 1 | | YR 8 | | YR 15 | |
| YR 2 | | YR 9 | | YR 16 | |
| YR 3 | | YR 10 | | YR 17 | |
| YR 4 | | YR 11 | | YR 18 | |
| YR 5 | | YR 12 | | YR 19 | |
| YR 6 | | YR 13 | | YR 20 | |
| YR 7 | | YR 14 | | | |

Figure 8

Figure 9 graphically depicts the model operation by displaying the interaction of the five areas described under model construction.

An important aspect of the model is the ability to review the outputs in both constant and discounted

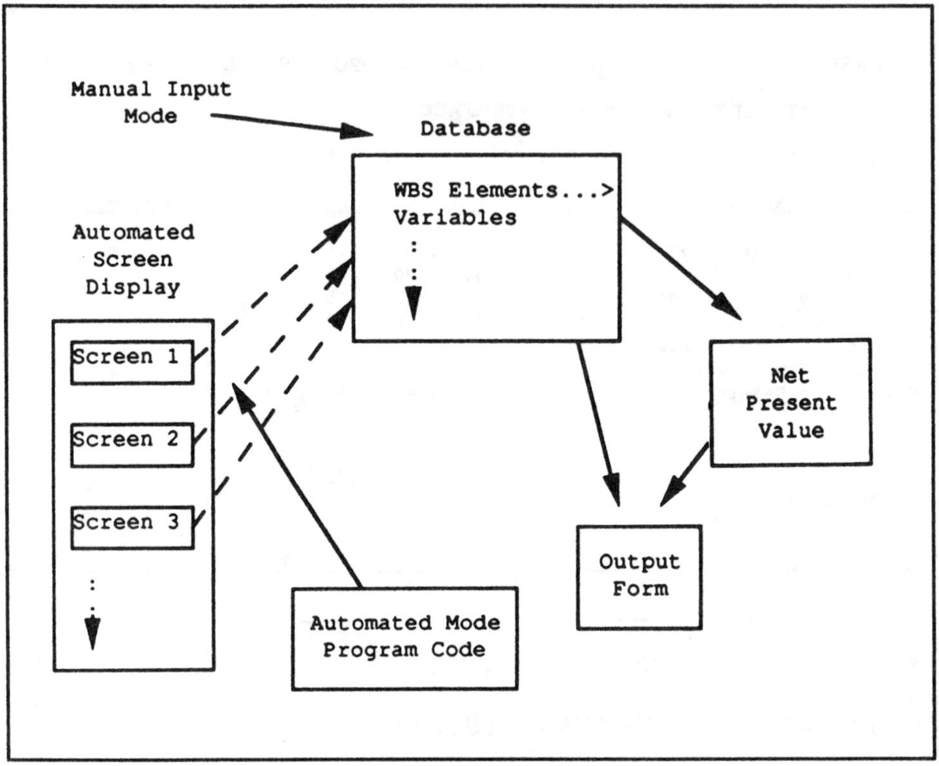


Figure 9

dollars. If the user provides a Calendar Year spread for each WBS element, the output form will provide both a detailed constant year cost comparison and a summary level discounted dollar cost comparison. The difference will incorporate the concept of Net Present Value, which says that the further out in time costs are incurred, the lower those costs are in present value terms.

## CASE STUDY

To illustrate the use of the model, the authors compared a commercially available DataBase Management System (DBMS) software product to a DBMS product developed in the Ada environment. They followed a disciplined approach to defining the estimate inputs and subsequent outputs, and obtained some interesting results.

In Part One, estimating the life-cycle cost of the commercial (COTS) product, software engineers determined that some amount of developed code was required to provide the "hooks" such that the commercial package could be integrated into the remainder of the system software; software engineers provided software sizing estimates for this custom software. In addition, Run-time licenses surprisingly turned out to be almost as expensive as Development licenses, based on vendor quotes. We also discovered that the vendor was unwilling to provide discounts on long-term maintenance agreements.

Software engineers provided sizing estimates and environmental modifiers for the functionally equivalent developed software written in Ada in Part Two of the model. Using the REVIC estimating model, the acquisition costs as well as the maintenance costs were estimated. Since the government customer was assumed to have the responsibility for maintaining the software, a different set of environmental modifiers was used to estimate maintenance costs.

By way of comparison in Part Three, the commercial software was much less expensive to acquire but much more expensive to maintain than the custom software over the life cycle. While total life-cycle costs in constant dollars were very close, the larger maintenance cost for the commercial software is spread over the 15-year maintenance life-cycle. When the net present value analysis was performed, the commercial product was clearly the lowest cost option. Figure 10 displays these

Comparitive Analysis

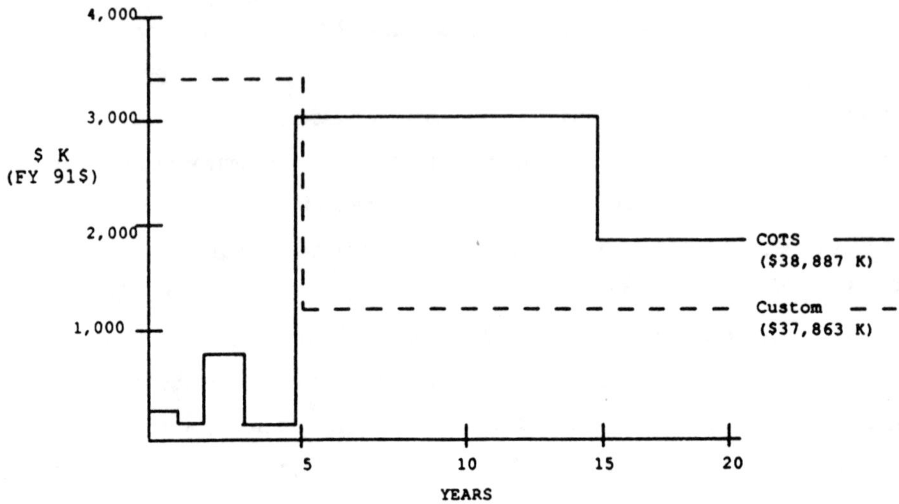


Comparative Analysis

| | COTS Software | Custom Software | Variance |
|---|---|---|---|
| Total LCC (Constant $) | $38,887,000 | $37,863,000 | $1,024,000 |
| Total LCC (Discounted$) | $14,022,000 | $20,804,000 | ($6,782,000) |

Figure 10

relative costs.

ISSUES

Some important issues uncovered in developing this model may not be readily apparent and deserve special exposure.

1) Accurately identify the COTS interfaces - COTS software packages can seldom be used for system requirements without designing custom software interfaces to

link the various custom and COTS packages together to form the system software. Insure that these interfaces are accurately defined; custom software development is generally much more costly than purchasing COTS software, so the interface software may be more costly than the entire COTS package!

2) The COTS versus custom software relative Life Cycle Costs can be misleading unless the Net Present Value concept is employed. In general, the further out that cost is incurred, the lower that cost is in present value terms. Thus a relatively large maintenance cost may not be as large as you may think if it is incurred in the out years.

3) The maintenance portion of many software estimating models has historically taken a back seat to the primary focus of estimating software development costs. The user should be aware that there are often different environmental modifiers that must be considered along with different labor categories in the maintenance phase. For example, a requirement for high software reliability in the development phase will drive up the development cost (large development environmental modifier); however, highly reliable software is easier to maintain, and maintenance costs are driven down (small maintenance environmental modifier). Likewise, while highly reliable software requires highly qualified developers, its maintenance may not require personnel of the same skill and salary level.

## CONCLUSION

The Software Cost Analysis Model described here provides a thorough, comprehensive method of analyzing the cost tradeoffs of commercial and custom software products. The model's user-friendly self-documenting characteristics make it ideal for performing quick "what-if" studies. By considering life-cycle impacts of spend profiles and net present value analysis, the lowest cost option may be different than the "obvious" choice.